ECHO OF A DISTANT DRUM

ECHO OF
A DISTANT DRUM

The Last Generation of Empire

Maurice Willoughby

The Book Guild Ltd
Sussex, England

First published in Great Britain in 2001 by
The Book Guild Ltd
25 High Street
Lewes, East Sussex
BN7 2LU

Typesetting in Times by
IML Typographers, Birkenhead, Merseyside

Printed in Great Britain by
Bookcraft (Bath) Ltd, Avon

A catalogue record for this book is available from
The British Library.

ISBN 1 85776 562 1

For my son Anthony and with thanks to Marion Henderson. Without the help and encouragement of both, this book would never have been written.

My thanks also to Major John Spreull MBE for his kindness and interest and for his glowing early review.

PREFACE

The entire British nation was intensely proud of its Empire, a huge area comprising a third of the world's land surface, shown on all our school maps in pink. It had come into existence some two hundred years earlier, either by war or by trade. Merchants, who afterwards became famous in India as '*box-wallahs*', set up trading posts. These came into conflict with local chiefs or kings, and had to be protected either by soldiers from Britain, or raised their own armies, which later turned into such organisations as the Indian Army. As more and more territory was acquired, its defenders and administrators were recruited and controlled from a very narrow section of British society, notably the gentry as opposed to the aristocracy.

The same families served in India for generation after generation; my father's for three and my mother's for five, for example. The Indian Civil Service, which needed a high degree of brains, were often educated at Winchester College, the others, not so much from schools such as Eton or Harrow, but rather from those like Rugby, Marlborough, Haileybury or Wellington. The education at these schools was rough and tough, the bullying horrendous, the food, comfort and welfare based on Sparta in 500 BC, centred around cold baths in every sort of weather, fresh air, extreme physical endurance, the worship of such games as rugby and cricket for their own sake, and leadership through the old Roman prefectorial system. Boys were taught that they were an elite, and as an elite, had an elite's responsibility, which was to lead, administer and if necessary die. They must be prepared to live under conditions of intolerable discomfort without complaint, to be incorruptible, and act with justice, only in the interests of those they governed. In fact, conditions at these schools were generally so dreadful that anything afterwards seemed like soft living.

After leaving school, those bound for the Indian Civil Service would go up to Oxford or Cambridge, those for the Army to Sandhurst, or 'The Shop' at Woolwich. Here, standards of drill, discipline and conduct were of the highest order, but especially at Sandhurst, the whole aim of the eighteen-month course was devised to ensure that anyone who had been through it, would never ever have to think for themselves again. This was achieved by marching cadets everywhere in a squad, in some cases not knowing where they were going, or what they would do when they got there, from the moment they arrived until the last one before they left. It was a splendid training to deal with Pathans or 'Fuzzy Wuzzies', even Zulus, but which failed miserably against sharp-shooting Boers. It was, however. still unchanged when I was at Sandhurst in 1932/33.

Most of the children were, like myself, born in India. Nobody would ever have dreamt of issuing us with a birth certificate. It was quite inconceivable that anybody would not know who you were. At the age of eight, children would be sent home to be educated at Preparatory schools and cared for by aunt or grand-mother. They would meet their parents, more or less as strangers, every third year, when they came home on long leave. It was a hard decision for a married couple, especially the wife; either to leave her husband and come back with her child, or stay in India. Most chose the latter.

Ostensibly, India was at peace, but on its North West Frontier, there were continual small wars going on with the Pathan tribes. These were greatly enjoyed by both sides, who had intense admiration and liking for each other. On the British side this was known as 'real soldiering'. Such events as the 1914–18 War did not really count. I often heard people say 'how nice it was to get back to some real soldiering'.

1

I was born at Bolarum in India, on 23 December 1913, and christened Maurice Frederick Vere. The name Vere denoted some mythical connection, the origin of which I have never managed to gather, with the Earls of Oxford, whose surname is Vere. It was the time of the peak of the British Empire, and my father, Douglas Vere Willoughby, was serving as a Captain in the 1st Brahmins, the oldest Infantry regiment in the Indian Army, and which, on later re-organisation, became the 1st Bn of the 1st Punjab Regiment. He was the younger son of Lt-Colonel Robert Willoughby, who had spent his career in the Royal Scots Fusiliers and had finished up commanding one of its two Regular battalions. I have a large photograph of him hanging in my study, in command of Queen Victoria's Guard at Balmoral in 1891. Robert had been ADC in the 1870s to Sir William Robertson, Governor of the Province of Madras, and like all good ADCs had married his daughter, my paternal grandmother.

They had two sons, Robin and my father, who was born in February 1882, at the Royal Scots Fusilier Depot in Ayr. Robertson was a School Governor of Haileybury College in Hertfordshire, and both boys were sent to Batten House there at the age of 13. Robin, some four years the elder, no good at games and slightly myopic – he wore glasses all his life – was a brilliant classical scholar and carried off all the prizes for Latin and Greek. He went on to Magdalen College at Oxford where he obtained a First in Classics. He then entered the Indian Civil Service. India at that time, and in fact until we left, was administered by a handful of British Civil Servants of the highest possible calibre; incorrupt and incorruptible. The examination for entry to the ICS was of a

1

higher standard than that of any other profession, including the Diplomatic. Its members were known as the 'Heaven Born'; and in the tight hierarchy of the British in India, they were at the very peak, even socially higher than officers of the British Cavalry regiments. The social ladder was definite, and clearly understood, but also on its rungs were the social differences between the Regiments themselves, acknowledged by everyone. Thus if two Cavalry regiments were stationed in the same place, their own standing in the Army social hierarchy would be never spoken of, but universally recognised. The system certainly continued until the outbreak of war in 1939, and probably until Independence in 1947.

Top of the pecking order were the 'Heaven Born' of the ICS. followed in roughly this sequence:

Officers in British Cavalry regiments in their own hierarchy
British Infantry regiments, Royal Artillery,
Royal Engineers, ditto.
British officers of Indian Army Cavalry regiments ditto.
Indian Army Infantry regiments, ditto.
Various Service Corps such as RASC, RIASC, RAOC.
(These were often disparagingly alluded to as 'sock smellers' or 'mechanics'.)
British officers of the Indian Police. These were followed by British officials running Government Farms and so on. Later on, and very low on the social scale, were the Royal Tank Corps and the RAF, both were considered to be mechanics or chauffeurs, likely to smell of oil and other unsavoury objects.

Apart from the Indian Civil Service, who 'only spoke to God' and were too far in the clouds for their interest, or otherwise, in it to be noticed, the system was based entirely on the horse, and how close was the connection with horses over the years of the unit as a whole. For instance, an officer of the Indian Police might own the best horse in the world. It could perhaps, greatly improve his own social standing in the Cantonment, but would do nothing to improve the general social opinion on the Police. This hierarchy

2

was accepted without resentment or rancour. It was just the way things were, and many probably did not even know of its existence or would have angrily denied it, if asked. Wives and other relatives of those involved shared the same social status as their menfolk, and the system was as rigid as a suit of armour. For generations it was accepted without question, and it worked. Everyone knew how they stood with everyone else. Funnily enough, nobody felt superior or inferior.

Amongst all this social plethora of soldiers and administrators, there was yet another category, that of the '*box-wallahs*'. These were people who indulged in trade; the inference being that like itinerant Indian vendors, they hawked their wares around in a box, and took them out for inspection and sale. *Box-wallahs* included bank managers and heads of large and important businesses trading in India. They mostly resided in big cities such as Calcutta, Bombay or Karachi. The social position of the *box-wallah* could not be exactly defined, and varied from place to place according to the influence they wielded; but it was never really much above par with the Indian Police. Few if any of the British in India actually lived there, and those who did were considered extremely odd. India was just the place where, on the whole, you spent a very pleasant working life. For one and all, 'Home' was Britain, and they passed their time in India longing for Home, and their retirement, usually to Camberley or Cheltenham, longing for India.

When my father was seven his mother died. It was a blow from which I do not think he ever recovered. He was handed over to the tender care of a Scots nanny, Miss Ellen Bullock, a stern and upright Presbyterian of impeccable credentials, and from what I could gather, no humanity or affection. As a result he was unable to make any display either of emotion or tenderness until he died. He was a man of enormous integrity with the stiffest upper lip I ever knew. His only code in life was to do his duty, with his own comfort and interests a long way last. As his family was his, their comfort and interest came a long way last as well, which was at times extremely disconcerting. Furthermore, such was the strictness of his upbringing under the aegis of Miss Bullock, that until his dying day he would never eat jam and butter together on a slice of bread. Ellen was eventually pensioned off and lived in a small house in Hove. Whilst at my preparatory school I was taken by him to see her, and was struck by the fact that although a Colonel in the Army at the time, this frail old lady turned him into a small boy again. It was 'Master Vere this and Master Vere that and Master Vere three bags full'. They were obviously completely devoted to each other and neither capable of showing the slightest sign of it.

Unlike his elder brother Robin, my father was a fine athlete who did well at games at Haileybury. To be 'good at games', notably rugby and cricket, was the be-all and end-all, and was the only thing that mattered. The bullying he received when he went there as a new boy or 'New Guvnor', he recounted to me with glee, when it was my own turn to endure the same fate. It was something that anyone who had to face it, never forgot or its perpetrators. From school he passed into the Royal Military College at Sandhurst, the Academy was then at Woolwich, and was eventually gazetted 2nd Lieutenant in the 21st Foot, The Royal Scots Fusiliers, his father's old regiment. He tried his best to get to the South African War against the Boers, but being only 19, was too young to go. One of his earliest experiences was conducting a draft of a hundred Jocks from the Regimental Depot at Ayr to the railway station, en route for Cape Town and the War. Except for himself, every single one was as blind drunk as only a Jock can be. Somehow, lurching, falling, being sick in the gutter, holding each other up, singing, shouting, swearing, he managed to shepherd them all onto the platform and into the train. A piper had been appointed to add a little martial glory to the event, but he was, if possible, drunker than the rest Every now and again he managed to coax a hideous wail from his bagpipes.

Instead of the War in South Africa, my father was sent to join the 2nd Battalion of his Regiment in India. His pay at the time was 5/- a day (25p). Although this was slightly increased in India, he had in addition an allowance of £100 a year from his father. Without a private allowance, no junior Regular Army officer could even pay his Mess bill. Although by 1998 standard some fifty times today's value, it was hard to exist. He found regimental soldiering stultifying, numbingly boring, and his brother officers so parochial as to be devoid of all interest in India, its languages or

4

people. Prospects of pay, promotion and responsibility were much better as an officer in the Indian Army. So when the opportunity arose, he with a great friend, Bill Browning, transferred from British Service into the Indian Army. Such postings were much sought after, and only those who passed out of Sandhurst in the highest categories were gazetted directly into it. Bill Browning and my father were appointed to the 1st Brahmins, where the Sepoys were entirely high-caste Hindus. As a small boy, I once inadvertently cast my defiling shadow across his food as one was eating, only to see him throw the whole lot onto the ground. Bill Browning was very good at languages and as well as the various Indian dialects, became a first class Russian interpreter. He was kept the entire 1914–18 War on garrison duty on a small, remote island off Aden at the entrance to the Red Sea. The more the British Army changes, the more it will always remain the same. The Spirit of Balaclava ever lingers. All the soldiers we so laboriously taught to ski in 1943 were used in boats around the Adriatic.

My father was far happier in the Indian Army. He had more responsibility, more pay, more interest and much quicker promotion. By the age of 28 he was a Captain, for which he would have had to wait at least another five years, and his Captain's pay was fully equal to that of a Lt-Colonel in British Service. Being a man of method, he decided he ought to get married. Perhaps in one of her many letters, Ellen Bullock told him it was high time to do so. 'What you need, Master Vere, is a good wife.' In the event, reality was the very anthesis of what he was seeking. Choice of girls in India was limited to the 'Fishing Fleet'. These were the women who came out to India at the beginning of each 'cold weather', with the express intention of finding the husband, that they were either too boring or too unattractive to find at home. With at least six panting young men, tongues hanging out, chasing every even remotely presentable female, their chances of catching one were better than odds on. In fact, unless they were as ugly as a water buffalo, they were onto a sure thing. Furthermore, even those who looked like water buffaloes usually managed to marry Gunner officers, these animals and Gunner's wives being reputed to be the ugliest two objects in India. The fishing fleet was not for

DVW. He was certain there was something better at Home. He would wait for his next long leave of eight months.

The leave given to British officials in India, right up to the 1939–45 War, was most generous and on full pay. Besides every weekend, Thursday was also a holiday. Then there was 'ten days local leave', which did not count against any leave quota and could be taken whenever possible. It would always be granted for example for a tiger-shoot, or the killing of almost any kind of wild animal for that matter, pig-sticking, a polo tournament or any such similar event which could be classed as strictly part of Military Training. It was much harder to get leave to travel, for example, to some social function, unless it was of a kind to bring credit to the Unit as a whole, such as maybe being seen around at a Viceregal Garden Party or other function. Leave for anything to do with the horse, hunting, shooting or fishing, would never be denied. By judicious use of Thursday at each end, the ten days could easily be stretched into a fortnight, and good juggling ensure you could be away on another 'ten days' almost as soon as you got back from the first. The official yearly leave entitlement was two months. This would be taken during the 'hot weather', in some local hill station such as Simla, Naini Tal or in the semi-independent State of Jammu and Kashmir at Srinagar or Gulmarg, where there was a fine golf course. Around April, directly there was the first whiff of heat down on the plains, where, until the following October the daytime temperature would remain at 110–114° Fahrenheit (45° C), and rarely dropped below 80° (27° C) at night, all the white women fled to the hills.

Even the barest hint of the summer heat was considered very bad for their complexions; likely to turn their skin yellow, crinkly and dry as parchment. For six months every year, the Garrison Cantonments became bachelor establishments, where people could concentrate in peace on training their polo ponies, not have to play mixed tennis at the Club, and be able to have dinner on the lawn there without female chatter. In the meantime up in the cool of the hills, the Memsahibs and the Miss-sahibs, wives and girl-friends, were having a whale of a time, as fresh relays of young men arrived every two months, hot and dusty from the Plains, eager for amorous adventure, known rather scornfully as 'poodle-

6

faking'. My father was dead against poodle-faking. From Ellen Bullock's teaching he had become convinced that the world's three greatest evils, were Sex, Constipation and the Pope. I never managed to discover in which order. Instead he would spend his leave trekking, photographing and shooting unfortunate animals in the Himalayas, such as bears, markhor, a kind of mountain sheep with huge horns, and snow leopards. All the heads, hooves, skins and other mementoes, were duly brought back as trophies; stuffed, mounted or cured by a well-known and celebrated firm of stuffers, mounters and curers called Roland Ward. They were then added to the already huge collection of trophies which littered every wall and floor of every bungalow in the Plains; to await ultimate destination in Camberley or Cheltenham, finally to crumble away from age and the depredations of clothes moths and fish insects. These seemed to find the red flannel, to which the skins were sewn, especially tasty.

Every third year, officers were entitled to Home Leave of eight months. The voyage took about a month each way, so they were left with six months at home. In 1911, my father, then aged 29, became eligible for Home Leave and decided he would look for a wife. He was a large handsome man, just under six feet in height, with thick brown hair, the conventional officer's bristly moustache, a muscular body, fit from hard exercise, trekking in the mountains and playing polo. He was a strong, if rather ungainly, horseman and a fine shot with any kind of weapon. He realised that as a married man he would not be able to continue to afford to play polo, but thought the sacrifice worthwhile. He used to tell me afterwards, with what regret he later wistfully saw the bachelors' ponies being led past his bungalow, down to the Maidan for the afternoon chukkas. He was of the very best type of British regimental officer it is possible to imagine, fearless, devoted to his men, their care and the minutiae of daily duty. He would accept any order, however preposterous, stupid or ridiculous without cavil or question, and make sure it was carried out better than anyone else could do it.

How, why, when and what, led him to discover my mother I never found out. She was the youngest child of future Lt-Colonel Frederick Birch of the Royal Artillery. He was commander of

7

No 3 (Kohat) Mountain Battery stationed on the North-West Frontier of India. Equipped with three-inch calibre portable guns carried on mules, they were in constant action against the wild Frontier tribes such as Afridis, Mahsuds, Wazirs and other such fierce and belligerent characters. Kohat was an armed camp, not far from Peshawar in what is now Pakistan, and was actually in tribal territory. Birch had just retired and had taken a house at Shanklin in the Isle of Wight. Two of his children, Gertrude and Colvin, were grown up and already in India. The third, Eileen, my mother, aged nearly 20 was with her parents. Colvin was an officer in the 9th Ghurkha Rifles and Gertrude – oh horror! – had married a *box-wallah*, a Director of the Alliance Bank in Calcutta. The Birches had served in India for generations and had taken an active part in the suppression of the Great Sepoy Mutiny of 1857. Frederick Birch was a good friend of 'Bobs', Lord Roberts of Kandahar, the future Commander-in-Chief in the Boer War.

Despite being a Gunner's wife, my grandmother was no water-buffalo; had been the Belle of the London Season of 1880. She was one of the innumerable children, I never found out how many, but at least eight, of Sir Reginald Leeds, Baronet of Croxton Hall in the Midlands. It is a large house, and all the work he ever did was to manage his estate; but he had a part-time occupation, more a hobby, that of Queen's Messenger, carrying the Diplomatic Bag from London to various foreign British Embassies. Of course he did not carry the bags himself, he would have men to do that, but he was in overall charge, and anything especially secret he would carry chained around his waist. His emblem of office was the diamond-studded brooch in the form of a greyhound, which all Queen's Messengers carry. He did all his travelling by ship, train or coach, and would be away, sometimes for months. He would return full of tales of hairbreadth escapes from brigands or wild animals such as wolves. I remember as a child my grandmother telling me how, on one occasion, he was chased by a huge pack of wolves as he was driven in a troika, a three-horse sleigh across the frozen and snowy steppes of Russia.

As the wolves got nearer his two companions began shooting at them, but the creatures only stopped long enough to devour their erstwhile companions and came on again, faster than ever. In the end they had to cut one of the horses loose from the troika for the wolves to eat, whilst they made their escape. Even then, this struck me as a daft sort of thing to do; for without the sleigh the loosed horse would go faster, and with only two horses, the sleigh would go slower. It was obvious whom the wolves would eat first. Personally I considered my great-grandfather Leeds nothing but a great fibber. Later he painted a picture of the incident, and we had it hanging on the wall at Snow View in Naini Tal. It had a dramatic effect on me as a child. It was dusk, and in the falling light there was the troika with the galloping horses driving across the flat, snow-covered steppe. Two long lines of wolves were converging on it, hundreds of them, their leaders with slavering jaws, snapping at the horses' heels. A man in the sleigh was desperately trying to cut one of the horses loose. Another was shooting at the wolves with a rifle, its discharge making a bright slash of crimson against the gathering darkness. The lines of relentless pursuers stretched far away into the corners of the picture; the eyes of the front runners glowing like red-hot coals and fading to flickering points of light in the endless stream of those behind. It quite put me off wolves for a long time. Of course I know now that I had been right all along. He was nothing but a great fibber, a line shooter. Wolves are rarely found in packs of more than about eight. They would never behave in the way he described, and their eyes only shine by reflected light. Furthermore, no wolf in its right mind would attack a sleigh full of armed men.

At sometime during 1880 or 1881, Frederick Birch, home on leave from his battery in Kohat, must have met my grandmother, Lilian Leeds, for in 1882 she followed him out to India and they were married in Peshawar Cathedral. By now he had made No 3 Battery very much his own, and when my grandmother arrived it became a family affair, with her riding at its head, alongside him, whenever they changed station. Two children, Gertrude the elder, and their son Colvin, were born within four years. Then there was a pause until my mother was born, she always claimed as an afterthought, in 1891. I do not know where she was educated, how she was educated or even if she was educated; but she was a clever, intelligent, extremely well-read woman, with an enormous variety of interests. She spent her childhood in Kohat, the pet of the Artillery Sepoys, and could speak Urdu and Pushtu better than English and would pass as a native in either. She could ride like a centaur and was a dead-eye shot with rifle, shotgun or revolver. She loved India. To her it was Home, and she longed for it all the long, rather miserable years she spent in England for the rest of her life; which for her, ended when she left.

Her marriage to my father was a failure from the start. He had come to meet her as she disembarked from the P & O liner at Bombay, and almost immediately dismayed her by his 'meaness', haggling with a flower seller on the quai over a bunch of roses for her. I once tackled him with this, and he was amazed. 'I only did it to show her how well I could speak Urdu,' he said. As it was exactly the kind of thing I would do myself, I could understand it. But he was undoubtedly mean. Ellen Bullock had instilled into into him from an early age the value of the bawbees. For him to spend money was as painful as having a tooth extracted.

I imagine at one time he and my mother must have been attracted to each other. Perhaps he just wanted a wife and thought this beautiful young girl of 20, soft and pliable, happened to be handy and came from the right background. Perhaps she just saw in him a way of getting away from her parents and back to India. Who knows, but they got married on 7 December 1912, her 21st birthday. It was the prelude to a disaster. All that remains of the event is a large silver tray, presented by the officers of the 1st Brahmins.

She told me that the only time they were happy together was for a couple of months early in 1913, when he was sent to command a detachment of his regiment, to guard a very outpost of Empire, a Beau Geste-like fort at Shabkadar on the NWFP in Mohmand Tribal territory; and it must have been here that I was conceived. The fort was under constant attack from tribesmen taking pot shots at it, just for amusement. All the windows were really loop-holes, and large armoured shutters could be pulled across them for protection. They would go to sleep with the occasional clang of a lead bullet against one of them, as a lullaby. Rations, fuel and garrison relief required a full Military Column. The shared danger was a powerful aphrodisiac.

On their return to regimental duty in Bolarum, in the 'Sloth

Belt' of Southern India, romance soon faded. She told me that she found him so physically unattractive she could not even bear him to touch her. My father had strict views on the control and behaviour of his wife. She should be demure and stay at home to attend to his whims. Furthermore, she was not allowed to read any book unless he had read it first and vetted it for anything he described as 'strong meat', such as vague allusions to sex or mild bad language. This censorship made her very angry, but being pregnant all that summer, there was nothing she could do about it. In the meantime, her father, Frederick Birch, had died, and my grandmother set off like a thunderclap to stay alternately with her married children, which she continued to do until her death in 1947. My father found this exceeding irksome.

2

Directly I was born, my grandmother took charge of me, jealously guarding me from my mother. At least this is what she told me herself, when I taxed her with lack of interest in her new-born child. My grandmother told a different tale, saying that my mother 'much preferred dachshunds to babies', and who can deny she had a viable point, with which I entirely agree; also that she was so tied up in the general social whirl of garrison life, she was only too thankful to have a squalling child taken off her hands. In fact no Memsahib, grandmother or otherwise, ever had to deal with a squalling child, as each one had its own Ayah or Indian nursemaid to look after it. No yells, smells or sleepless nights for Memsahibs.

I imagine the truth is halfway between the two. My grandmother wished somehow to renew her lost youth by once more having a baby in her arms, whilst my mother was enjoying herself too much to care much either way. It must have been a heady time for her, an attractive, intelligent, athletic girl of 22, let loose in the almost endless social round of an Indian Cantonment during the cold weather, with at least six officers to each female. There was a curious and set code of behaviour to all this. Unmarried girls were fair game, and most went around with a 'tail' of young men, reminiscent of a Highland Chieftain. There was both safety and self-esteem in numbers. Directly a girl became engaged, she was taboo and all pursuit ceased, even if her fiancé was posted away or sent on a long course, such as signalling or machine gun, which could last three months. I suppose there was some logic in this. She must love the man, or she would not have agreed to marry him; so what was the point of pursuing a lost cause? Flogging a dead horse, as it were. Besides, it was considered 'damned bad form'. Furthermore, it might happen to you one day, and it was comforting to know no-one would be chasing your own girl bow-legged, whilst you were away. However once married, she became fair game again, especially if her husband was posted away or on a signalling or machine gun course. So it can be seen that such courses were not popular with the newly married, except perhaps for their wives, footloose and fancy-free once more.

From this it might be assumed that life in India at this time was one great heaving brothel. The exact opposite was the case. Most of the flirtations were nothing more than romantic friendships, platonic in the extreme, though some might result in hand-holding and chaste kissing. People who were not married going to bed with each other was highly frowned upon, and if discovered, led to social ostracism. Any unmarried girl so 'compromised', or even under suspicion of being compromised, would find her chances of attracting and landing a future husband very difficult. Word would get about that 'she did it', and girls with such a reputation were deemed to be ruined, and the man concerned a 'cad', unless he made amends by marrying her. If not, she was no longer marriage-able material, and in an age when marriage was the only career open to a woman, this was a very serious business.

There was great ignorance on matters sexual altogether, and fear of pregnancy kept many women as chaste and pure as snow and maybe more so. My mother was completely ignorant of all such matters, and on the night of her wedding found, to her indignation and amazement, that the rather charming companion of rides, picnics and dances had turned into a slightly evil-smelling, naked, hairy monster in bed with her, doing quite unmentionable things, of which she had never even dreamt. Besides, it hurt like hell. Furthermore, I doubt my father was any great shakes when it came to sex anyway.

But by far the greatest obstacle to promiscuity was sheer lack of opportunity. There was nowhere anybody could go without being discovered by one or more of the horde of Indian servants who watched, waited upon, and were on call 24 hours a day in case they were needed for some trivial duty. And servants talk. Someone's Ayah or bearer would hear or see something suspicious, and it would be all round the Cantonment quicker than

13

the speed of light. Through their servants, every European in the Station knew what every other was doing, thinking or saying almost before they knew what they were doing, thinking or saying themselves. A clandestine affair would be as difficult for a gold-fish in a bowl. As for adultery, anyone having an adulterous affair with a brother officer's wife would be put on the next train and boat Home, and made to resign his commission.

A further protection for everybody was the very much greater formality in use. Christian names were only used by intimates, such as husband and wife or engaged couples. Men called the women Miss, Mrs or Lady so and so. They called each other simply by their surname, or a nickname, of which there were a host of stereotypes. Women called the men Mr followed by their surname, or Captain, Major, Colonel and so on. It was a great thrill, almost like a first kiss, when a man she liked, 'inadvertently by accident', called a girl by her Christian name, to test the temperature of the water as it were. My Uncle Robin, who was by no means a slouch when it came to romantic friendships, had been going around with the same girl for some months, a rarity for him. 'Do you know, Mr Willoughby,' she said, 'everyone is saying we are engaged.' 'Ah,' he replied, 'but we know better, don't we'! Which, I gather, brought the romantic friendship to a close.

For my mother, there were compensations for her rather stolid married life, in the way of a non stop round of routs, balls, dances, mixed hockey, tennis, riding picnics, both by day and in the moon-light, local shooting, continual flattery and pursuit by an unending coterie of attractive young men. What girl could have failed to have had her head turned, or to regard my father as rather serious-minded and a bit of a bore? It was convenient, too, to let her mother take care of her new-born son, but by doing so, she lost me altogether. My grandmother took her place entirely in my affections. Directly Turkey entered the Great War, sometime in 1915, my father went off with his Regiment to fight in Mesopotamia, where he won a very good DSO; so the problem of coping and pleasing him was solved for a bit.

My earliest recollection of life must have been in 1917, when I was four, and we were all living in a large house called Snow View in Naini Tal. My tooth glass on the bathroom shelf bore a picture

14

of a bearded King George V dressed in Admiral's uniform. Night and morning as I cleaned my teeth, I used to stand to attention and salute the 'King-Emperor'. By this time I had two cousins, Awdry, born in 1910 to the *box-wallah* named Stuart and my grandmother's elder daughter Gertrude, and 'Twig', son of Colvin Birch of the 9th Ghurkha Rifles. who was eighteen months younger than myself. Colvin had somewhat foolishly stayed in a house where a girl called Marjorie was also staying. She was so terrified of a raging thunderstorm that somehow she found herself fleeing for protection to his bed. In those days and in such circumstances, there was only one honourable thing the poor fellow could do, and that was to marry her. It was a disaster and he died some ten years later of pneumonia, thankful to escape. On a one to ten scale of horrendous women, Marjorie Birch would have certainly rated about nine and a half.

In the meantime my Aunt Gertie had ditched her *box-wallah* and taken up with a young cavalry officer called James Logan, who had won an MC in France and been posted back to India to recover. *Box-wallah* Stuart's Alliance Bank of India, of which he was a Director, had folded. and the not inconsiderable amount of money the Birchs had in it had gone too. They were highly incensed that, knowing it was about to become bankrupt, he had not warned them in time to get their money out. Had he done so, the situation would merely have become worse more quickly.

Naini Tal was the hill station for most of the garrison Cantonments of the United Provinces (UP), now Uttar Pradesh, which included such places as Cawnpore, Lucknow, Fategarh and Bareilly. It had been built around a lake – the word *tal* – means a lake in the hollow of the mountains which rose steeply all round it. Snow View was at the top of a ridge, some thousand feet above the lakeside and on its Northern side. From it could be seen all the big peaks of the Nepal Himalayas. There cannot be any view in the world to compare with it. In the evening, all the long wonderful chain of enormous mountains would glow pink in the setting sun.

Living semi-permanently at Snow View were my grandmother, Aunt Gertrude, known as 'Auntie', with her small daughter, my first cousin, Awdry, James Logan, who had now become Uncle Jimmy, and seemed to be on perpetual leave, and myself.

15

Occasional visitors were my father, back on short leave from Mespot, and my mother complete with the usual quota of dachshunds and various 'uncles' she brought with her from time to time. She also kept a very nice horse in the stables, a grey, which I was occasionally allowed to ride. Other visitors were Colvin Birch with Marjorie and their little son 'Twig', whom I am afraid Awdry and I used to gang up on and bully.

It was a large rambling house with deep verandahs, set in about eight acres of garden and a ramshackle tennis court. Beyond the ridge, sweeping away from the main gate, were three high peaks, Cheena, Liriakanta and Alma, thickly wooded and rising to some 9000 feet. All round the 'compound', as the garden was called, was a fence, made from long wooden beams fitted into large, white-painted, stone pillars, some five feet high and a yard square. It was the habit of the local monkeys, grey in colour with black faces, called lungoors, to sit on these pillars and watch the house. Any food or shiny object was immediately seized and carried off. The dining room had large doors facing onto the verandah, and the animals would be in and out like a flash, even grabbing food from one's plate. *Khidmatgars* and other servants would rush out, wave sticks and shout at the creatures, who took it all in good heart, and waited for the next opportunity. The house was painted white and had a red tin roof, the red colour being the rust with which it was covered. The roof leaked like a sieve from all the bolt holes which held it in place. Every time it rained, water poured through and there were basins and jugs all over the floor below to catch the drips. Directly the rain stopped, countless men would be sent up with putty in an attempt to caulk up the holes. It was my great delight to go with them and make myself a general nuisance, but as all Indians love children, and tolerate them to an almost impossible extent, nobody seemed to mind.

The most impressive thing about the house was the huge ball-room. which we used as the drawing room. At least it seemed huge to me, as if you could fit two normal-sized houses into it. Folding doors led into the dining room, where we sat around a table which could take at least 14 guests for dinner parties. From the dining room, various doors led off into the living accommodation. Each person had their own set of rooms, consisting of a big bedroom, dressing room and bathroom or '*ghussal khana*'. There must have been a considerable number of these rooms, for my grandmother, in whose room I slept, had one set, Aunt Gertie, another which she shared with my cousin Awdry, and to maintain appearances, Uncle Jimmy had a third. There were also always guests or visitors of one kind and another, such as my mother, who had come up to stay, and had their own suite of rooms. The place was like a rabbit warren, probably in more ways than one.

By this time, what with tales of Little Red Riding Hood, and my grandfather fleeing from the beasts across the snowy wastes of Russia, I was into wolves in a big way; simply terrified of the animals. There was an alcove in my grandmother's room where I was convinced a wolf was hiding every night, just about to jump out and devour me. As long as the dining room door was left slightly ajar and I could hear the grown-ups talking at dinner, I knew the wolf would keep off. Aunt Gertie, 'Auntie', knew this because my grandmother had told her of my fears, and the reason for leaving the door ajar. This made no difference. The first thing Auntie did on coming into dinner was to take a rather vicious pleasure in closing the door, 'to teach me not to be a little coward'. Now 80 years later, I can still remember lying shivering with terror every night, until I finally fell asleep, waiting for the wolf to jump out and gobble me up.

There was no running water, flush sanitation or electric light at Snow View. The bath in the *ghussal khana* consisted of a large tin tub, set in a tiled area with a raised rim around it, and a hole at one end for the water to drain out. This hole was also an open invitation to snakes, for whom the *ghussal khana* was always cool and you would often find them wrapped around the large iron container for the cold water. On one occasion, a highly poisonous small snake, called a krait, which could kill in two minutes flat, fell into my bath from the ceiling. How it climbed up there was a mystery, and I do not know which of us was the more astonished, the snake or myself; but I certainly did a record leap out of that bath. Water for baths was prepared by a servant called a '*bhisti*', or water-carrier. Only *bhistis* were allowed to touch or prepare water, and he would bring in the drinking water in a large goatskin bag. There was a tap somewhere in the compound from which the water was drawn. It had been purified by the lakeside and pumped up to an intermediate pumping station and container tank, which we passed halfway up the hill to the house, the water hissing and gurgling in the most fascinating way.

The *bhisti* kept the bathwater in old kerosene tins, holding some four gallons each. These he heated over a large log fire, and brought in to pour into the bath, adding cold water as required. This would be finger tested by the Sahib's bearer for correct temperature, before he would report to his master '*ghussl tiar hai Huzoor*'. 'your bath is ready, Sir'. It can be imagined that with five or six Sahibs all calling for their baths at the same time, how difficult this was for the *bhisti*. He usually had a couple of boys working under him to help, and I can never remember anyone having to wait for their bath. The most extraordinary thing about Indian servants was their adaptability, the way they rose to each and every occasion. However many baths were required, they were always ready, even if double the usual number. One could come home two hours after the correct time of the evening meal, with 14 unexpected guests, tell the cook you wanted food and within an hour the most delicious five-course dinner would appear, soft footed *khidmatgars* serving the dishes and liveried bearers standing behind each Sahib's chair.

There was respect and friendship between master and servant, but no familiarity of any kind. Apart from officers of British regiments, who were either too ignorant, too stupid or too stuck up and prejudiced to learn Urdu, except for enough to order a whisky and soda, or 'bring my horse', it was a deadly insult for a native to address a Sahib in English. As a small boy of five or six, I was exempt from any of this ritual. Not only were the servants my friends, but I was on familiar terms with every one of them, played with their children and spoke their language better than English; speaking it even to my parents. The dog boys were my especial friends. Not only did each Sahib have his own personal servant, but each of his dogs had its own personal dog boy, who fed it, groomed it and generally cared for its welfare. Most of the dogs were extremely snobbish and took it all as a matter of course, followed their white masters everywhere, and only went back to their dog boy when it suited them. Besides, dogs are not fools.

Before every meal its bowl of food had to be shown to its master, to be sure it was up to standard. Dogs knew exactly to whom they owed their allegiance. The most popular breed of dog was the smooth-haired, white fox terrier. They appeared in every photograph in every issue of every regimental magazine, sitting in front of the Regimental Polo team. In fact as all British officers looked exactly like each other, the same photograph was used, year after year, merely the captions and names being changed. No one was any the wiser, and it made the Editor's life much easier.

On the very lowest rung of the Hindu caste system was the 'untouchable', from which came the '*maitar*', the sweeper. There were several at Snow View. As there was no flush sanitation, it was their job to clear out the thunder-boxes, with their Welsh-hat-shaped receptacles. It was also his job to collect, empty and clean every chamber pot beneath the beds. The Indian servant system was that each individual could only do specific tasks within the competence of his caste. Thus only a *maitar* could clean lavatories, only a *bhisti* deal with water, only a *mali* work in the garden. It was in fact a huge trades union which safeguarded jobs and ensured full employment. Its real drawback was that a *maitar* could never be anything else. He was an untouchable, born to such work all his life. There was no alternative. He was untouchable and despised for it. There were also certain jobs that Muslims, who have no caste system, could be employed upon, such as in the kitchen as cook or washer-up, serve at table, or best of all be a Sahib's bearer or personal attendant and oriental Jeeves.

The cook or *khansama* was lord of the kitchen. The words *khan saman* mean 'lord of the things'. Under him would be a boy, possibly son, nephew or cousin, being trained as a cook. With the exception of hot curries, the food was completely English. Also in the kitchen would be employed a couple of '*masolchies*', who did all the washing-up and kept the place clean and tidy for Memsahib's daily inspection, and no Commanding Officer ever inspected his regiment more closely than the average English Memsahib on her kitchen rampage. Dysentery, typhoid, enteric and cholera were rife, not to mention the usual local 'Rajah's Revenge'. There were few if any antidotes other than constant vigilance that things were kept as clean as they should be. Serving

19

at the table were the *'khidmatgars'*, *khidmat* meaning service. They were usually Muslims, and they would be dressed in the house livery whilst waiting at table. As there was no electricity, it was also their job to clean and prepare the lovely paraffin (kerosene) oil lamps. It was my delight and joy to 'help' them do this every morning, polishing the chimneys until they shone, and buffing up the brass bases with metal polish until they gleamed like burnished gold. I have always loved the light from an oil lamp ever since. Perhaps it reminds me of my childhood, but its glow seems to have a softness and a clarity that electricity can never equal.

Bearers were always middle-aged and stately, full of their own and their Sahib's dignity, which they jealously guarded. They were usually Muslims, often old soldiers from an Indian Regiment and almost invariably came from the District of Poonch in North-West India. In fact, after Independence in 1947 with all the Sahibs gone, one wonders what happened to the inhabitants of this area, whose only source of employment was supplying bearers to British officers? Everybody had a bearer. It was impossible not to have one. He was at the top of the salary scale with about 22 rupees a month (£1.80p). You can imagine what the others got. However with 16 annas to the rupee, it was possible to live quite well on 4 annas a day and the bearer was comparatively rich. I never heard anyone complain, and I certainly would have done, living among them as it were. The bearer would wear his master's regimental or other livery, stand behind his chair at meals, put out and put away his clothes, be responsible for his packing and welfare when he travelled and generally be at his beck and call for 24 hours a day. My father brought a Turkish prisoner of war, called Abdullah, back with him after the fighting was finished in Mesopotamia, as a bearer, who was with him for years and kept up a correspondence with him through letter-writers until my father died in 1949. He was devoted to him.

Other servants were the *syces* or grooms, one to each horse. They were either Muslims or Hindus. Perhaps one of the most important member of the staff was the *chowkidar* or night-watchman. Old India hands often allude to the Coldstream Guards as the *'Tunda pani Chowkidars'* or 'coldwater night watchmen'.

20

The *chowkidar* was almost invariably an old man, past doing any other work, and a Muslim. His task was to defend the house against thieves and robbers, '*budmarshes*' as they were called. To do this and show willing he carried a long stick, a '*lathi*', about an inch thick and six feet long, bound with a brass collar at one end. The Indian Police can be seen wielding them with great effect from time to time on the television. In fact all the defending the *chowkidar* ever did was to sleep all night on a string bed or '*charpoy*', on the verandah. On cold nights he would bring along a small boy or even two, sons of nephews, cousins or friends, to share his bed and keep him warm. Nobody even considered it strange. A *chowkidar* was an essential form of house insurance which also ensured employment for old men in the twilight of their years. Woe betide any Sahib whose house did not have a *chowkidar*. He would wake up one morning to find every stitch of clothing, jewellery and furniture had disappeared during the night.

Many *chowkidars* were Pathans from the fierce tribes along the North-West Frontier, whose propensity for boys was well-known, and probably why they liked one or two sharing their beds. A popular Pathan song, the '*Zakhmi Dhil* or Wounded Heart', starts off with the words, 'There's a boy across the river with a bottom like a peach, but alas I cannot swim!'. They also have a saying, 'A woman for necessity, a goat for pleasure, but a boy for sheer delight'. When the Royal Welsh Fusiliers, whose Regimental Mascot is a large white goat, arrived at Landi Kotal in the heart of Pathan Afridi country, the locals were puzzled and amazed. 'What! Only one goat among so many?' Later the Goat-Corporal was the subject of one of the most celebrated court martials in the British Army; that of being charged, 'Contrary to Good Order and Military Discipline, he did upon certain dates, Prostitute the King's Goat'. Apparently he had found himself a nice little earner, hiring the animal out to local tribesmen. His defence was that he had only done so for the animal's delectation and pleasure, being sorry for it in its celibate state. Furthermore, he had been wise enough to place its earnings, the amount was impossible to assess, in the correct Regimental Goat Fund Account. His plea was accepted, probably because no member of the Court could keep a straight face.

21

Finally there were the Ayahs, the only women servants. There was an Ayah who cared for and tended each European child in the same way as a Nanny would at Home. Most Memsahibs also had their own personal Ayah, who acted as ladies maid, and did much the same for her as the bearer would for his master. She would take care of her clothes, laying them out for the innumerable changes during the day and evening. Some Memsahibs had a bearer as well; the Ayah doing duty looking after a child. My grandmother had a Christian couple by the original name of Mary and Joseph, Hindu converts, which led to endless difficulties with the other servants, who regarded them with suspicion and dismay. Mary would look after me, but I do not think that Joseph was ever a very good bearer. Awdry had a Tibetan Ayah, recruited in Darjeeling where she was born, and considered vastly superior to my Mary. It was not everyone who could boast a Tibetan Ayah.

For some reason, my grandmother had become too infirm to ride a horse. I don't quite know why this should have been, as she was only about 60 at the time, and lived to a great age; and could walk extremely well. However, she used to be carried up and down the hill to Naini Tal and around Snow View in a kind of open sedan chair or palanquin called a 'dandy'. It was white in colour, made of wood with basket sides and shaped like a canoe with cross-carrying poles at each end. The whole contraption was carried by four men known as 'jomponnies', recruited from the local hillmen and very strong. There were always five jomponnies with a Sirdar or Captain, who took his turn at carrying with the others. They were all dressed in her livery with the Royal Artillery badge in their pugaries or turbans. They were invariably Muslims. I usually found them also my especial friends, and used to play football with their children on our disused tennis court. Whenever my grandmother was taken out in the dandy, I used to trot along beside it, chatting to the men.

On one such occasion we had a particularly unpleasant experience. My grandmother had a small, very dark brown Pekinese dog called Mowgli. Wherever she went the dog would go too, and when she went out riding in the dandy, the little dog used to sit beside her or on her lap, snuffling and panting in the way that Pekinese love to do. It was far too proud and Chinese as to do anything as common as walking. One afternoon we were all out for a walk, 'sniffing the air' as the Indians say, with my grandmother in the dandy, the little dog sitting on her lap and my cousin Awdry and I trotting along beside. Just outside our main gates lay the dirt road to old Government House, standing rather grandly in its huge deserted compound. The road skirted the edge of the thickly wooded hillside, known as the 'cud'. On its inner side was a high stone wall, along which in wet weather crawled many fascinating coloured snails, which I used to collect and keep in a tin and wonder why they all died. The cud itself was jungle, home to every kind of wild animal: brown bears, langoor monkeys, leopards, even the occasional tiger. Man-eating ones appeared from time to time to kill the odd villager, but none had been rash enough to try out a Sahib, or even worse, a Memsahib. I quiver at its subsequent fate had it eaten a Memsahib. The entire Indian Army would have been called out to dispose of it.

When we were about a mile down the road, there was suddenly a noise as if some big animal was breaking through the undergrowth, and we could see the form of a large leopard about 20 feet away, level with us at the edge of the jungle. Mowgli must have seen it too, for with a terrific growl he leapt straight out of the dandy and charged, barking madly, his one thought to defend his mistress. I can think of few more unequal contests. With a single snap of its jaws, the leopard took Mowgli and made off. There was deathly silence. Now of course if there is one thing a leopard enjoys above all else, it is a good juicy, fattened-up European dog, and this one must have been very surprised to find its dinner arriving like that out of thin air, on a plate as it were. If anyone deserves a VC perhaps it was that little dog, its gallantry and effectiveness equal to that of Colonel Jones in the Falklands, living up to the motto of my grandmother's regiment, the Royal Artillery, '*Quo fas et gloria ducunt*' 'Where duty and glory lead'.

Whenever tales of self-sacrifice and heroism are told, there will loom up in my memory through the mists of time, the wraith of Mowgli leaping from the dandy to lay down his life in defence of his people, for we were all part of his pack. Perhaps he has achieved a kind of immortality too; for Awdry and I remember what he did all these years later, and my nine-year-old granddaughter says she will remember it all her life. To me, Mowgli will never be Kipling's small village boy, rescued and bought up by the Seonee wolf pack, but Mowgli the little dog who died to protect us from a leopard. However, it does emphasise the folly of volunteering for anything, especially if it is dangerous. You are more than likely to end up in a pickle, such as being shot or maybe eaten. At my prep school I was much impressed by a story from Daudet's *'Lettres de Mon Moulin'* which always made me think of Mowgli. In it, a certain Monsieur Seguin had a goat, which, tired of its placid existence in his field, escaped to the hills, and spent the night battling with the local wolf. It got eaten in the end, but the moral of the tale is 'that a single hour of glorious life is worth an age without a name'. Mowgli the dog and Monsieur Seguin's goat are among the immortals.

As for the leopard, it was probably after one of the big grey lungoor monkeys which were everywhere and formed part of its regular diet. It could have mistaken Awdry or myself for small monkeys, and that was why it was following us. A single rush and away with one of us, probably me as I was the smaller, in its jaws, before anyone could do anything. Instead it got Mowgli. It was more than just for his mistress that he died. The monkeys loathed and despised leopards at all times. On one occasion I thought I would give them a surprise by covering myself in one of the innumerable leopard skins which littered Snow View and go into the jungle wearing it. Within minutes I was surrounded by a chattering, snarling group of big males, who made it very obvious that they did not like me at all and were going to do something about it, such as tear me into small pieces and enjoy doing it. Fortunately my plight was seen by the *jomponnies*, who rushed to my rescue, shouting and waving *lathis*. If there is one thing it taught me, was that you should never monkey around with monkeys.

3

Kite flying in Naini Tal was the great local sport, as it still is all over India. Kite battles took place throughout the country, the object being to cut one's opponent's kite loose with the powdered-glass-covered, cutting string which connected the first 30 feet to one's own. As he was trying to do exactly the same thing to you, a single moment's inattention or tightening of the string would end in its being cut and the loss of your kite. They were expensive, 4 to 8 annas each (2p to 4p), but when it is realised that this was equal to many a man's daily wage, the loss of a kite was a serious business. They were beautiful things and I loved them. Not unnaturally they were kite-shaped, but almost square, and measured about two feet across the shoulders. Made of very thin, light delicate paper, almost like tissue or rice paper, they tore easily and you kept a supply of the paper handy to mend the holes. The glue used was starch from rice and you made it up yourself. It was the colours and the smell of the kites in the bazaar that was so fascinating, green, blue, red, yellow or variegated. Each one you saw you wanted to own. There they were hanging from rails on the stalls, swinging and rustling gently in the wind. Below were balls of the flying and cutting string.

From the *jomponnies'* children, I learnt how to make my own kites. You bought the paper and the thin bamboo struts, cut to regulation size, in the bazaar. First there was the central rib, and tied to this, a crosspiece, two-thirds of the way up; bent in the form of a bow and fixed to the sides with the rice paste. They fitted into a pocket formed from spare paper. Similar pockets were made to hold the central rib at top and bottom. The fixing string was now attached. It had to be in the form of a right-angled triangle, with

25

the point of the triangle exactly over the point of balance, which was a third of the length of the kite. This measurement was absolutely vital or it would not fly true, but merely dive into the ground.

Flying a kite was an art which took years to learn. In the beginning you needed a good wind to get it to fly, but an expert could get one up in apparently no wind at all. The novice needed someone to hold the kite about 30 feet away and let go; those who knew how merely held it up at arm's length and released it. It would then take to the air, and the flyer raised it further by a series of jerks on the string. In a tournament, the object was to make your kite swoop down on your opponent's and cut its string by a sawing action of your own. The trophy was then yours if you could find where it had fluttered down. Small boys made a good living, finding and selling them. When I came home in 1922, my grand-father, knowing my interest in kites, bought me a large cloth one, and we went flying it on the front at Hove. A good stiff offshore breeze was blowing, and I had got it up a couple of hundred feet to the extent of its string, which was fastened to a wooden handle. 'Let me fly it,' said my grandfather, and promptly let go. The last I saw of my kite was it flying out to sea on its way to France. The water pressure on the wooden handle gave enough tension to keep it flying. It was also the last time I ever flew a kite.

The town of Naini itself straggled around the lake. There was the usual bazaar and native part of the town, quite separate from the European. Two big shops I remember vividly. They were Whiteaway Laidlaws and Valerios. Whiteaway Laidlaw was a huge emporium based on the Army and Navy Stores in London, where you could buy anything from clockwork train sets to camping gear, clothes and high-velocity rifles. Valerios was quite different. It was kept by an Italian and sold ice cream, sticky buns and all kinds of delicious foods. It was also a very good restaurant, and the trysting place of many officers up on leave from the plains, and whoever it was they were romancing at the time. Every Thursday, when my mother was in Naini we would ride down from Snow View for lunch at Valerios, past the hissing '*bumba*' or water-pumping station and large water tank half way up the hill. I would ride my 20-year-old, rather lifeless, pony and long to exchange it for my mother's magnificent grey. Lunch always consisted of everything I liked best and invariably finished with a huge ice cream. Afterwards we would visit the bazaar, where if I were lucky, she would buy me a new kite. I loved Thursdays, but what I liked best was that she spoke and treated me as if I were a fellow grown-up.

Everywhere the British went throughout their Empire, there was always The Club. Much mud has been slung at them for supposedly putting up notices at the gates of these clubs such as 'No natives or dogs'. Which of course is utter nonsense, because there could never have been any ban on dogs, and no native would be rash enough to dare to go in unless working there. Besides, few, if any, could read their own language, let alone a notice in English. The Club was the centre of social life. People could stay there, it served excellent meals, and there were dances in the ballroom every Saturday. During wartime, officers would be in uniform, but any civilians would have to wear 'white tie and tails'. Only officers and those of a similar status could be members of the Club, and certainly no Indians, even Maharajahs. It was quite impossible to imagine the consequences of one even dancing with a white girl. In Naini Tal, The Club owned the polo ground and organised the polo games. It also ran the Yacht Club. The lake was quite large, a couple of miles long and there was wonderful sailing, most of the yachts being of the dinghy type, not unlike a modern Wayfarer. Being in the hollow of the mountains, the wind on the lake could change suddenly and without warning. The yachtsmen were often inexperienced to the point of complete ignorance. They would take a boat out, it would capsize and they would drown. Everyone said 'How sad, such a charming young man' and carry on as before. Nobody tried to stop the yachting because it was dangerous or inflicted any of the innumerable rules and regulations which would be enforced today. You were informed of the danger and what the wind could do. If you ignored it and got yourself drowned ... well too bad!

Looking back I cannot help a feeling of guilt that more was not done for the British soldier, the Other Rank, for whom there was nothing at all, yet there were many thousands of them sweltering on the plains all year round. There was nothing more for them in the way of amusement than their unit could provide, such as football, athletics, occasional swimming pool, unit libraries and rest rooms. From time to time, units would arrange Sergeants' and All Ranks' dances. There were few girls other than the daughters of the many Eurasian families who ran all the Indian Railways. Muslim and Hindu parents guarded their own womenfolk with the utmost jealousy. Thus there were only the raddled whores in the local brothels, who cost about 4 annas (2p) a time. No wonder venereal disease was a problem. As a six-year-old at the time however, I was scarcely concerned with such matters.

In garrison towns served by the railways, many British soldiers met and often married girls whose fathers themselves had either married Indian or Eurasian girls. They spoke English with a curious Welsh-like lilt, called '*chi chi*', and always talked of England as 'Home', although none had ever been, or were likely to go there. Most of the girls were breathtakingly beautiful. Merle Oberon, the film star, was one. They would flock to the Sergeants' and All Ranks' dances, their faces covered with powder to look as white as possible. There were many unkind jokes and stories told of them. One was about such a girl at a Sergeants' dance, being asked rather pompously, 'For the pleasure of this dance', and replying 'Dance you may have, but for pleasure,' nodding towards her companion, 'you must ask my sister, I am for matrimonial purpose onlee.'

On one occasion in Naini Tal I did something which I have regretted ever since. Somewhere, somehow, I had acquired a dud 8 anna piece, half a rupee (about 4p); and was determined to spend it somehow, such as maybe on a couple of kites. India was full of dud coins, mostly counterfeited in some alloy mixed with lead. Every bank had large flat stones on the counter, upon which the teller would ring each coin he received and upon which every customer did the same with the coins he was given. Seeing an old man of the '*babu*' or clerk type with an umbrella – they always carried an umbrella as a mark of status, sitting on a bench by the lake – I went up to him and asked if he would change my 8 anna piece. '*Ap kelie mujko burri khush hoga*' he said, 'for you it would please me greatly.' Producing two 4 anna pieces, he gave them to me and pocketed my coin without question. It was money for old rope. He didn't even bite or ring it. As obviously the son of a Sahib, he trusted me not to cheat him. The incident has haunted me with shame, not so much perhaps the actual swindle, but the fact that I had destroyed in an old man the faith that 'the British Sahib never cheated'. Furthermore I had deprived him of enough to live on for a couple of days. I wish I could remember what I did with the two 4 anna pieces he gave me. Perhaps I bought a couple of kites after all. It would be a pity not to.

The belief that a Sahib never cheated and that his word was his bond, was very real and was reflected in the chit or chitty system. No officer ever carried more than a few annas around with him, enough to give the beggars who were everywhere. All other payments were made by chits, even for something as trivial as a 'tonga' or pony trap ride. These chits would pass from hand to hand, being used as actual currency, possibly for months, even years, until they finally fetched up at the signer's Club, where he would find them put on his monthly bill. To meet such a bill with a dud cheque was a very serious affair, resulting in court martial and cashiering. Had I been grown-up and found cheating that old man, I would have been in real trouble. At the time I kept very quiet about it, or I would have received a well-deserved beating. My father only beat me once, when I must have been about seven. For some reason I had found some matches and lit a fire which nearly set the surrounding jungle alight, and could have burnt down the house. It certainly cured me of wishing to light a fire ever since.

Forest fires were always a problem around Naini Tal. Every summer it seemed the jungle would blaze, and at night one could see the fires raging on the hills on the other side of the lake and on our own Cheena and Alma. Men were hired to put out these fires, and were paid a rupee a day for doing so, untold wealth. Directly they put one out, they would light another. The opportunity was too good to miss, as were the wages. Another problem was endemic, that of rabies amongst the dogs. Everyone had a dog, and in addition there were the innumerable pariah or pi-dogs scavenging in every bazaar. I was bitten once by a rabid Airedale puppy, and have disliked the breed ever since. Rabies is death, and anyone who has seen a rabid dog will never forget it, the rolling bloodshot eyes full of terror, the slavering jaws, the weaving from side to side of the head, the unsteady gait and the attack upon any and every living thing within reach.

Any warm-blooded animal can get rabies. In India the danger came from domestic dogs and cats, but even more so from those which had no homes and were semi-wild. Jackals too were great carriers of the disease. Wild animals lose all fear of man and often become quite tame. The infection is spread by bite or lick of a scratch or small wound, the organisms being contained in the saliva, which has to enter the bloodstream and then finishes up in the brain. The slightest touch with a scratched hand is enough. Therefore anyone who had been in the remotest contact with a rabid animal, whether bitten or not, had to have the Pasteur treatment. Once the symptoms develop there is no cure, only an end in a dreadful, terrifying painful death after ten days. Furthermore the incubation period is very long, and the threat could hang over one for at least six months.

There are two types of rabies, dumb and rage. With dumb rabies, the animal will crawl away into a corner and does not attack, but will bite anything that disturbs it. With rage it will attack all in sight, and often runs and runs for miles with weaving head, its jaws dripping saliva, biting everything in its path. The first sign that a dog is developing the disease is a change in character, snapping at imaginary flies, and a dislike of water which will develop into a terror as the sickness progresses. A quiet dog will often become unexpectedly vicious and vice versa. The terror of water, even though desperately thirsty, is strange and occurs as well with humans. Rabies was generally known at that time as hydrophobia, hatred of water.

There is still only one antidote, by no means absolutely sure, and that is inoculation. At the time of which I am writing there was only one place where this could be done, at the Pasteur Institute in Kasauli, near Simla, seemingly at the other end of India, a two-day train journey from Naini Tal. As it was essential to get treatment as soon as possible after being bitten, the delay was worrying. So off we set. We had all been in contact with the Airedale, and either been bitten or licked by it, my grandmother, Auntie, Awdry and Uncle Jimmy, not to mention the various servants such as

30

the dog boy, who had been looking after it; accompanied by the usual retinue of assorted bearers and ayahs without which no-one could move a step. The treatment was long, painful and took 28 days.

The Institute was in a large red-brick building with an avenue of dusty neem trees in front of it. Every morning we all went there, lay on a couch and bared our stomachs. On alternate sides each day, a huge and agonising needle was stuck into them, reminiscent of those formerly used to blow up footballs. Very soon our midriffs resembled pin cushions. Everyone was frightfully brave, and as the grown-ups were done first to show an example, we children could not cry either. I don't think the needles were thrust in very far, merely into the stomach muscles, but it seemed at the time about a teacup full of the vaccine was being pumped in, consisting of millions of dead rabies organisms, 'negroid bodies' as they were called, which triggered one's own immune system to destroy anything which looked like them. These negroid bodies are found, on autopsy, in the brains of all creatures who have died of the illness and are a certain sign of its presence. If there was any doubt as to how a dog had died, its brain was sent to Kasauli for analysis, and if found to be positive, the sooner you got the treatment the better. In fact anyone with the brains to grease a gimlet would take the dog's brain along with him, and start the treatment whilst they were still busy doing the analysing. I believe nowadays this anti-rabies treatment remains much the same, but only lasts a fortnight. In these times of Political Correctness, I imagine other words have been found for the negroid bodies. It would hardly do to have a Negro wandering around in one's brain.

In much the same way as children are now taught never to accept sweets from strangers, we were taught never to stroke, pet or have anything to do with a strange dog. It could be incubating rabies and not develop it until long afterwards. No-one really knew when it became infectious. The warnings of childhood and the experience have made me terrified of rabies all my life. I have an irrational fear of the disease, and whenever I am abroad will never allow myself to touch a stray dog or cat. The fear is just as irrational as that which some have of spiders, snakes or mice. It is possible that everybody has some secret phobia. Mine is a mad

31

dog, and anyone who has seen one will perhaps agree that it is the most terrifying sight they are ever likely to witness.

All arrangements with Kasauli had to be made by telegram. In these days of instant communication, it is hard to imagine a time or place without a telephone. Perhaps then, only 80 years ago, there might have been telephones in vice-regal circles, but there were certainly no others. Telegrams or wires, '*tar*' in Urdu, had to be used in any kind of emergency, or if you wanted a quick answer. The telegraph lines were carried on long poles alongside the railway lines. The *tar* had to be written out on a special form, and given to one's bearer or other servant, with the necessary money, to take to the telegraph office. Here he would hand it over to the '*babu*' in charge, usually a rather fat Hindu, teeth and lips stained bright red from chewing betel-nut leaves or '*bhang*', with a very high-flown knowledge of the English language. A *babu* always used the longest word possible, such as some Americans do today, in order to impress or to make a meaning impossible to mistake. For instance he would always say 'proceeding on furlough' instead of 'going on leave'. Often he would get his words mixed up, leading to many apocryphal stories; such as the one of a *babu* asking another, 'Who is that venereal gentleman with horn-rimmed testicle?' and getting the reply, in the wonderful sing-song lilt they affected, 'Oh, but you are ignorant and rumbunctious fellow, that is Rectum, come and be seduced.' As there is no definite article in Urdu, this would usually be left out. I am glad to say the tradition lingers on, and even quite recently, my heart was made glad, '*mera dhil khush hogia*', when I heard a *babu*'s modern counterpart threaten a hotel with 'I am prostituting you with sexual relation', when he meant 'prosecuting for racial discrimination'.

Babus were always incredibly myopic, wore glasses as thick as the bottom of wine bottles, holding anything to read about an inch from one eye. Despite this, telegrams were usually tapped out in Morse code with great accuracy. Every now and again, the operator would pause to spit, a stream of scarlet betel-juice shooting out like a chameleon's tongue, to slaughter, with deadly aim, some unfortunate fly or other insect on the floor. The same process took place at the other end, from where it was delivered by

32

a smart uniformed orderly of the Indian Post Office, who would wait for an answer. It was of course also possible to telegraph Home, and all the business of Empire was conducted from London in this way.

The postal system was very good, all letters being carried by the official mail trains. It took three weeks for a letter to reach England and a further three weeks for a reply. Letters from Home arrived once a week as the P&O liners came in. Thus although you could get a letter regularly once a week, the news it contained was always three weeks old. In addition to the telegram and the post, there was the very extensively used chit system. 'Chit' really meant a letter in Urdu before it became corrupted to mean any piece of paper with something written on it. Invitations to dinner or other functions were sent out in this way. A note would be given to a servant to take round to a neighbour and wait for an answer. 'So and so has just arrived, do come and have dinner with us this evening to meet him'. *Syces* were often used as such messengers, for they could exercise the Sahib's horse at the same time. In plays and films about the British Raj, the deplorable habit is prevalent of calling Sahibs, 'Sar-heeb'. The word should always be pronounced to rhyme with garb, or Saab, the Swedish motor car, for that matter.

In addition to running the mail, the Indian Post Office had a wonderful system of *dak* bungalows, throughout the country. *Dak* means post, and is pronounced 'dork'. They dated to the days before the railways, when they were staging posts for the horse or bullock-drawn mail, and were never done away with. They could only be used by Europeans and their servants for whom quarters were also provided, and consisted of two or three bedrooms, *ghussal khanas* and a dining room. The whole was surrounded by a deep verandah. They were often thatched, a home for innumerable snakes, lizards, birds, civet cats and insects of every description. *Charpoys* or wooden string beds were provided to sleep on, often full of fleas and bedbugs, plus chairs and tables. You had to bring your own bedding and everything else. Standard procedure on arrival was to disinfect everything in sight by a liberal use of Keatings Powder.

The *dak* bungalow had its own permanent staff, consisting of

33

khansama, maitar or sweeper, and the *mali* who cared for the garden, usually a few poor shrivelled-up weeds. The food was invariably the same throughout: porridge, eggs and bacon for breakfast, and for all other meals, mulligatawny soup, very tough roast or curried chicken and caramel custard. The object of this was for ease of administration and to dissuade guests from staying too long. In any case, 48 hours was the longest anyone was allowed to stay, for *dak* bungalows were essentially places of transit. They were extensively used by Deputy Commissioners of the ICS on their rounds of their Districts, usually about the size of Wales.

There was no train to Naini Tal. The railway stopped short at Kathgodam, some 25 miles away, in the foothills at the edge of the plains. This usually meant a night's stop in the *dak* bungalow on the way down. Everything had to be carried by *tonga* or bullock cart. There were no motor cars or lorries. *Tongas* or pony traps were the universal method for any local journey. The trap consisted of a two-wheeled vehicle with a canopy over it. The driver sat in front and there was a padded bench behind for the passengers. It was pulled by a single horse, often lame, nearly always underfed, with its ribs showing, and chafed by harness galls. They were normally hideously overloaded with natives. As the *tonga-wallah* or driver usually earned so little that he was as hungry as his horse, it was difficult not to accept things as they were, which everyone did. *Tongas* were the taxis of India. Without them one could not have moved.

The railhead at Kathgodam was on the narrow 3 foot 6 inch gauge of the RKR, the Rohilkund & Kumaon Railway. It went down to Bareilly and met the broad gauge 5 foot 3 inch BB&CI, the Bombay Baroda & Central India Railway, at the huge rail junction at Shahjehanpore. As the standard 4 foot $8^1/_2$ inch gauge in Britain and Europe had long been established before any were built in India, it is difficult to understand why these particular gauges were chosen, and if they were, why one of them could not have been made the standard. The diversity led to much confusion and endless delay.

For Europeans, even Indians who could afford it, rail travel was very comfortable, though they could never be mixed in the same

34

carriage. The compartments were the size of a small room and contained four let-down bunks, two of which were permanently down for people to sit on during the day, but could be raised if they wished to use camp chairs instead. A door led into a small *ghussal khana*, with a tin tub in the middle, a shower, and also the loo with the usual exhortation 'Not to be used whilst the train is standing in the station'. In the middle of the compartment was a table which people could sit around on their camp chairs, and eat the food from their Fortnum & Mason picnic hampers, set out by their bearers. Fans played cool air from the roof, and a block of ice was often put in the tin tub from the *ghussal khana*, a kind of primitive air conditioning. As journeys often meant more than two nights on the train, the universal bedding roll everyone had, was spread out on one of the bunks. Like the *dak* bungalows, the carriages were full of fleas and other even more unpleasant biting insects. The first action on getting in was a general sprinkling of Keatings Powder, without which, the British Empire, instead of ending as it did, would undoubtedly have been bitten to extinction.

The carriages had pull-up glass windows with slatted blinds to keep out the glare. It was a wise precaution to keep them up during the night, as well as making sure all doors were securely locked. Every railway station was infested by the most expert thieves in the world, barring of course the Pathans, who are in a class of their own. These thieves could get into a Sahib's railway compartment and remove every single thing he possessed, even his bedclothes, without waking him. They could probably have given him a bath as well if they had tried. As for the Pathans, a man was heard at the Club in Peshawar, boasting that 'No Pathan could steal from him', only to wake up the next morning to find himself in his bed on his lawn, with all his furniture arranged around him exactly as it had been indoors. Railway thieves too were expert 'fishers'. If they failed to get into a compartment, they would insert a thin rod through the lattice work of the shutters, with a line and a hook at the end of it. With this they were able to fish almost any object through the window. Nothing loose could be left around for them to get at.

Every station, day or night, was thronged with people, jostling for places on the train. Vendors walked up and down the platform

35

shouting their wares: '*Dudh gurram dudh*' milk warm milk, '*Pani Hindu! Pani Mussalman*'. Water Hindu! Water Muslim! There was no way in which the two would drink the same water. Any European attempting to drink it would probably get dysentery or typhoid, or at best a severe go of the local form of 'Delhi belly'.

Indians seemed to have no sense of time. If they wished to travel, they would merely go to the nearest railway station, buy a ticket and wait there for a train, perhaps for days before a suitable one arrived. Whole families camped on the platforms, brought their brass cooking pots along and lit fires to make their meals. Directly a train came in, a concerted rush would be made for it. The third-class compartments, which consisted merely of wooden benches, were soon crammed to overflowing. People climbed onto the roof and travelled there, ducking low as the train went through a tunnel; others stood on the carriage footboards and clung onto door handles. Every train was festooned with them hanging on like this. Naturally such conduct was not permitted on the Sahib's portion of the train. Inevitably under such crowded conditions passengers would fall off, but it was all taken in good heart and nobody seemed to mind. Every locomotive was fitted with a cowcatcher in front, I imagine to sweep up the bodies of those who had fallen off a previous train, for I certainly never saw a cow on the line or heard of one that had been swept off it.

4

Every year on 23 December, my birthday, we all went down to
Kheri-Luckinpore for my Uncle Robin's annual camp and tiger
shoot. It meant spending a night on the train, and a special one
used to be laid on for us and our huge retinue of servants, for
nearly everyone from Snow View would be accompanying their
Sahibs down to the plains. Above all things in the world I loved
travelling by train, and if it stopped during the night would lie
awake, praying and hoping it would start again, not wanting to
drop off to sleep once more and miss hearing it puffing along. I
loved the smell of the smoke, the clicking of the wheels, the sight
of the countryside rushing by outside, and the rise and dip of the
telegraph lines as they floated past the window. The Eurasians
who ran all the railways were intensely sensitive about their
European birth, and the engine driver, who always had a coolie to
shovel the coal, wore his solar topi as a badge of office and to
show he was not a native, even at midnight. To me he was some
kind of god, standing up there in his cab, controlling the power of
that hissing monster. On occasion I was taken onto the footplate,
and allowed, to my joy, to ride on the engine to the next station.

The British in India were terrified of the sun and avoided it at all
times, considering it very dangerous. Later they transferred their
terror to polluted water. Apparently the sunshine contained a very
evil substance called actinic rays. These rays only began quite
suddenly, East of Suez. To protect against the actinic ray, a huge,
thick, khaki or white, pith helmet was worn, called a 'solar
topi', *topi* being the Urdu for a hat. Governors and high ICS
officials wore white ceremonial pith helmets with a spike, and
often ornamented at the side with a bunch of feathers pulled from

37

the tail of some unfortunate exotic tropical bird. So sure were people that this mysterious ray only existed East of Suez, that they would go happily hatless through the Suez Canal, only to dash to their cabins for their solar topis directly they got into the Red Sea. On the voyage home, topis were ceremoniously cast into the water on reaching Suez, until every ship looked as if it were floating on a sheet of grotesque water weeds. Those returning to India at the end of their leave would buy a new topi at Simon Arzt General Store at Port Said. In addition to the pith helmet, many wore spine pads, pleats along the back of their uniform and plain clothes jackets, to protect against this vicious ray which killed white people by sunstroke, but apparently did not affect the natives, especially Hindus who often went bareheaded 'because the shape of their heads was different'.

I am reliably told that there is no such thing as sunstroke, only heat exhaustion, when the body's natural heat control methods fail to keep its temperature within acceptable limits, and one is more or less cooked to death. But fear of sunstroke and the actinic ray was very real, and everyone believed implicitly in its existence. There were many accounts of hospitals being built, always in some far-off cantonment, with such a thin roof that the actinic ray was able to penetrate and all the patients died of sunstroke.

Dress was always as formal as possible, and worn on the theory that directly it got a bit cooler in the evening, you put on something extra just to make you hot again. On the plains during the hot weather, shorts and shirts would be worn with stockings, but of course everyone changed for dinner, complete with starched boiled shirt and black tie. It was very cheap and very easy to get clothes made in India. They were made up by the '*darzi*' or tailor, who, given a copy, pattern, or shown an illustration, would cut a suit or jacket as well as anything from Savile Row. A *darzi* would copy exactly, and if the original had a patch or a moth hole, he would include that as well in the new garment. Much material was sent out from home to be made up in this way. Nor was it a complicated business. A servant would be sent to the bazaar to fetch the *darzi*, (pronounced 'durzi'), who would set up his workshop on your verandah, sitting cross-legged to use his scissors or ancient Singer sewing machine, the wheel of which he often turned with his big toe. A complete and perfectly cut and made suit or lady's dress could be ready within 24 hours. At times of the many fancy-dress dances and balls at clubs during the cold weather, *darzis* were much in demand, concocting outlandish creations for the Memsahibs, taken from magazines or books and copied to perfection. I whiled away many happy hours, squatting on my hunkers like any small Indian boy, watching the *darzi* at work making some fancy-dress for my mother or Aunt Gertie, giving helpful advice from time to time or discussing the latest gossip.

My uncle, Robin Willoughby, was Deputy Commissioner for the District of Kheri-Luckinpore, north of Lucknow. It was about the size of Yorkshire, and he presided over it in some splendour, dispensing justice at various perambulatory courts, and generally being in charge of the Administration. He was helped by a British officer of the Indian Police who maintained law and order through a force of Indian constables. Uncle Robin lived in state in a large comfortable house with many servants, but it must have been a lonely existence as the only other European was the policeman. Most of the time he was out on tour and was too busy to wonder if he was lonely or not. At some time or other, whilst my father was away at the War, my mother fell desperately in love with Robin. Whether he reciprocated her affection or whether they were lovers, I shall never know. But human nature being what it is, I am more than willing to bet six to five that the answer would be yes!

Whatever the case, they soon became talked about, the subject of much conjecture and gossip. Uncle Robin was an exceptionally gifted man and would have gone far in the ICS. There was talk of him being a future Viceroy. Rumour of any such affair, true or false, would certainly have put paid to his further advancement. In a closed society, where everyone knew everybody else, for some-one to have an affair with his brother's wife, whilst he was away at the Front, fighting for King-Emperor and Country, was considered extremely bad form, to say the least of it. It would be described as 'a damned poor show, would never have thought him capable of it'. My mother was obviously besotted with him, and I often heard her say that she just liked to sit for hours and listen to him talk on

39

any subject. Personally, I consider this an extremely high level of besottment.

One of the chief reasons for the outstanding success of British Colonial Administration, and resounding success it certainly was, is because nobody was in it for the money – the pay was very poor – but from a sense of duty. It was carried out by people from an exactly similar background, who had been educated at public schools and spoke each other's language with all its hidden nuances, understatements and secret meanings. From the middle of the 19th century the whole system of education at the public schools had been devised to train future leaders of the Empire. Thus the emphasis was on character, physical fitness, endurance, pride in duty, integrity, justice, a sense of honour, belief in hierarchy from the prefect system, intense unspoken patriotism, and the inherent conviction that they were natural leaders, that the British Empire would last forever because it had the blessing of God, and that it would never occur to them to do anything else but manage it. My own school, Haileybury, used to be the old East India Company's training college, their equivalent of Sandhurst, where cadets were trained for their duties in administering, soldiering and policing huge areas of India. After the Mutiny in 1857, the Company was taken over by the Crown, and in 1870, under Disraeli, Parliament voted Queen Victoria Empress. Not only were the same kind of people recruited, mostly younger sons from the Gentry, running India, but many were from the same families, who for two or even three generations had been doing so. Their sons born there as I was, going Home at eight to prep and public schools, spending their holidays with grandparents or relations, then going to university or Sandhurst and coming out to carry on where their parents had left off, as ill-paid as they had been.

The system had its reverse side. It bred intense snobbery, a sense of privilege and effortless superiority, of infallibility, self-righteousness, and a belief in a God-given right to rule and command others. Above all it gave rise to a very high degree of intolerance towards those who were not exactly like themselves. Anyone who did not fit in, whether by birth, speech, clothes or in any other way, would be given a very hard time. This was

40

especially the case in the Army. Nobody ever carried any kind of proof of identity. The very idea of others not knowing who you were would be absurd, almost laughable. In any case, everywhere there would be friends, friends of friends or those who were at school with you, to confirm you were who you said you were. To such a degree was this the case, that birth certificates were not given to those born in India. Only their baptism was recorded in the local garrison church. It was not considered necessary to have a piece of paper to prove you had been born, or who your parents were, because everybody knew. I myself have no birth certificate, and if I want proof of my birth would have to obtain a photo copy of the baptismal register from the old garrison church at Secunderabad, which I believe no longer exists, so it might pose a problem. I was lucky in that my father had been born in Ayr. Had he, too, been born in India I might have found it difficult to obtain a British passport. Field Marshal, former Viceroy, Lord Wavell of the Black Watch, whose father as well was born in India, was refused a passport in 1949, and informed he was an alien. The Field Marshal told me this himself, and of the difficulty he had in eventually obtaining one.

In 1932, my cousin Awdry eloped with a wild young man called Kendrick Hughes, whom Aunt Gertie and Uncle Jimmy, now married, considered highly unsuitable. In fact, as far as they were concerned, the only thing to be said in his favour was that he had been to Eton. Kendrick later won a DFC in the RAF in the war, and was killed flying over Italy in 1943. He had bought a marriage licence and they went to a registry office to get married. 'Birth certificates please,' the official asked. Kendrick produced his, but Awdry looked nonplussed, and explained that having been born in India, 'she hadn't got one.' 'In that case' replied the Registrar, sadly shaking his head, 'you cannot get married. You will have to write to wherever you were christened and get a certified copy of the appropriate page of the baptismal register. Funnily enough,' he went on, 'we had one in only yesterday for a similar situation; here it is.' Awdry looked at it, and to her astonishment there was her name at the top of the page. Of all the churches, and all the pages, and all the registry offices this had to be the one! They were married and returned to face the wrath of the Logans. Uncle

Jimmy was standing on the doorstep, a riding crop in his hands, ready to thrash the fellow to within an inch of his life. He never used it. Kendrick was a lot bigger than he was anyway, and less than half his age. In the end they all became very friendly, especially after Kendrick won his DFC. The marriage was a great success, and the 1930s were enlivened for me by the phenomenal and wonderful parties they threw.

The annual shoot in the Kheri-Luckinpore District was subsidised by the Indian Government, and was a form of pest control. Uncle Robin could never have afforded it on his own, nor would he have been allowed to have a private shoot. The District consisted mainly of thick jungle: trees interspersed with areas of scrub and criss-crossed by rivers and streams. It abounded in tigers, leopards, bears, crocodiles, deer, jungle fowl and all kinds of game. The object of the shoot was to control the number of tigers and leopards. The rest of the shooting was either for the pot or for sport. Throughout the year, reports would be coming in from outlying villages to say that 'Tigers had taken cattle and goats here, and leopards done the same thing there. Would the Sahibs please come out and shoot them.' The best time to do this was around Christmas, when the weather was at its pleasantest. During the summer it was unbearably hot, a fairly steady 110 to 114° fahrenheit in the shade (43 to 46°C), much too hot for the elephants to be used.

'Guns' were invited for the Christmas shoot, and would be limited to some five or six. There would be Uncle Robin himslf, my mother and aunt, both crack shots, Uncle Jimmy, and only one other I can recall, a Mr Joplin, and the main reason I can remember him is because he loved a pudding called 'spotted dick'. In fact he loved it so much that we called it 'Joplin-pudding' instead. The rifles used were of the large calibre express type, such as the Westley-Richards .375 inch. The bullet had a very flat trajectory due to its high velocity and delivered the fearful punch needed instantly to kill a big animal. A wounded tiger or leopard is a dangerous beast to have around, and it was a point of honour, even at risk of your own life, that if you wounded one, to track it down and kill it, so as not to leave it in further pain and a menace to other people.

42

The animals were hunted in two ways; either by an organised 'beat', or by sitting up for them, deep in the jungle, on a string bed fastened high in a tree. A live bait was tied up below, such as a goat, which bleated incessantly in terror, and obviously hoped you would shoot the tiger before it got eaten itself. I often sat up with my mother in one of these '*machaons*', along with the unarmed native *shikari* or professional hunter. The *charpoy* we sat on was uncomfortable, full of bedbugs or fleas, no matter how much Keatings was used. It was difficult not to fidget. Then suddenly the goat would stop bleating, and there would be the tiger standing majestically in the bright moonlight of the jungle clearing. The *shikari* would barely breathe the words '*Bagh agia, maro Memsahib maro!*', (The tiger is there, shoot Lady, shoot!) There would be the shattering crack of her rifle, followed by the sight of the tiger lying dead on the ground, much to the relief of the tethered goat. I always felt terribly sad and sorry for the tiger. It looked such a magnificent creature, and I could not see why the villagers should grudge it the odd cow or goat from time to time. Only once in about ten waits in a *machaon* did an animal appear. It was mostly all a big scratch until the dawn, when a pad elephant would appear to carry us back to camp.

Although one was safe from tigers in a *machaon*, this was far from being the case with leopards, who are much better than raw hands when it comes to climbing trees, being able to go up them as quickly as monkeys. On one occasion sitting up with my mother, a leopard appeared. Something must have alarmed it, for it suddenly made off. She took a quick shot as it left and missed. On coming down from the tree at dawn, we followed the direction the leopard had taken and found it lying as dead as a doornail, some 50 yards off, a bullet hole exactly in the centre of its forehead. My mother had missed all right, but the animal must have turned its head round for a second, to receive the full impact of the bullet as it fled, and died instantly. I considered it to be just about the unluckiest leopard in all India.

A beat for tiger always took place during the day and usually began about ten o'clock, in time for breakfasts to settle and beaters to assemble in the jungle, of which a large area had been selected and cordoned off. Spread out in a line, possibly a mile

43

long, they would beat trees, bushes and grass with *lathis*, sound gongs, shout and sing to frighten the animals towards the Sahibs mounted on elephants, advancing in the opposite direction. The 'guns' would be sitting in *howdahs*, a kind of double armchair in tandem, fastened on the elephant's back. Other elephants carried pads, thick mattresses, on which sat the Indian *shikaris*, clinging onto straps and shouting encouragement. Although not armed, my grandmother also rode in one of the *howdahs*, generally giving back-seat advice to the *mahout* sitting astride the animal's head in front, and to the gun with her, on how to shoot the tiger. I can only once remember seeing a tiger during one of these beats: it looked like an enormous black flea as it fled for its life through the long grass, and I felt intensely glad when it got away.

Our camp was always pitched in a large clearing in the jungle, near a river where the elephants, some 20 of them, could have their daily bath and mud wallow. Indian elephants are much more amenable to training in captivity than their African counterparts. They also have smaller ears. The reason for this is because they were originally forest dwellers, mostly living in the shade, whilst African elephants lived on open savannah, where they felt the full force of the African sunshine. Huge ears were developed through evolution to act as radiators. Plentifully supplied with blood vessels in its ears, an African elephant flaps them to create a cooling breeze and carry the heat away from its body. Living in shade, this was not necessary for the Indian. Both varieties love wallowing in water and cool mud, which also kills insect parasites on their skin, stops it cracking and is regarded by them in much the same way as women regard moisturising cream. Indian elephants too are smaller, making it easier for them to avoid low-hanging jungle branches.

To most people, an elephant is just an elephant, and all they know about them is that it is a large animal with a leg at each corner and a long trunk, also that 'an elephant never forgets'. There are, however, three distinct species. One is Asiatic and the other two are African. The Asiatic type is the one most frequently seen in zoos and circuses. African elephants are not often seen in captivity, and can rarely be broken in for work. There are four distinct races of Asiatic elephant – Indian or Burman, Ceylonese,

44

Malayan and Sumatran. They are all very similar in appearance, and differ from the African in having smaller ears and smooth tapering trunks, with only one finger at the end. With the Ceylonese, neither the male nor the female has tusks, and with the other three Asiatic races only the male has them.

The African elephant is taller, heavier and more lanky, with the large ears described, and a segmented trunk. It differs also from the Asiatic in having a well-defined hollow back, whilst Asian elephants have a distinctly rounded one. There are four races of African elephant the Sudanese, Central, Eastern and Southern varieties. There is also an African pygmy, now limited to the Equatorial and Congo basin. This never exceeds eight feet at the shoulder, and once was plentiful at the foot of the Atlas Mountains and in Southern Tunisia. It was this type which was used by Hannibal against the Romans when he invaded Italy in 218 BC. It is believed that he crossed the Alps by the Little St Bernard Pass – over 9000 feet high – with an army of 38,000 foot soldiers, 8000 horse and 37 elephants. In spite of losing half his force on the way, and all but three of his elephants, he burst upon Northern Italy with all the impact and surprise of the German attack through the Ardennes in 1940. Of his 37 elephants, only one was Asiatic, and was Hannibal's own private transport. We even know its name – The Syrian. The rest were African pygmy elephants, and their size is clearly shown by comparison with their riders on ancient coins. The Syrian was a present to Hannibal from the Egyptians, who were actively backing Carthage in her war with Rome.

Elephants had been used in war for some centuries before this, and whenever they were used, the devastating effect of the Asian elephant in battle had been clearly shown. Inevitably one must think of an armoured elephant in terms of the modern tank, but that was far from the case, and their main use was to strike terror into an enemy who had never seen them before. In reality they were very much a two-edged weapon, easily frightened and likely to turn their backs on the enemy and stampede through the ranks of their own army. Normally a brave creature in its proper surroundings, an elephant could see no point in fighting for humans, whom it loathed and despised at all times. They were extensively used in wars in India from around AD 1000, but mainly in siege operations as battering rams, pulling siege guns, supply wagons and so on. During the days of the British Raj, elephants were used to haul the heavy guns of the Royal Artillery, and for general work by the Royal Engineers. The last elephant on the British War Establishment was called Daisy, and she died in 1895.

The elephant is a lovely creature, magnificent in its strength and power, in the length of its life, which is the same as our own, and its love and care for its young. It is the only animal which will help another, and will even face rifle fire to help a wounded comrade get away, propping it up on either side. Elephants deserve a better fate that that which is being meted out to them by mankind. In the wild, elephants live in herds of about 30 to 50 animals. Theirs is a matriarchal society and the herd is led and controlled by a dominant female; my grandmother would have been a tip-top matriarch. They cover great distances in search of fodder and water. The bulls mostly remain outside the herd, and mating is a very private affair. The female comes out to where she knows the bull is likely to be, giving the herd the slip at dusk and rejoining it at dawn. Very often a rival bull will interfere, and then the two will fight it out. Female elephants never fight – they have too much sense. The bulls fight head-on, and rarely to the death, but death often results for the weaker, who usually breaks and gets a mortal wound by exposing the most vulnerable part of his body. The deadly blow is the thrust of one tusk between the hind legs into the loins, the intestines and the testicles. These are carried inside the body.

Some males never grow tusks, but as with the red deer hummel, or hornless stag, this appears to be no disadvantage in a fight, for it gives the animal a much greater power of manoeuvre. Furthermore a tuskless elephant seems to compensate by being more aggressive in a fight and is often actually physically stronger than his rival; for from the age of about three, the strength required to build his tusks has gone into building his body instead. The extra strength seems mainly concentrated in the trunk, whose size and girth is so much increased that it can be used to smash an opponent's solid ivory tusk as though it were a twig. Some females prefer a tuskless bull.

There is no particular season for mating. Two animals are attracted to each other and fall in love. Days and weeks are spent in courtship. Elephants seem to enjoy mating in water, hardly surprising, for the male can weigh up to seven and a half tons. But if it is done on land, he takes nearly all the weight on his hind legs. He mounts the female with ease and grace, his forefeet resting gently on her hindquarters. Eventually mating is comsummated, the act lasting some five to ten minutes, and is repeated three or four times in 24 hours. The pair graze and keep together for months, the honeymoon lasting all that time. Working elephants in Asia call each other after knocking off work and go into the jungle together until it is time to start work again the next morning.

The honeymoon goes on for ten or twelve months, until the cow suspects she is pregnant. The average female first mates between the ages of 17 and 20. She has no particular season like other animals, but feels some natural urge. The gestation period is 23 months. Directly the female knows she is pregnant, she will have nothing further to do with the bull, and replaces him with a female friend or 'Auntie'. Auntie is the actual name by which this friend is known among those who train and look after elephants. The two females become inseparable, grazing together, and always keeping the calf between them to protect it from predators. Most females have some four calves, often twins, during their lifetime. The baby calf follows its mother around for three or four years, being suckled for all that time from two breasts between her forelegs. This position affords the calf complete protection, and it drinks about 24 pints a day. The trunk of the baby is kept to one side for suckling and is not flexible for three or four months. When the fabled and sacred White Elephant of the Mandalay Palace was a calf, its mother died, and it was suckled by 20 Burmese girls taking turns daily to act as wet nurses.

The oldest recorded female giving birth to a live calf was, curiously enough, called Sarah, and she had her baby at the age of 61. Young elephants stay with their mother long after they are weaned, until the age of 16 or 17 and often she will have two or three calves of different ages at foot at the same time. Their devotion and intense love for each other and for their family is striking. Imagine the effect the selling of captive calves to other working stations must have on them, and even worse, the so called 'culling' of herds that takes place in the African game parks. At the age of five or six the calf learns to gather its own fodder, and at around 16 they start flirting with each other. At about 20, the bull is fully grown, and begins an annual condition known as 'going on musth', when he is particularly savage and uncertain in temper, and is a danger to one and all, including other elephants. The period of musth is accompanied by a discharge of strongly smelling fluid from the musth glands near the eyes. Musth occurs every year until the animal is over 50.

Their lifespan is much the same as that of humans, about 70 years. Once they roamed every continent save South America and Australia. A big African bull will grow to as much as eleven feet at the shoulder, his tusks weighing over 200 pounds each. They drink some 50 gallons of water a day. If an elephant manages to live out its life span, it will usually die of starvation in the end. During its life it has six separate sets of teeth, unlike our two. When these finally wear out it can no longer chew the grass and branches which are its food, for it is entirely vegetarian. As their teeth begin to wear out, old elephants tend to foregather more and more in places where the food is easier to eat, and die there, giving rise to the belief that elephants all go to the same place to die. This of course is no more true than the idea that old ladies go to Eastbourne or Worthing to die. It merely means that the weather and other conditions suit the old best.

But there is now definite evidence to show that when it is time for a female elephant to die, the herd will accompany her to her last resting place, and will take a final and loving farewell of her. This does not apply to the bulls, for by this time they will have become solitary. As the old female lays herself down to die, each of the herd in turn will rest its trunk upon her, as though in blessing and farewell. The whole herd then stands around her in vigil for some hours to make sure she is dead, before leaving her body to the hyenas and the vultures.

But it is for their zest in life that elephants are best remembered, for that and for small things like being right- or left-tusked just as we are right- or left-handed. Nowhere is their love of life better seen than when a herd is bathing together. Not only do they have

48

to drink their 50 gallons of water a day, but bathing is essential to their health or their skins will harden and crack. The entire herd bathes together, the young ones squealing with delight as they squirt their elders with water and mud. The whole affair takes on the aspect of a family outing in its simple fun and the obvious pleasure they all take in it.

5

All our elephants in the camp were females. It would never have done to have had a bull which suddenly came on musth. The matriarch of the herd was Latchmi, an elderly matron of about 45, whom I got to know very well, and who used to sway on her forelegs and trumpet with pleasure whenever she saw me. The rest were flighty young things in their twenties or thirties. Five or six would have been trained to carry a *howdah*. The rest were pad animals. Each elephant had its own *mahout* (pronounced 'mahowt' to rhyme with 'nowt'!). He would take take charge of his elephant when it was young and he was young, and they would grow old together, becoming an inseparable and formidable team.

Whilst in camp, Awdry and I used to spend as much time as possible with the elephants, learning the special language which is used to speak to them, watch them being bathed, cleaned and fed. The amount of food they got through was enormous: huge piles of fodder consisting of branches of trees, leaves and grass. They also eat a great number of *chupattis*, but these were no ordinary *chupattis*, being elephant-sized in every way. The *chupatti* was the staple diet of all native inhabitants of India, and probably still is. Pancake-like, it is made of flour and water, flattened between the hands into a thin disc about a foot across and a quarter of an inch thick. Usually cooked by being placed on a red hot stone over an open fire, it had a delicious smokey taste. Everything was eaten with the fingers, and food was placed on *chupattis*, scooped up with them used as a spoon, wrapped up in them, carried in them. They were used as plates and eaten afterwards, rather as in Europe in medieval times, food was placed on a bread 'trencher', which was also eaten afterwards or given to the poor. Elephant *chupattis*

50

were at least two feet across and about an inch thick. I used to love breaking bits off and eating them myself, or giving pieces to one of the elephants, who would take it very delicately from my fingers with her trunk, and put it in her mouth.

The *mahout* sits astride the neck, just behind the ears. To mount, he orders the elephant to kneel. The front legs bend forwards at the elbow and the hind legs backwards at the knees, just as a human would be, crouching on all fours. The *mahout* climbs onto a fore-leg and is hoisted into position by the trunk. After years of being together, elephant and *mahout* almost become one animal. Once on its head, the *mahout* guides and directs it by means of an '*ankh*', a heavy iron goad. This has a blunt spike at one end and a large hook ending in another spike, coming from the middle. The whole is about 14 to 18 inches long. The stems were often beautifully chased with lines and designs. *Ankhs* were great status symbols, and many Maharajahs equipped their state elephants with solid gold or silver ones. For some mysterious reason nobody ever seemed to steal them.

I was often taken up on an elephant's head and allowed to drive it, sitting astride in front of the *mahout*. I always thought they treated their charges very roughly, banging their heads with the *ankh* or even driving the point of it into the flesh. Most of the elephants had suppurating sores from this treatment, on which some concoction was put daily. If he wanted it to go left or right he caught the appropriate ear with the hook and tugged in the direction required. The elephants were our friends, and seeing them banged around like this was very distressing. I used to beg the *mahouts* not to do it, but they only laughed and said the elephants didn't mind. Nor did they seem to, either.

The Asiatic elephant has passed into a form of slavery, not unlike that suffered by the American Negro and others in the 18th and 19th centuries. The wild herds are rounded up and driven into an enclosure called a '*keddah*', where they are broken and finally trained by 'Uncle Toms', animals already old in the service of man. For the rest of their lives and of their children, they will be used piling teak, dragging huge logs in the forest camps, often in chains or in leg irons. They will be humiliated in zoos and circuses doing silly tricks, eating buns and giving boring, futile rides. They will have had to face tigers and other perils in the jungle, but what of course terrifies them most is a mouse, which they fear will run up their trunk. They also loathe and despise horses at all times. As loving, family herd animals, they will see their young sold off to unknown humans, never to have news of them again. On one occasion, quite by accident, a young replacement female was brought to Kheri. She turned out to be one of Latchmi's daughters, whom she had not seen for 20 years. The joy of that reunion has ever remained with me – the love and pleasure of the animals at seeing each other again and the excitement of the rest of the herd, squealing and trumpeting a welcome home.

Most evenings in camp, two or three elephants would be 'padded up' and some of the 'guns' would go out into the jungle, ostensibly to 'shoot something for the pot' – actually to kill anything that moved. The *howdahs* were reserved for the big organised tiger shoots, where the shooting was done from the *howdah* itself. It was not possible to shoot from a pad, as you were too busy clinging on. As has been described, the pad was a thick mattress girthed onto the elephant. There were straps across it, onto which you clung or you would get thrown off as your mount walked along. In order to shoot, you had to dismount, and on these 'pad shoots' three animals were usually deployed. There would be the Sahib 'guns' on one, *shikaris* or gun bearers on another. and the third would be used to bring back the game, mostly deer such as sambhur, nilghai or cheetal. The *shikaris* would carry the guns, rifle or shot, until they dismounted, and then hand over whichever type was needed to their Sahib. Shotguns were used for jungle fowl which were delicious to eat. To be a gun bearer was a coveted and honourable occupation.

These evening expeditions on elephants were always a delight for us children. As evening fell there would be a breathless hush over the jungle. The shooting would have been done, and as dusk fell we would make our way home. Kipling describes it perfectly with the lines, 'when Mang the bat brings home the night that Cheel the kite sets free'. It was a time of sadness too, of memories of sambhur or nilghai being shot, lying there on the ground. At first its eyes would be as bright as they were when alive, then slowly they would glaze over, and you knew that whatever had been there, had made the animal what it was, had gone, departed to some unknown place from whence it could never return, for surely it must have gone somewhere. Now 80 years later, I can still see those animals dying in the falling light of the Kheri jungle. On one of these evening shoots, somebody shot a crocodile, which was duly tied up and hoisted onto the game pad elephant. Back in camp it was laid out on the ground and measured. It was a big one, over ten feet from tip of its nose to its tail. Suddenly, just as I was about a foot away from its head, it opened its jaws and roared. I fled to my tent and crawled under the bed, convinced it was coming after me and that my last hour had come. It was some time before I would again go near any dead animal.

Because of possible quicksands, walking along the edge of a river was a dangerous occupation for any elephant. Uncle Robin was always deluged with requests for us to come and deal with the 'muggers', crocodiles which infested the rivers. There were two types of crocodile, in Urdu 'mugger', and the gharial, a long-jawed reptile, but like a crocodile in all other respects, which only eats fish. The mugger will take anything, cattle, goats, children, even the odd full-grown villager. All the water for a village came from the river. The women would wash clothes in it and the children would play and bathe. The whole set-up was a mugger's bonanza. Thus if you shot one, a self-righteous glow would come over you, striking a blow in the cause of humanity. Besides, the hides made wonderful strong suitcases. I still have several I inherited, which are so heavy that even empty, they would exceed any airline baggage allowance. I often wonder if the modern words 'mugger' and 'being mugged' originated with the old Indian crocodile. The activity is so similar.

Far more dangerous than the muggers were the quicksands or 'fussan'. From the outside, a fussan looked exactly like any area of wet sand near the river. It had a firm crust on the top, but below was a gluey mess of sand and water into which any heavy object, such as an elephant, horse or man, would sink and slowly disappear. The more they struggled to get free, the more surely they sank. Fussans were to be found along sandy river banks and around almost any ford. The elephants were terrified of them. You could always tell when you were on quicksand; the ground below your elephant's feet began to quake, and the animal would squeal with terror and start dashing across. If it was caught it was a serious business, for as it gradually sank it would, as like as not, tear off those riding on its back to trample under its feet to make the ground firmer.

Whenever a place was reached where quicksand was suspected, an elephant would be sent forward first with only its *mahout* on board to test out the ground. With such a light load, it could turn back in time. It was no good sending a man to do this, for what was firm ground for him might turn out to be *fussan* for an elephant. If one got stuck, the *mahout* would be off its back like lightning. The other elephants would then be brought up, their pads taken off and pushed out so that the one caught in the *fussan* could use them as a kind of raft to step on. It usually worked, and with a squelch the animal would extricate itself from the gluey substance and get onto firmer ground. On one occasion, however, it did not, and in spite of every effort, the throwing down of pads and anything else that could be thought of, the elephant sank lower and lower into the *fussan*, until at last all that could be seen of it was the despairing tip of its trunk, and then that disappeared as well. Quite apart from the tragedy, Uncle Robin was faced with a difficult explanation and a possible hefty bill for the loss of a Government elephant.

Such worries did not concern us children. When we were not with the elephants or out on the shoots we spent our time sliding down the sides of the tents, some of which were as big as marquees. My uncle had a great deal of administrative work to do for his district wherever he was, or whatever he was doing. For this he had a large office tent with a double flap. One day we thought it a good idea to crawl up the inner flap and slide down that. We got to the top of the tent, where the canvas was not very strong. Suddenly it gave way and Awdry fell through a large hole, smack onto his desk. In those days everyone wrote with a pen dipped in ink from an inkwell, and all the ink went flying in every direction, all over his papers, petitions, bills and unanswered letters. Awdry tore her knickers and the incident was a laugh for several days.

Directly we were old enough to hold a gun, we were taught to

54

shoot, both with a rifle and a revolver of small .22 calibres. Learning to shoot properly was considered a very important part of our education. My mother taught me with a small rifle she had, called a Quackenbush. The shooting was invariably at paper targets over distances up to 50 yards. I was shown the correct way to lie, to sight and to use available cover as a rest to take steadier aim. It was interesting and it was fun. We were never allowed to shoot at any animal, however small, for fear of wounding it. Above all and everything else was safety.

> Never ever let your gun
> pointed be at anyone.
> All the pheasants ever bred,
> are not worth one man dead.

Not only did we never point a gun, but it became a matter of habit always to open the breech before handling it, and always passing it to another with the muzzle to the sky, breech open. The way I was taught to shoot was in almost unbelievable contrast to the mind-numbingly boring way I found the subject handled in the Army some 15 years later.

The camp at Kheri-Luckinpore usually lasted some three weeks. The rest of the cold weather was spent at one of the garrison cantonments such as Lucknow, Bareilly or Fategarh, until April when it was time to go back to Naini Tal again at the start of the hot weather. We lived in the shadow of the Great Indian Mutiny of 1857, which was at that time, within living memory. At Lucknow, my Ayah used to take me for walks in the grounds of the Residency, scene of the famous siege. It had remained untouched with the flag still flying over it, day and night, never to be lowered until Independence Day in 1948. The buildings remained battered and holed from the incessant shelling, and cannonballs lay about everywhere. My grandmother had many friends, including Field Marshal Lord Roberts, 'Bobs' to one and all, who had taken part in the fiercest of the fighting. My great-grandfather, her husband's father, had been in the column which relieved Cawnpore, too late to prevent the massacre there. He was an officer in the 79th Cameron Highlanders, and his dirk lies on a table in my hall.

55

At Cawnpore, the British garrison had been promised safe conduct by the Nana Sahib, leader of the mutineers. They were lured into boats on the Ganges and massacred by artillery and musket fire from ambushes on the bank. The men who were not killed were suitably dispatched afterwards, the women and children taken to a place called the Bibi-garh, the House of Women. Here some ten days later, after terrible privations they were done to death, cut to pieces with swords and their bodies thrown down a well. It was over 50 feet deep, and the bodies filled it to within six feet of the top. The commander of the relieving force, General Havelock, gave orders that every man should be given a piece of one of the women's dresses, accompanied with the words 'Remember Cawnpore'. I still have the piece given to my great-grandfather, a small square of fawnish silk. Unfortunately at some time, somebody washed the blood off.

As a child, I felt that the aura of mutiny was still strong. The implicit trust that the British officers had in their men had been broken. Although prior to 1857 signs that all was not well were very evident, every officer was convinced that, whatever the circumstances, 'the men of his own regiment could never be other than loyal'. They regarded the men as their children, their *'baba-logue'*. Whatever the men of other regiments might do, it could never happen with them. Thus they took no precautions, for to do so would be to suspect their own people. It was impossible to contemplate, until it happened; over and over again. For ever after, Indian Sepoys, although no-one would have dared admit it, were still objects of covert suspicion. They were never again given access to the heavy artillery with which they had done so much damage.

On that fateful Sunday of 10 May 1857, when the Mutiny first broke out at Meerut, the 60th Rifles had been on Church Parade and were caught without their arms. In the future, certainly until the outbreak of war in 1939, British regiments always attended the ceremonial parades to church every Sunday fully armed, their rifle magazines charged with ball ammunition. Nobody ever doubted the loyalty of the Indian Army, but it was wiser perhaps to make sure. Even with daily news of the terrible carnage taking place in France during those years of the Great War, we were still under the influence of what had happened only 60 years earlier, a time equal to writing this and the start of World War Two – a mere footstep in human memory which I remember as though it were yesterday. The Indian Army fought magnificently in Burma during that War and were largely our instrument of victory over the Japanese. Even so, after the fall of Singapore, any number of Sepoys enlisted under Chandra Bose, to fight against us with the Japanese, in the Indian Liberation Army. So perhaps our former fears were not altogether groundless. I always had this somewhat vague feeling that the grown-ups were under some threat and had to be constantly on their guard, always vigilant.

Whether we were in the hills or on the plains, the meals were always the same and were a ritual, shared and loved by Sahib and servant alike. The day began at about 7 a.m. with 'chota-hazri' (little-breakfast), brought to one's bed by the bearer or ayah. It consisted of a pot of tea, milk, sugar and a banana, always a banana, not toast, marmalade or any other kind of fruit, but only a banana. Without one, chota hazri would be unthinkable. Around nine o'clock there was 'hazri' or proper breakfast, which was what would be described as 'fully English'. It began with porridge or cereals. I used to love Grapenuts, which came in a round, golden-coloured tin with writing on it. It was quite unlike modern Grape Nuts, being dark brown with a delicious malty taste. Then there were eggs cooked in different ways, with bacon. Kedgeree was a very popular dish, and our word for it is the original Urdu. Then of course there was toast and thick-cut Oxford marmalade in beautiful white jars, followed by fruit such as mangoes or lychees. The grown-ups drank tea. We had cold milk. It was unpasteurised and had been through many hands, probably containing every germ known to the human race but by now we were immune. As an infant I had already had pneumonia and enteric fever. A lot of children died in India, and it was accepted as just one of those unfortunate things. Attitudes have changed. Then, children were the adjuncts of their parents instead of being the end-all and reason for their being allowed to exist.

At one o'clock there would be 'tiffin' or lunch. It was always called tiffin. There was usually a curry, probably chicken, beef or goat heavily disguised with hot sauce and called mutton. It was eaten with piles of rice, white as snow, each grain separate from the rest. This would be followed by traditional English puddings, such as suet with treacle, joplin or baked apple. For us children there would be disgusting rice puddings with skin on the top, which we loathed. After lunch, everyone went off for a siesta until teatime or '*char*', with buttered toast, scones, cake, and cucumber sandwiches thin as wafers. Dinner or '*khana*' – the word means 'food' in Urdu was the formal meal of the day. It took place at eight or eight-thirty, and we were in bed long before then. Even in camp, everyone changed for dinner – the men into dinner jackets with stand-up collar, black tie and boiled shirt, and the women would wear long dresses. The food resembled as closely as possible that served at home. The one concession to India was mulligatawny soup.

Back in Naini, life was becoming grim and earnest. I was sent to a kindergarten school, run by a Mrs O' Halloran, halfway down the hill into the town. Gone were the leisurely mornings when I could ride my tricycle around the verandahs of Snow View, pretending I was an engine on the Rohilkand and Kumaon Railway, with a genuine white engine driver complete with solar topi. Instead I was made to do something called 'Pothooks and Hangers', a form of primitive writing, which was not only difficult, but deadly boring. Feigning a bad headache, I was taken by a sympathetic Mrs O'Halloran to a bedroom and told to lie down until I felt better. Directly her back was turned I was out of the window and away up the hill to Snow View like a flash. My reception there was hostile. Uncle Jimmy threatened to beat me, my grandmother, to whom I had fled in desperation, was unenthusiastic at my appearance. I was put in a dandy and taken back to school, yelling my head off, 'Take me to my dear old home, my dear old home is Graneee!' It was some years before I was allowed to live that down. Eventually I must have settled at my kindergarten, for there were no more such episodes, and I was soon able to read and write quite well.

My grandmother was a deeply religious woman, stalwart in her conviction that only the faith of the Church of England was the true one. Thus every Sunday, morning and evening, we attended the church which, like Mrs O'Halloran's school, was halfway down the hill to Naini, and not far from the hissing *'bumba'*, the auxiliary pumping station. For church, I was made to wear the disgusting little silk tussore suit that I loathed so much. It made me feel a cissie and a ponce. My hair was a mass of blonde curls, and to be told I looked sweet by elderly ladies made things even worse. One evening in church, I had a desperate urge to pee. 'What am I to do?' I whispered to Awdry, sitting beside me. Without a word, she pointed to the hassock we used for kneeling. It was a large one filled with sawdust, ideal for the job. Hidden by Awdry from the rest, I peed away into it and not a drop appeared. Quick thinking on her part had saved me from an embarrassing situation.

Only one other encounter did I have with a tiger and that took place from Naini Tal itself. A man-eater had been reported wreaking havoc among the villagers at Rani Khet, some 20 miles away. I have never been able to understand why a tiger which eats humans should be considered such an embodiment of evil. To it, they are no different from any other form of prey, except, being rather slow and defenceless, easier to catch. Furthermore it is often some man's fault that a tiger has turned maneater in the first place, It could have been wounded and incapacitated by some villager's shot from an ancient muzzle-loading rifle, a *'jezail'*, or it could have a poisoned foot from a porcupine quill. No longer being able to catch its normal prey, it looks for something slower and easier, a grass cutter or a herdsman tending his flock. Once having acquired a taste for human flesh, tigers seemed to relish it.

Now of course if there is one thing which would give British rule in India a bad name, it would be to allow villagers to be eaten by tigers, so a *'bandabast'* (pronounced 'bunderbust') was made to shoot it. *Bandabast* is a lovely Urdu word meaning 'to make all arrangements to do a certain thing'. It could be having a picnic, moving house, or shooting a tiger. Whatever the occasion, it merely meant informing your bearer of what was afoot and leaving the rest to him and the servants. It was an ideal form of existence. In this case, my mother's bearer was told there would be three guns, she being one of them, and myself, going to the *dak* bungalow at Rani Khet, to stay there until the tiger was dead. Bedding rolls, food, servants, *tongas* for transport were all prepared and sent on ahead. We rode out the following day to find all prepared, our beds made up, Keatings liberally sprayed, and a smiling *khansama* to meet us with the news that *'Aplogan ka tiffin tiar hai'*, lunch is ready, and would consist of mulligatawny soup, roast chicken and caramel custard.

That afternoon, after our siesta, my mother and I set off for a walk down one of the dusty jungle paths. She carried a gun, naturally, for without one she would have felt naked, but we hoped to shoot something for the evening meal instead of the inevitable tough roast chicken. On the way home, after a fruitless hunt, we saw the pug marks of a large tiger alongside our own in the thick dust of the forest path. All the way along where we had been walking, he had been following us, perhaps a hundred or so yards behind. It was an eerie walk back – my mother, her quite inadequate 12-bore at the ready, both of us wondering when the tiger would leap at us out of the undergrowth. I had this feeling that being so much the smaller and easier, it would be me he would choose. Just before we reached the *dak* bungalow, we saw the place where he had left the jungle to follow us. And that was the last that anybody heard of that particular tiger. It just disappeared, and the villagers around were able to continue their lives without being eaten. As for the tiger he probably realised that if my mother was after him, then it was time to move on.

In August 1920 Uncle Robin was murdered at his desk in Luckinpore. The first I knew anything was wrong, was when my mother, who was with us in Naini Tal, came rushing to me, shouting 'Pray for Uncle Robin, pray for him as you've never prayed before.' I wondered what he could have done wrong that I should pray for him, so I ran as usual to my grandmother for advice. She told me that a telegram had just arrived to say that he had been attacked and was gravely ill. He died the next day. Only the weekend before he had been staying with us, and had been warned not to go back to his district as there was trouble brewing, until the Army and more police had been drafted in. He laughed it off and went back. On 20 August, three men armed with *talwars*, curved sabres, moved in on his bungalow during the morning. The red-coated *chuprassies* or orderlies who sat on the verandah to supervise the throng of petitioners, slunk away. Nor were there any petitioners that day, a strange phenomenon. He was left alone. They attacked him as he worked, slashing at him with their swords. He ran from room to room, hoping to find at least a golf club to protect himself. It was no good. He was cut up and left for dead. Carving people up with *talwars* is an old Indian custom in which they seem to take great pride as something they have always done. It was prevalent during the Mutiny and throughout the time of the British Raj, whenever there were communal riots, During the rioting after the Partition of India and Pakistan in 1948, at least a million were killed in this way. It still seems a highly favoured weapon during the internecine quarrels between Hindu and Moslem to this day.

My uncle's murderers were caught, tried and hanged. They were Muslim extremists who were working to get the British out of India. Freedom fighters they would be called today, or terrorists, depending upon which way you looked on them. Before they died, they said they had no grudge against him, and that he was a good man, respected by everybody. But they wished to murder the most important British official around. He just happened to be that, and at hand. I have no doubt that in India they are regarded as 'martyrs'.

My uncle's death changed our lives completely. My mother was distraught for months. Even her dachshunds appealed to her no longer. Gone were the Christmas elephant tiger-shooting camps, gone were the special trains on my birthday. Gone also was the problem for my father of what to do about his wife and his brother. At least for the time being that had been resolved. He had been given command of his battalion of the 1st Punjab Regiment, and was now a Lt-Colonel. His great friend, Dick Browning, the Russian interpreter who had been kept throughout the war guarding a small island off Aden, was his second in command. Hockey was, and is, the national game of India, and his battalion team won the All-India championship, thanks to the wizadry of their centre forward, Dyan Chand. They were stationed at Fategarh. My grandmother and I spent the cold weather with him. For several years over this period my mother disappeared altogether, and other than knowing she was still in India, I had no idea where she was. I believe she and my father met again and tried to live together in a form of reconciliation and to make a new start. It was a hopeless failure. Two more different people it would be hard to find.

My chief recollection of Fategarh was being taught reading, writing and arithmetic by my grandmother, and the civet cats which ran about the ceiling of our bungalow. She used to teach me spelling by means of small lettered squares like those used for Scrabble. One day she asked me to spell 'axe', and when I did so, produced a little tomahawk with a big hook at the back of it, as a present. It would have gladdened the heart of Hiawatha himself. I used it to dig a big hole in the garden, and it was my most prized possession for years.

The bungalow was thatched, and each room, as a protection from all the rodents and other creatures which lived in the thatch, had a thick canvas ceiling, painted white. This also helped keep the place cool during the heat of the day. Among the other roof inhabitants were these civet cats, which when scared let off a stench which can make even a genuine red-blooded, Fourth of July American skunk envious. To do this they squirt an obnoxious fluid from glands at the base of their tail. These particular civet cats seemed to be frightened all the time, and there were yellow patches all over the cloth ceilings. In the end you got used to it, and the smell seemed to keep the mosquitoes away. By this time I had become a great walker and thought nothing of covering 15 miles or so in a day. My father used to take me crocodile-shooting along the banks of the Ganges. I would chatter away to him in Urdu as we walked. For a picnic lunch we would inevitably have hard-boiled eggs, and now, whenever I put salt on a hard-boiled egg on a picnic, it takes me back to those crocodile shoots with my father along the banks of the Ganges.

I was now some seven years old. It was time for me to be sent home to start my education at boarding school. This was the pattern of nearly all children born to British officials and officers in India. They would stay with their parents until they were about eight and then be sent Home to live with retired uncles and aunts or grandparents during the holidays, and the rest of the year as boarders at school. Some even had to spend their holidays at school as well. There were a number of schools which catered especially for this. Every third year their parents would come home on eight months leave, some six weeks of which would be taken up with the voyage, and most of the rest by school terms. Thus most children after the age of about eight scarcely ever saw their parents again other than as strangers. There were so many of us in the same boat that it seemed the normal state of affairs.

One more hot weather did I spend at Snow View. Then it was everything being packed up and leaving India for good. My grandmother was coming home to look after me. She had another Pekingese by now, to replace Mowgli. It was called Tingaling or 'Tinngy', and along with Awdry's dog Belinda, a mongrel bull terrier, would have to spend six months in quarantine for rabies. Uncle Jimmy was retiring from the Army and coming with us, along with Awdry and her mother, my Aunt Gertie, who was trying to get a divorce from her *box-wallah*. They had a large and very beautiful Afghan wolfhound which would also have to go into quarantine. Eventually the dreadful day arrived when we had to leave. All the servants came with us to railhead at Kathgodam. There were tears and wailing, garlands of flowers around the necks of the grown-ups. By this time I was too excited to mind much. I was on the Night Mail to Bombay and would soon be realising a dream, one day to travel on the BB&CI, the Bombay and Baroda Central Indian Railway. A wide-gauge train at last.

6

One of the ship's officers was whistling 'Yes, We Have no Bananas', the hit song of the moment, as we climbed up the gang-plank onto SS *Scindia* at Bombay, that morning of January 1922. She was a small ship of only some 5000 tons, with a long slender black funnel amidships. She belonged to the Anchor Line, and all their ships had black funnels. To me she looked quite immense. Her cruising speed was about ten knots, and what with coaling stops on the way, the voyage back to England would take about a month. Awdry, her mother and Uncle Jimmy, by now what would be described as 'an item', were going all the way home. My grandmother and I were to disembark at Marseille and join my father to spend a couple of months at Menton on the French Riviera. She felt she could not yet face the bone-chilling reality of an English winter. He was on long leave, and had been in Florence looking at the pictures, regarding the place as his cultural home, being into art in a considerable way at the time. My mother had disappeared somewhere in India and was staying there indefinitely. For her it must have been the Golden Years.

Many of the more important servants, such as bearers and ayahs, had come with us to Bombay, and there were further tearful farewells and garlands of flowers on the dockside. Besides ourselves, the three dogs and their kennels, an absolute mountain of our luggage had to be loaded on board. Most of it would go into store on arrival, waiting to be used 'one day', which would never come. Clothes, uniforms, shooting trophies such as tiger and leopard skins and heads, antlers, blankets, sheets, camping gear, all packed into large wooden crates, with convenient ill-fitting joints at top and side for the moths to get in. With my grandmother especially, nothing could be thrown away, everything hoarded, in case 'it might come in handy one day'. You could almost hear the moths and silver fish sharpening up their teeth in anticipation.

Luggage had to be carefully marked, not only with its owner's name, but where in the ship it was to be carried. Labels were issued to that effect, marked 'Cabin', 'Wanted on Voyage', and 'Hold'. Cabin luggage usually consisted of suitcases and a cabin trunk, containing those clothes needed for immediate wear on the ship. Even on a small liner like the *Scindia*, decorum still prevailed and all passengers had to change for dinner, men into dinner jackets and black tie, the women into evening dresses, and be suitably dressed during the day. What was needed changed during the voyage as the climate changed. Such clothes were kept in long black tin trunks, securely padlocked and marked with the 'Wanted on Voyage' labels. Access to them was made available once or twice a week, the items which were no longer required being packed away instead. Any box marked 'Hold' went into the hold and would not be seen again until unloaded in the home port. All the luggage was loaded on board by means of the ship's derricks, hinged to the base of the two masts. These derricks could be raised and lowered like cranes and were worked by steam driven donkey engines. There was very little deck space on the *Scindia*, and what there was seemed to be taken up by the derricks and the tops of the holds which were covered by a tarpaulin. She was really a cargo ship which took passengers, and there could not have been more than 20 of us aboard. Awdry and I were the only children and ran wild. Among the passengers was a huge German. How and why he came to be there, nobody knew.

I shared a cabin with my grandmother. It was rather dark, with a small porthole, and beautifully panelled in wood. There was a small washbasin with running hot and cold water. All cabins had electric light. This was a great novelty as we had known nothing but oil lamps. Admittedly the train compartments were lit by electricity – it was called '*bijli*', the Urdu for lightning but to find it everywhere was wonderful, as was constant running water. Huge, white enamel baths, instead of the tin tubs we were accustomed to in the *ghussal khana*, were to be found down the corridor. The water was salt and showers were provided to wash it off as you got out. The ship was about 20 years old, built on the Clyde, registered in Glasgow and most lovely withal in every respect. The crew were all lascars, seamen from the south of India, and mostly spoke Tamil. When we tried them in Urdu, they merely smiled and shook their heads. The officers were all Scots or appeared to be. One, the third officer was an especial favourite. He told us that Scotland was 'full of mountains'. It seemed a nice place to live, as we had heard that England was completely flat, there was no cold or hot weather, only nine months winter and the rest of the time rather dismal and wet. We were not looking forward to it.

The Anchor Line was the proudest of shipping companies in those days when three-quarters of the world's mercantile trade was carried in British ships. Its emblem, an anchor, was stamped on everything, even the soap in the cabins. It was Pears soap, in transparent cakes, a beautiful red-gold in colour, and was advertised by a picture called 'Bubbles', of a small, curly-haired boy blowing soap bubbles from a white clay pipe. It had been painted by a famous contemporary artist, Millais. The inference was that the child's exquisite complexion was obviously the direct result of the exclusive use of Pears soap.

The big German became the immediate object of hate and suspicion to one and all. It was rumoured that 'he had been in the Prussian Guards', that final apogee of evil. The Great War had only finished some three years previously, and feelings were still running very high. In Naini Tal there had been an unfortunate Mrs Olifant, a German married to a British official in the Forestry Department. She was reputed to have not one, but 'two brothers in the Prussian Guards', as if that in itself was a crime. Personally I always considered that if I were a German, I too would have liked to have been in the Prussian Guards. It sounded splendid.

I suppose as a small boy of eight, on the Richter scale of obnoxious unpleasantness I would have made a grade of about nine. I was deliberately egged on by Uncle Jimmy and others to make this unfortunate German's life aboard an absolute misery. Wherever he sat on deck I would go and play, make rude noises, trip over his feet and generally be a complete pest, to the delight and encouragement of the grown-ups, who in normal circumstances would not have tolerated such behaviour for a moment. In the end he could bear it no longer. Grabbing me by the top of my shorts with one hand, he held me over the railings. I could see the water and foam from the ship's prow passing below, and thought any minute he was going to let me drop. After what seemed an eternity he put me back on the deck. As with the crocodile in the camp at Kheri which opened its mouth and roared, I never went near that man again. For some reason, his quite justifiable action caused great indignation, and he was made to leave the *Scindia* at our first stop which was Port Sudan. Looking back, I did not want to bait him and only did it to please my elders who encouraged my reptilian behaviour. In fact I rather admired him for being in the Prussian Guards, especially after he had hung me over the side with one hand. I felt very sorry and guilty at his being put ashore with his luggage at Port Sudan. He gave me an ironic wave as he left, clicked his heels and bowed.

One of the best things on the ship was the ice cream. It was made by one of the lascars every day on the deck outside the cook's galley. The mixture was put in a long metal tube, the top of which was connected to a long winding handle. The whole lot was put into a wooden bucket and packed all round with ice from the refrigeration plant, and salt was added. It was then whizzed round with the winding handle. I learnt later, doing physics at Haileybury, that the salt lowered the melting point of ice, which in order to turn into water had to get its heat from somewhere, and where better than the tube containing the ice cream, causing it obligingly to freeze to the right consistency. Ice cream made like this tastes better than anything that can even be imagined today.

On one memorable occasion, the Chief Engineer took us round the engine room. This was located just behind the funnel, a huge space going from the deck to the bottom of the ship. It was full of latticed steel walkways on different levels, connected by steel stairs. The whole place gleamed with cleanliness and efficiency. At the bottom were two large boilers, continually stoked by sweating, half-naked lascars, shovelling the best quality Welsh steam coal from bunkers behind them. Pipes from the boilers took the steam to the cylinders some 30 feet above the propeller shaft.

There were no leaks, no hissing of steam and little more noise than a sewing machine, a continual whirring hum. Long steel conrods connected the pistons to the crank shaft, gleaming in the electric light as they slid up and down. The propeller shaft seemed to be about a foot across and was revolving steadily. It ran through sets of constantly lubricated bearings to the stern of the ship. Even by Red Sea standards it was hot in the engine room. We were particularly struck by the refrigerating plant, a huge black object on one of the upper stair levels, coated all over in ice, despite the heat.

Port Sudan was our first coaling stop. All night long by the light of electric flares, the coolies humped large bags of coal on board. The tops of the coal holds had been opened and the men carried the bags from the dock up a narrow plank, dumped their load and went down another plank with the empty sack. The planks were only about a foot wide, and the height of the ship above the ground considerable. There were no safety ropes, and why some of the men did not fall off is a mystery. They probably did. No-one would have minded very much, and another coolie was instantly available to take their place. The men sang all the time they worked. I can still hear the endless monotony of it, 'Haile Dumka! Haile Dumka!', was what it sounded like, and was probably an invocation to Allah to protect them from the perils of walking the plank. As the coaling progressed, the whole ship became coated with a fine black dust, and took days to get clean again. I was fascinated by the clarity of the water in Port Sudan harbour. You could see all the fish swimming around amidst the beautiful corals. It made me wish to be down there in the water amongst them; an ambition which was fulfilled almost exactly 35 years later, when I was Military Attaché to our Embassy in the Sudan.

Port Sudan lies halfway up the Red Sea, on the left-hand or African side if you are going north. The top of the Red Sea breaks into two long fingers of water one leads to Aqaba, and the more westerly one, the Gulf of Suez, leads to the town of that name and the Suez Canal. Ever since it had been opened in the latter part of the 19th century, the Canal had been the main artery of the British Empire to India and the Far East, and Whitehall's most important political consideration. Any threat to the Suez Canal was a direct threat to our Empire. To guard it, we kept a large garrison in Egypt, and though ostensibly free, Egypt was entirely under British control. Mostly, throughout the Empire, we liked and admired the native peoples we ruled. The exception was the Egyptians, or 'Gyppos', whom everyone, from General to Private, cordially loathed and despised at all times. The feeling was reciprocated equally heartily. Egypt had claimed enormous resources during the Great War, and had been the base for our campaigns against the Turks in Palestine and Syria.

The Canal begins at Suez and finishes some hundred miles further north at Port Said. As we sailed up the Gulf of Suez, everyone got ready for the ceremonial dumping of our solar topis over the side. For here the dreaded actinic ray from the sun began and ended. 'One! Two! Three! Go!' All the topis went over the side together, floating rather forlornly around the ship, as if unwilling to be parted, whilst we waited to join the north-bound convoy. The width of the waterway is only some 50 yards, certainly not enough for ships to pass each other. Thus there are two convoys every day, one north- and the other south-bound. Ships queued up in turn to join a convoy. Each took a pilot on board, either French or British; no Egyptian could be considered fit for such a task. The Canal was still ostensibly a French Company, with the British as the main shareholder. Disraeli, when Prime Minister in the 1870s, had bought the shares for Britain with money loaned by Baron de Rothschild. Halfway to Port Said, the northern entrance, ships enter the Great Bitter Lakes, where the two convoys can pass each other before starting the second, for us, north-bound stage at Ismailia.

We sailed through the Suez Canal by night, so I remember little about it. Next morning we were moored in the harbour at Port Said. Passengers who wished, were taken ashore in boats to see the town and to visit Simon Arzt, the famous store with a reputation equal to that of Harrods today. However, all the goods it sold were free of duty, and especially attractive things to buy were watches, cameras and binoculars. Receipts for them were made out at considerably less than the price actually paid, the invoices being marked 'surplus stock' or 'slightly water damaged', so that even if duty had to be paid, it was much less than buying the same article in England. As long as the goods were obviously for personal use or as a present, and not on a commercial scale, the British Customs were perfectly willing to accept things at their face value. Moreover it encouraged people to declare what they had bought rather than try to smuggle them through.

Cameras were especially popular. Everybody took photographs, but it was a very much more skilful business than that of the point-and-shoot variety of today, which is itself rapidly changing to electronic imaging. In a very few years, film will be as antiquated as the cameras of the 1920s. All the film then was known as roll film. The now universal 35mm perforated cine-type film cassette did not come into use until the 1930s. With roll film, light-sensitised coated celluloid was fastened to an opaque paper backing, red on one side and black on the other, to which the celluloid film was attached. The system meant that the camera could be loaded in daylight. Before that it had to be done in a dark-room, lit by a dim red light, to which the primitive coating was not sensitive. The roll film spool was put into one side of the camera body and the paper leader inserted into the empty spool on the other. The camera was then closed and the film wound on. Its progress had to be watched through a little red window on the back. First would appear a hand with a finger pointing forwards. This was a warning that the first frame would soon appear. Then the magical figure 1 would materialise, and all was ready for the first picture. After each exposure the film had to be wound on, and it was very easy to forget to do this, causing double or even treble exposures. It always seemed to happen with the most important, crucial and unrepeatable shots.

Each film gave eight exposures, which were oblong in shape. The smallest size was the 127, giving a picture of about $2\frac{3}{4} \times 1\frac{3}{4}$ inches (7 × 4.5 cms). This was followed by the 120 with a negative of $3\frac{1}{2} \times 2\frac{1}{4}$ inches (9 × 6 cms). The next size up was the 620 with a big negative of 6 × 4 inches (15.5 × 10 cms). Of these roll films, the only one which remains today is the 120, used mainly by professionals. There was only one 'point-and-shoot' camera, and that was the Kodak Box Brownie. It consisted of a small wooden box covered with thin black leather. It had a simple lens, a single shutter speed of $\frac{1}{25}$th of a second and a lever for time exposures.

You simply pointed the box at the subject, looked down and framed it in the tiny glass viewfinder and pressed down the shutter with a click. The results were usually amazingly good, and I cut my own photographic teeth on a Box Brownie.

Nearly all serious amateur cameras were made by Kodak. They folded into a compact size and were carried in a canvas or leather case. My mother had hers made out of part of the skin of a tiger she had shot. You pressed a button on the camera and the lens assembly sprang out, rather like a jack-in-the-box, at the end of black leather bellows. The lenses, rarely wider than F=6.3 in aperture, gave superlative definition, aided by the large size of the negatives. Many of the lenses were made by Ross of London. The distance to the subject had to be guessed and set on the rotating lens dial, as did the exposure. There were usually three shutter speeds, $\frac{1}{25}$th, $\frac{1}{50}$th and $\frac{1}{100}$th of a second. On each film box there was printed a list of suggested shutter speeds and stop openings for various conditions of light. One of the main difficulties was getting what you wanted to take into the tiny viewfinder, resulting in any number of people appearing without heads. To be technical, I understand that the viewfinders were actually reversed telescopes of the Galileo type, with the image reflected in a mirror. You can get a similar effect by looking the wrong way through binoculars. The viewfinder was attached to the front of the camera, alongside the lens. Photographs were taken from waist height and you had to peer into the viewfinder, hoping you had got everything in. The most famous and best loved of this type of camera was the Vest Pocket Kodak, known as the VPK, which took size 127 film.

Having remembered to guess the distance and the exposure, set both on the camera, taken the picture and wound on the film, it was time to get it processed, winding it on until the little red window was empty, open the camera, take out the film and lick and fasten down the little glued tab to make sure it did not unroll. In England the film was then taken to the nearest chemist and handed across the counter with the immortal and immutable words, 'One of each glossy please'. In India it was different. In every hill station and cantonment, there was the local photographer, the most famous of all being Mahatta of the Bund at

Srinagar in Kashmir. Here the film would be removed from its paper backing, developed and printed. The operator would sit cross-legged on the floor, rocking one of the chemical dishes with a toe whilst doing some other part of the process with his hands. Having made the print, the most important thing was to 'fix it' against further effect from light. This was done by placing it in a dish of 'hypo', after which it had to be washed to remove every trace of the hypo from the rather absorbent paper. Usually the washing was not thorough enough and this is the reason why over the years, so many photographs have turned yellow, faded and eventually disappeared.

For those like ourselves, who remained on board at Port Said, there was endless haggling and buying from the horde of local merchants, hawking their goods from boats surrounding the ship. It was nearly all local ware, camel saddles as seats, animal bladders made into reading lamps, prayer mats, carpets, ivory figures, paper knives, Arab daggers, necklaces, mosqui glassware rough and opaque, coloured blue or green, Egyptian fezes, small red conical hats with a red tassel, and pocket knives made in Birmingham. There was endless shouting from the boats. 'Hey Johnny – you look! Mighty fine – mighty cheap – you want nice camel saddle?' If anything was sold, the money was passed down in a bucket on a rope, and the goods pulled up in the same way.

The only Egyptians allowed on board were the '*gulli-gulli*' men, sleight-of-hand conjurers. They gave shows for us on the deck, surrounded by spectators only a few feet away. We were enthralled. Every so often one would produce a live chick from under his fez, out of his sleeve, or from somebody's pocket, until at the end the deck was practically a farmyard with at least a dozen of the little creatures running about cheeping. Their skill was of the highest order and would have done credit to any top-grade London music hall of the time. After the show they would pass their fezes round, but the audience seemed to melt away, and they would be lucky if they got more than a few piastres. The *gulli-gulli* men were also fortune tellers and made a bit on the side in this way as well. They also made money from the 'three-fez trick' – under which fez was the chick? Six or seven of them

72

would be working each ship in the harbour, and would set up their show on different parts of the deck. If you got bored with what one was doing you could stroll along to watch another. It must have paid off, or so many would not have been doing it. The art was passed down from father to son, and some had been conjurers for generations. As a sideline, they seemed anxious to invite people to meet their little brothers and sisters. 'You want see my sister?' they would enquire politely of their audience. Apparently you had to go into the town for this. My grandmother was extremely evasive when I asked her if we couldn't go ashore to meet the nice man's little sister, and told me to stop talking nonsense. The *gulli-gulli* men insisted it 'was all same like Queen Victoria', so it must have been all right, though I wondered what Queen Victoria had to do with it. Perhaps at some time she had given a tea party for them at Port Said.

The Mediterranean was very rough, and except for Awdry and myself, everyone was seasick. We ate huge hot curries in the almost empty dining room. To make matters worse, my poor grandmother had bad toothache from a large hole in a back molar out of which the stopping had fallen. With no prospect of seeing a dentist for at least a week, she would plug the hole with cotton wool soaked in brandy and became quite tipsy. The only remedy for the seasickness appeared to be endless glasses of fizzing Eno's Fruit Salts, that universal panacea for almost any and every complaint. As it was too rough and stormy to go out on deck, she spent much time reading to us, or continuing with our lessons. Uncle Jimmy told us we were going to land at Marseille, in a country called France, where all the natives were white, or anyway whiteish, and did not speak Urdu but a language called French. However, if you shouted at them loudly enough in Urdu, they would certainly understand. I imagine that from handling generations of British officers, anxious to shorten their journey home by disembarking at Marseille and taking the train instead of going all the way round via Gibraltar and the Bay of Biscay, by word and gesture, the French porters and officials managed to make out what was required of them. Many years later, as a journalist, writing up a ski resort in France, I heard an English visitor yelling at a ski lift attendant in whatever language it is that they speak in Nigeria, and he understood perfectly. So perhaps Uncle Jimmy was right after all.

My father met us on the docks, and we said goodbye to the others who were going on in the *Scindia*. They would also deal with our heavy luggage from the hold. I was very sorry to be leaving Awdry behind, and wished she could have come with us. We had been booked into a hotel by the sea at Menton, exactly on the border with Italy, near Bordighera. Here we stayed until the end of March, when my grandmother considered the English climate possibly warm enough for her to face.

At Menton, my father and I used to spend many hours on the beach. I especially remember using his pocket knife to prise limpets off the rocks. Just behind out hotel lay the coastal railway line, along which clanked enormously long goods trains, of anything up to 120 trucks. The locomotives were of the old- fashioned type, probably built 50 years previously, with very long funnels. We used to stand on bridges and try to drop pebbles down them as the engines passed below at about 20 miles per hour. French goods trains travel extremely slowly. We also went for long walks of 10 to 15 miles in the hills above the coast, talking all the while in Urdu. We often spoke about the Army and the recent fighting during the Great War. When I repeated the popular myth that the 'Germans were all brutes and cowards who ran away all the time', he asked 'Why then was it that it had taken four and a half years to beat them?' He was full of praise for the bravery of both the Germans and the Turks, but said there were really only three efficient (*larai ka bandabast tik karne wale*), fighting races in the world, the British, the French and the Germans. I have long wondered what exactly he meant by the words for 'efficient'.

7

The first thing which impressed me on arrival in England was the immaculate steam engine coupled to our train at Dover. We had been hauled across France at breakneck speed, by a huge, black, rather dirty monster, hissing from leaky steam pipes fixed to its boiler. For all its huge size, it would let forth from time to time a curiously effeminate little squeak, instead of the full-throated roaring whistle one would expect from such a gigantic creature. This English engine was much smaller, sleek with a squat funnel, altogether a joy to behold. It leaked no steam and was spotlessly clean. In 1922 the London Chatham and Dover Railway, affectionately known as the London Smashem and Turnover, served the Channel ports of Dover and Folkestone. Their locomotives were painted dark brown with gold piping. They had a brass rim to their short funnels, and these were kept burnished like gold.

Our final destination was East Clevedon in Somerset, where the rest of the family had installed itself in a small house called Barry y va, which we always called 'Barry why va'. The Welsh influence was still strong from just across the water of the Bristol channel in that part of the county. Here we were to stay for a couple of years. The day we arrived in early April was brilliantly fine and sunny, although some six inches of freshly fallen snow lay thick everywhere. It was my first experience of the obsession the British have with all aspects of their weather, providing them with an endless source of conversation. Life was full of surprises. For instance, I was amazed to see white people doing menial tasks. True, they had also done them in France, but there they had somehow still been natives and that did not really count, even though a Frenchman, Georges Carpentier, was heavy weight-boxing champion of the world and had just knocked out the fearsome Battling Bill Siki. Then I saw my first aeroplane. Apart from Uncle Jimmy, who had seen them over the trenches in Flanders, none of us had ever seen an aeroplane, and we all rushed out of the house in great excitement. It was a single-engine biplane, with two large wheels dangling below the fuselage. Later this feature was to give rise to a popular music hall joke. Old lady to yokel: 'Tell me my man, is that a Mail plane up there?' 'No lidy, them's only wheels.' As *Punch* ended so many of its jokes at the time, 'Collapse of old lady.'

It was at Clevedon that I was introduced to two childrens' magazines, *The Rainbow*, and *Tiger Tim's Weekly*. *The Rainbow* came out every Thursday and cost tuppence ($\frac{1}{2}$p). It consisted of brightly coloured cartoons of anthropomorphical animals in human dress, and centred around Mrs Bruin's school. Mrs Bruin was a large and matronly brown bear who ran the school with an iron hand in a velvet paw. Her nephew, Bobby Bruin was a pupil, but the principal character was Tiger Tim, leader of all the japes and escapades the animals got up to. Other pupils were Georgie Giraffe, Willy Ostrich and Joey Parrot. The most unpopular animal in the school was Porky Boy, a large pig who was continually getting hampers of food from home, which he refused to share with the others, who always found a method of getting it away from him. Poor Porky Boy had a truly miserable time at Mrs Bruin's, and certainly today there would have been an outcry about bullying, with the magazine probably being forced to cease publication. I vividly remember one episode when Mrs Bruin had taken her school down to the seaside for a holiday. Porky Boy had got his hamper away from the rest, spread a cloth on the sand and was just about to tuck in. But the other animals had been busy digging a tunnel under the beach towards him. A picture, in cutaway, showed them all inside it. They then came to the surface exactly under the hamper and carried it off in triumph, just as poor Porky Boy was about to take his first mouthful. Again I can hear today's outcry of 'encouraging children to dig tunnels in the sand which might fall in and kill them'. I cannot remember any dying as a result of reading *The*

76

Rainbow, or even *Tiger Tim's Weekly* for that matter, which came out on Tuesdays instead.

At Clevedon I was sent as a day boy to my first preparatory school. Walton Lodge. The headmaster and owner was a young man called R.F. Gwynne, fresh from the trenches and newly married. Before the outbreak of War in 1914 he had been to Emanuel College at Cambridge, where he had obtained a very high degree in Classics and a University Blue for hockey. To see him bounce a ball on one end of a hockey stick and run with it from one end of the field to the other was a revelation. He was a fresh-complexioned, earnest young man in his early thirties when I went to Walton Lodge, and had only been married about a year, His wife, Helen, was a tall, rather thin blonde, and for some reason we were all terrified of her. To us, she was as warm and cuddlesome as an iceberg.

Displayed on the school gate was a large brass plate, grandiloquently inscribed 'Walton Lodge. Preparatory School for the Sons of Gentlemen'. There was an outcry when Mr Gwynne, probably strapped for cash, allowed the son of the local auctioneer to join us. The school colours were blue and silver, and we wore its crest, also Mr Gwynne's, of a severed horse's head impaled on a sword, on our blue school caps. The school was housed in a large, rambling old mansion with a big barn attached, used as a gymnasium and general playroom. It was lit entirely by gas, and all the pipes leaked. Mr Gwynne was constantly going round mending leaks with a paste he made out of soap. The whole place reeked of coal gas and carbolic soap. There were some 25 of us boys, about half a dozen of whom were day boys like myself. I quickly made great friends with one called John Reynolds. The teaching staff consisted of Mr Gwynne and a Mr Richards, an ex-Captain in the Coldstream Guards with only one arm and a permanent grudge against life. He and the Matron, universally known as 'the Hag', shared a common living room and loathed each other with a deadly hatred. Mr Richards used to take us for drill and made us come to attention by lifting one knee almost up to our chin and slamming it down beside the other foot. Not only did it hurt, but it seemed to me a very long way to go about such a short manoeuvre. Mr Richards only lasted a term and

77

was replaced by a weird little man with a ferrety face called Mr Pell.

My two heroes at the school, both about 13, were Curtis and 'Pip' Poncione, son of a man who made ice cream on Clevedon's seafront. How he managed to slip past the brass plate on the school gate I never discovered. Curtis was captain of the school cricket XI, and Pip was a brilliant football player as well as being vice-captain of cricket. Mind you, with only 25 pupils, it was not too difficult to get into the school teams. But to me, aged eight, they were gods. In addition to being cricket captain, Curtis was a wonderful neat writer of 'script', a new form of unjoined writing taught at the school, and the latest educational fad. He was also a great swimmer, and was able to swim out to 'the point' at Lady Bay, the little beach where we were taken to bathe once a week during that summer term. Lying on the Bristol Channel, the tidal currents around the Point at Lady Bay were always uncertain and dangerous. The water was invariably full of silt and mud as well as being horribly cold. Accustomed as I was to the warmth of India, I regarded our bathes with loathing and trepidation, especially as I could not swim and no-one made any attempt to teach me. Mr Richards shepherded us down to the pebble beach, where we undressed behind a rock and were then driven into the water. Those of us who could not swim shivered and splashed each other at the edge. The swimmers made great display of their prowess further out. Before I left the school in 1925 I could swim quite well and even reached the Point.

At Walton Lodge there were only two classes, an Upper and a Lower. Naturally I found myself in the Lower with some 12 others. Mr Gwynne took us for Classics and Languages. He always wore modish 'plus-fours', large baggy trousers cut short at the knee and worn with stockings. They were much in favour with golfers, eventually finishing up as the correct wear for grouse or pheasant shooting in Scotland, where they are still highly favoured by gamekeepers, and standard undress for stage performances of 'Lady Chatterley's Lover'. I began to learn Latin and French. Mr Richards took us for Maths.

There was a curious system of punishments and awards, called Stars and Stripes. If you did particularly well at anything you were awarded an Alpha. Four Alphas made a Star. If you got ten Stars you got a prize. During my time there I never knew anyone who got ten Stars. Stripes were awarded for almost any and every kind of misdemeanour, from inattention in class, not doing your prep, or failing to finish your food. One Stripe cancelled out a Star. If you got ten Stripes it automatically meant a caning. The catch was that although Stripes cancelled Stars, the reverse was not the case, academic excellence could not save you from a beating. There was a large wall chart in the Upper classroom, showing the Star and Stripe position of everyone, with two horizontal columns after each name, Red for Stars and blue for Stripes. When you got to nine, you knew a visit after breakfast to the headmaster's study was not far away.

Besides the Stars and Stripes wall chart there was another, 'Matron's Constipation Checklist'. Each day you had to mark this to show whether you had 'been' or not, so that if necessary you could be given the appropriate dose of medicine. Thus the state of everyone's bowel movements was a matter for conversation and conjecture throughout the school. As the standard remedy was a delicious concoction called 'Californian Syrup of Figs', doled out every evening by the old Hag, many of us left unnecessary blanks in the daily marking of our checklist. It was a close-run thing, for if you left too many blanks, you were as likely as not to get a large dose of castor oil instead.

One of the wonders of that first term at my preparatory school was my introduction to wireless and the first early transmissions by the BBC from their station in London, called 2LO. Mr Gwynne was an enthusiastic innovator and had one of the first receiving sets. He had set up a very long aerial of some 30 yards across the kitchen garden. This led into what was called a crystal set, where a very thin wire, or 'cat's whisker' was put into gentle contact by means of a weak spring, with a small crystal. Tuning was done by moving a coil of fine copper wire wrapped around a cardboard tube. Reception was through headphones. The sound was so weak as to be almost inaudible, but it seemed to us, both wonderful and incredible that we could hear speech and music, however faint, all the way from London with nothing in between other than the aerial wire in the kitchen garden.

Another wonder of that first and summer term was my introduction to cricket; a game which appeared to make no sense at all, but in a very short time became almost a religion. My father took me into Weston super Mare and bought me a cricket bat called a Cobbett. It was heavy, unwieldy, far too big and quite useless. To me it became a treasured totem. I stood it in linseed oil which was supposed to make it drive the ball better and stop it stinging your hands when you hit it. The oil achieved nothing, the bat stung like a wasp and had no drive at all. It was about this time that I found I could run quite fast and won a cricket ball in the 100 yards sprint at the school sports. Mr Richards was the starter, firing blanks from a huge army pistol; Mr Gwynne was Chief Judge, and his wife presented the prizes. The Sports Day was also open to our deadly rivals in Clevedon, Darcy's School. My chief recollection of it was seeing hordes of little boys racing off into the distance as if loosed into battle, never to be seen again.

At the end of that summer my father's leave was up, and he went back to his regiment in India. It would be three years before I saw him again. In the meantime I was left in the charge of my grandmother. The next term I became a boarder, and loathed it. The food was quite horrible, especially the midday meal. Breakfast consisted of lumpy porridge with hot milk, thick with skin, followed by a boiled egg. For some reason I hated egg yolk, as I thought it looked disgusting, and used to bore a hole through the bottom of the egg so that the yolk could drain off into the cup. This little dodge earned me many a Stripe. Lunch usually consisted of very tough, overcooked meat full of gristle, blood vessels and other such stringy objects, potatoes and watery cabbage. followed by some kind of fruit pudding with gluey custard, that staple dish of the English. Sometimes we had semolina instead. The worst day of all was Friday, when we had fish pie; which always tasted rancid and smelt to high heaven. The general opinion was that it had walked all the way by itself from Grimsby. I usually managed to scrape it undetected into an old envelope to dispose of later. Once I forgot, and going through my pockets some three weeks later, Matron found it. All hell was let loose. We always claimed it went back into the next Friday's fish pie.

Mr Richards had gone, his place being taken by a small, ferrety, thin and weasel-faced little man called Mr Pell. At first, he and I took an instant dislike to each other, until in a moment of extreme exasperation, I began to swear at him in Urdu, calling him 'the off-spring of a pig's sister's genitals' and other choice epithets with which that language abounds. Instead of being angry, he was entranced. From being his most unpopular scholar I became in an instant his favourite. I really did not know what was going on. Of course in these days of the child sex abuse industry, nobody can get anywhere, especially in America, unless they have been sexually abused as a child. I wish I could lay the blame for my defects of character upon the unfortunate little Mr Pell, who, although he never did anything that could be construed as abuse, certainly acted in a most peculiar manner. For instance he would come up to my dormitory at night, give me piggy-back rides and continually call me 'little boy'. At half term he got permission from my grandmother at Barry y va to take me to the fun fair at Weston super Mare, where we spent a happy afternoon eating ice cream and riding such things as the big dipper and merry-go-round. I accepted it all in good part, found it difficult to understand why Mr Pell, very sensibly of course, should prefer me to others, but was aware all the time of some unknown, ulterior motive, and always slightly apprehensive of what he might do next.

The following term Mr Pell had gone. I imagine the Gwynnes had become suspicious. He was replaced by Mr Simpkins. There are two people who were perhaps the greatest influence upon my future life. One was Mr Simpkins, and the other was L.A. Speakman, my teacher in the Army Class at Haileybury. Both imbued in me an abiding interest and love of history. Mr Simpkins – I can never think of him by any other name than complete with the Mr – was in his early thirties, tall and thin with a crop of unruly hair brushed over his forehead. He had been a Captain and a Company Commander in the Leicestershire Regiment and was fiercely proud of having commanded 120 men in action. He used to enthral us with tales of the Great War. He had been one of the first into the huge craters we blew up with mines on the Messines ridge. He would recount with gory detail of the bodies of dead German infantry they found lying around after the explosions, and of how his Company had mown down hundreds more with their rifles and Lewis guns when they counter-attacked to try and retake the position.

Now it is a curious fact that the only people who ever complain about the Great War, calling it a bloodbath and saying how stupid and uncaring were the Generals, are those who never took part in it. Moreover the further away in time they are from it, the more vehement becomes their horror and criticism. I was brought up under the shadow of that war and it clouded my whole outlook. I never heard anyone call it a bloodbath or even complain about it. They were all immensely proud of having taken part, seemed to miss the intense comradeship of the trenches, and most actually seemed to have enjoyed themselves. At Walton Lodge we were all sorry we had not been in it, and hoped there would be another fairly soon so that we too could take part.

Mr Simpkins told us of the 'Archers of Mons'. During the retreat of the British Expeditionary Force from that city in 1914, the ghosts of ancient English archers had obligingly descended from the skies with their bows to help their stricken descendants pursued by hordes of Germans. He added that although he had not seen dead enemy with arrow wounds, himself, he knew others who had friends who had actually seen them: the yard shafts, fletched with grey goose quills, sticking from their chests, steel points coming out at the back. The retreat was taking place almost across the old battlefields of Crecy and Agincourt, hardly a step out of the way for the ghostly archers. They could zoom down from the sky, shoot up a few Huns and be back in time for tea. In the parlance of a later war, it was a piece of cake. With help like this, who needed machine guns, of which the BEF had woefully few? What they lacked in machine guns, however, the soldiers made up for by the accuracy and speed of their rifle fire. Every man could get off 15 to 20 aimed rounds a minute with devastating effect upon an enemy who advanced en masse, shoulder to shoulder. Although extremely helpful, heavenly intervention had undoubtedly been useful, but not essential, more of a bonus.

Mr Simpkins used to read to us at weekends and often in the evenings as well. He was a romantic, steeped in English history, in heraldry and chivalry, especially of the Hundred Years War with

France during the 14th and 15th centuries. He read to us from Conan Doyle's *The White Company*, of the adventures of Sir Guy Mannering and his fighting against the French at Poitiers, where he won his spurs as a knight, being awarded them by the Black Prince himself, son of the great Edward III. The victory had been gained from the near-annihilation of the French by the English archers.

During a long truce afterwards, 30 English and Breton knights, out of general boredom and lack of something to do, challenged an equal number of French knights in a contest to the death. It took place ten miles from Josselin in Brittany, and the field where they fought, marked with an obelisk, can still be seen. I visited it some 60 years after leaving Walton Lodge, and could almost hear Mr Simpkins reading to us of 'the Battle of the Thirty', or 'le combat des trentes', as the French call it. Rules were drawn up, and it had been agreed that they all should fight dismounted. The contest began at dawn and lasted all day with a suitable break at midday for light refreshments, when the combatants met on the most comradely terms, 'in friendship most wondrous to behold', before continuing to kill and wound each other, an hour or so later.

They fought on until late afternoon, when only three or four on each side were still upright, and those barely able to stand through loss of blood and exhaustion. Breaking his pledge to fight on foot, it was then that one of the French knights slunk away to mount his horse and charge the remaining English and Bretons, knocking them down and dispatching them with ease. The French have always claimed the Battle of the Thirty as a victory. We considered it nothing but by cheating, not the behaviour of a knight at all.

For 200 years the English bowmen remained masters of every battlefield. The best archers came from the Welsh borders and Cheshire. It took years to train an archer, and in all towns and villages throughout England from around AD 1300 onwards, every young man after church on Sunday would have to practise at the archery butts. The marks where they sharpened their arrow heads on church walls can be seen in many places to this day. The bows were six feet long, hence the name 'longbow', and made of yew. It took great strength to pull the string back, and bowmen developed enormous chest and arm muscles, their bones also increasing in size to meet the challenge. At close range and for piercing armour, the archer would hold the string and bend the bow by stepping forward 'into it', thus adding his own weight to the overall power.

The arrows were exactly a 'cloth yard' in length. As so much emphasis was put on the cloth yard, there must have been different measurements for other 'yards'. They were fletched with feathers from the grey goose, and the point was made from hardened steel so shaped as to best penetrate the plate armour worn by knights. This shape was such that the hole it made, facilitated the entry of the arrow shaft in a similar way to armour-piercing shells in the 1939–45 war. Such was the power of the bow that an arrow could penetrate a 6-inch oak door, and at ranges of less than a hundred yards it would go through plate armour as though it were paper. The effective range was 300 yards, and at this distance the arrow flight would trace a parabolic curve, picking up tremendous velocity and kinetic energy as it descended. A trained bowman could shoot off five or six aimed shots a minute and have at least three or four arrows all in the air at the same time. The English longbow was undoubtedly the most devastating infantry weapon in the world, until the invention of the breech-loading magazine rifle of the late 19th century. It was not ousted by the muzzle-loading musket on grounds of effectiveness, but because a musketeer could be trained in less than a tenth of the time.

In battle the English fought on foot, the knights and men at arms formed a solid block in the centre. The archers were posted on the wings, probably some 5000 on each flank. They were pulled slightly forward to take the advancing foe in enfilade. Each archer also carried a sharpened stake which he dug into the ground, pointing forwards. Thus a wall of stakes would protect them from cavalry attack. Besides their bows, each man had a short sword. In addition to those slung on his back in his quiver, the bowman would have a pile of arrows at his feet within easy reach. More arrows were continually fed forward from carts full of them in the supply train. To this day, the British Army has always used this system, 'that men should never have to go back for ammunition, it must always be brought forward to them'. Once men start going back for any reason, you never know how many will follow.

Directly the enemy came within range, the archers would open fire. With 10,000 men loosing off, there would never be less than 30,000 or 40,000 thousand arrows in the air with their terrible whistling, and the sky would be black with them 'so that the very earth was darkened'. Men advancing through this 'arrow storm' would be bending forwards as if walking through a blizzard. Arrows penetrated every joint in the armour, and no horse could live for five minutes without becoming a pin cushion, as the French quickly found out to their cost at Crecy. Another disadvantage they soon discovered was that they always had to attack an enemy on ground of his own choosing. The initiative was ever with the English. If the French did not attack, then the archers would simply advance to a safe distance and shoot them to pieces. From Halidon Hill in 1333 against the Scots, to the victories against the French during the Hundred Years War, and the destruction of the Scots at Flodden in 1513 and Pinkie in 1547, the English bowmen were the ultimate factor that dominated every field. The French knights considered the use of archers as both cowardly and unfair. War was the business of knights and gentlemen, not for low-born archers. Perhaps this helps to explain the conduct of the French knight at the Battle of the Thirty. Maybe he wished to show that he, too, could cheat.

Mr Simpkins, that paladin among pedagogues, also taught us all about heraldry: how the coat of arms, borne on a knight's shield would tell all those who could read it, exactly whom he was, where he came from and what his lineage. We learnt of the heraldic 'colours' and of the 'metals', gold and silver, of how you could never have a 'metal upon a metal', or a 'colour upon a colour'; of how when a knight died, his effigy in his church would bear a lion at its feet. If he died in his bed, it would be a dog. We all hoped we would die with a lion at our feet. One day we awoke to find he had been working out all our family coats of arms, and had produced exquisitely painted, large shields made of thick cardboard, emblazoned with them. Those he could not find, he invented, and many a small boy found himself a bearer of coat armour of which he had no knowledge, and to which he was not entitled. The work must have taken months to complete. To go with the shields were painted cardboard swords and helmets, replicas of those used by English knights in the 14th century. Being boys, we regarded swords and shields only for fighting, and with hoops of delight were soon hammering away at each other with them. In no time at all, everything he had so carefully made was a battered wreck.

But Mr Simpkins was not all sweetness and light. He had a famous little switch called 'Skeeter' and you would do well to keep out of its reach. We wore shorts, and Skeeter's favourite place of attack was just behind the knee. Every boy had a bath once a week, supervised by Matron, but in addition as we went to bed at 8 p.m., we would have to wash thoroughly at the row of basins in the bathroom. Stripped to the waist, we scrubbed our hands, faces and necks with the carbolic soap provided. Woe betide the boy who was idling or not doing it properly. Skeeter would catch him with a crack across the back and raise a shriek and a fine weal. I remember on one occasion, watching fascinated as two delightful, dirty little trickles of water spread down from my neck on to my chest, only to be brought to my senses by the stinging bite of Skeeter and a roar from Mr Simpkins. 'What are you dawdling for, Willoughby? Wake up! You look half-asleep!' To me, being half-asleep just as you were going to bed seemed as good an idea as any other, but there was no accounting for school-masters. Funnily enough, no-one bore him any grudge over Skeeter, and the little switch became almost as popular as he was. People would exchange Skeeter tales and experiences, just as years later they would swap 'bomb stories' during the Blitz. Furthermore Mr Simpkins was doubly popular for never dishing out Stripes. He let Skeeter do it for him.

8

Our school day began with breakfast at 8 a.m. At 8.45 there were daily prayers led by Mr Gwynne, who had a fine baritone voice, accompanying himself on the piano for the hymn, which was usually of the stirring martial kind, such as 'Fight the Good Fight' or maybe 'Onward Christian Soldiers'. A great favourite was 'From Greenland's icy mountains to India's coral strand', in which blind heathens bowed down to wood and stone. This I could never understand, for although I had actually seen Hindus doing such things, none seemed to be blind. I had even argued with one who had found a curiously shaped stone in the Kheri jungle, which he wished to take home and pray to. 'Don't you Christians believe God made everything?' he asked. 'Yes, of course,' I replied. 'Well then,' he continued, 'what is wrong with praying to a stone, surely that is praying to God?' There was a flaw somewhere in his logic, but I could not pinpoint it.

What with breakfast, morning prayers and the start of work at 9 a.m., there was little enough time to do the necessary to fill in Matron's Constipation Checklist. There was always a big run on the five or so cubicles in the school bogs. These were situated in an old greenhouse next to the upper classroom, and got unbearably hot in summer and freezing cold in winter. They were of the old-fashioned high cistern type called Niagara, and when the plug was pulled the ferocious rush of water was not unlike that famous waterfall – though I cannot imagine anyone going to the Walton Lodge bogs for their honeymoon. In fact a favourite trick was to lean over the wall and pull the plug whilst someone was sitting on the seat, when the water pressure would lift him about a foot in the air.

Work periods were of 40 minutes each with a five-minute break between. There was a mid-morning break of 15 minutes, and lunch was at 1 p.m. After lunch we played games such as football or cricket. In winter, lessons began again at 4 p.m. and lasted until 6.15. Supper was at 7 p.m. and we were in bed by 8. There were half-holidays on Wednesday and Saturday. During the summer, lessons began immediately after lunch, leaving the rest of the time free for cricket. The Easter term began about 19 January and lasted until early April. The summer term started around 3 May and continued until the 20 July, and the winter term lasted from about 20 September until 19 December.

In all three terms Sundays were free. In the morning we would be taken by Mr Simpkins to the little church at Walton, just down the road for the Matins Service; after which we would, led by him in crocodile two by two, go for our Sunday morning walk. As he was the only assistant master, he was permanently on duty, though he would often have time off in the afternoon, when Mr Gwynne used to take us for games. It was on one such walk on a Sunday, it must have been in May 1924, that I experienced something that has remained with me ever since. It was the most perfect morning, fresh as only summer can bring. We had walked up to the old ruined Walton Castle, set in a woodland glade. The birds were singing, butterflies were everywhere, the meadows were ablaze with wild flowers. It was a scene that now could not be found anywhere in insecticide-polluted Britain. To me it will be a memory that will never fade. For sometime I had been boring poor Mr Simpkins with jungle tales of India, how beautiful it was and how wonderful the climate; he would often relieve his boredom with a quick flick of Skeeter. That Sunday he just said 'Look around you Willoughby! Look around you, and you will know why we love England.' But then, can even that morning equal the memory of the hush in the Kheri Jungle as evening fell, and for a brief moment all was still except for the soft thud of Latchmi's feet and the swish of the high tiger grass against her flanks, as we rode on her back, swaying to the rhythm of her tread, home to camp?

During the summer term we played cricket. I found I was quite a good bowler and soon got into the cricket XI. I would run madly up to the wicket, then stop dead and bowl the ball. No-one

Left to right: Gertrude Birch (Auntie), Lilian Birch (Granny), Eileen Birch (My mother), 1893

Field Marshal Lord Roberts signed portrait. Friend of Col. Frederick Birch, R.A., husband of Mrs L.E. Birch (Granny)

British and Indian Officers 1st Brahmins 1903. Seated far left, D.V. Willoughby, just joined still in R.S.F. uniform. Standing just behind, 'Bill' Browning also Scots Fusiliers

D.V. Willoughby 2/Lt on joining 1st Brahmins 1903, still in R. Scots Fusilier uniform

D.V. Willoughby's
'Shikari' 1908

From wedding group: Charles Stewart - Gertrude Birch 1909. Seated left to right:
Eileen Birch (my mother), Col Frederick Birch, Bride, Groom, Mrs Lilian Birch. Standing
behind groom D.V. Willoughby (best man?) my father

Awdry Stuart, Darjeeling, 1913

Capt. A.F. Logan 'Uncle Jimmy'
1917

Me with Rouge (mother's dog)
1917

Mrs L.E. Birch 'Granny' with
Mowgli, 1918. This was the dog
that sacrificed itself to protect its
mistress from the leopard in
Naini-Tal

Latchmi the herd matriarch with 'Pad'. Kheri Jungles 1918

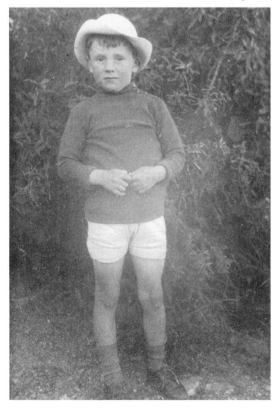

Me in 1919

Rouge the dog, Eileen Willoughby
and her Sister Gertrude Stuart
1919

D.V. Willoughby 'Uncle Pug'
to Awdry Stuart

Tiger shoot 1919, Kheri Jungles. Left to right: elephant, Latchmi, Shikaris, Eileen Willoughby, Gertrude Stuart, dead tiger

Gertrude Stuart 1919, Kheri Jungles, Westley Richards 'Express' double barrel rifle

Jimmy Logan 1919 with kill - Kheri Jungles

Kheri Jungles 1919, end of shoot bag, on left Gertrude Stuart, other guns unknown

Kheri Jungles. Going out for Tiger, Latchmi in the lead

Snow View 1920

1920 group Snow View, Naini-Tal. Top row left to right: Gertrude Stuart (Auntie), Mrs L.E. Birch (Granny), R Willoughby (Uncle Robin). Front row: Maurice Willoughby, Awdry Stuart, Eileen Willoughby.This was the last photo to be taken of Uncle Robin before he was murdered in Aug 1920. He stayed with us the week before going back to Luckinpore

Awdry Stuart 1920

Me 1923/4, Walton Lodge, Clevedon

Me at Windlesham House School 1926

'Twig' Birch my first cousin 1926

Awdry Stuart and me

Left to right: Twig Birch, myself climbing on sealskins

Miss Ski, 1929

Emil, ski instructor, Park Hotel Schönegg. Note very long skis and sticks with huge baskets, Grindelwald 1929

Jan 1929 group outside Hotel (Park Schönegg) Grindelwald. Left to right: ?, Desmond Wakely, Gladys Parsons, ?, my father, myself, ?, extreme right: Joyce Parsons

La Matholière 1929. The Baron and Baroness de Moncuit de Boiscuillé

La Matholière L'étang des puits. Left to right: Moussa, Raudi, Robert de Moncuit, ?, Yves, ?

1929 excursion to Chartres. Left to right: three Swedes, Robert, Jacques, myself, David Renton

explained how I could do better. Once I took six wickets against Darcy's. At batting I was pretty useless until I learnt that the best way was to block everything unless it was miles clear of the wicket. This had the added advantage of infuriating the other side, and at the same time winning approving noises from Mr Gwynne for staying in a long time. In the winter term we played soccer, where for a time I was the school goalkeeper, until promoted to right back and then centre forward. For the Easter term it was hockey and showman tricks by R.F. Gwynne. A curious feature of sport in those days was that nobody ever explained or showed you how to do anything. As an English boy and according to the brass plate at the school entrance, 'a Gentleman's son', you were expected instinctively to know. Throughout my entire education at both prep schools, at Haileybury and at Sandhurst, I was never coached or taught anything about games, about cricket, rugby football, soccer, tennis or athletics. You were either good at games or bad. If you were good, you watched those better and improved. If you were bad you were miserable and generally despised. To this day I have no idea what a 'long hop' is, or a 'good-length ball' at cricket, other than knowing that a good-length ball is more likely to get someone out and a bad length be hit to the boundary. But I still have no idea where a 'good length' should pitch on the wicket. Had we the present knowledge and custom of 'picking the seam', or scuffing one side of the ball to make it swerve or even greasing one side, we would undoubtedly have cheated with the best of them. It was sheer ignorance, not intention, which kept us honest.

There was usually a match against some other school every Saturday afternoon. Some were at home, but the best ones were away. We travelled by hired bus, called a charabanc, often open to the weather with just a hood for protection. At other times we used the Somerset and Dorset Joint Railway, affectionately known as the 'Slow and Dirty'. By modern standards it was a paragon of punctuality and cleanliness. The passenger carriages in those days were divided into a number of compartments. Passengers sat opposite each other, four to a side in the third class, three in the first. Folding arm rests separated each seat. Second class had already disappeared due to lack of demand. Above the seats were photographs of scenic parts of the Line. Each compartment had a door giving onto the station platform and a sliding one leading into the corridor which ran the full length of the coach. The coaches were connected to each other by a kind of flexible bellows. Such trains were known as 'corridor trains'. On branch lines or local journeys, carriages often had no corridor and the compartments ran the full width, providing an extra seat. Each door had a window which was opened or shut by pulling it up or down by means of a leather strap which had holes punched along its length. These would be pushed over a stud protruding from the door to keep the window in the desired position. Even tight shut, the draught from every window was penetrating, especially in winter.

Each time the engine was stoked, it would belch forth a plume of acrid smoke, full of hot sparks and smuts. At such times it was dangerous to lean out of the window, and notices telling you so were screwed to each door. If the window was open as the train entered a tunnel, the compartment was instantly filled with sulphurous yellow smoke which covered everything in grime. In fact a feature of steam travel was the filthy condition in which one finished every journey. In the top right-hand corner of each compartment was a horizontal chain, which in emergency could be pulled down, immediately applying all the brakes and stopping the train. Below the chain was a notice in red, 'Penalty for improper use £5'. This would equal about two weeks average wage at the time.

Being a very small school we were almost invariably beaten in these matches, played mostly against rather grand preparatory schools of 50 and more pupils to choose from. In fact I often thought they really only played us because it was a match they would be sure of winning and look good in the school magazine. As goalkeeper I would get intensely cold and bored pacing the goalmouth, hoping against hope to see the opposing forwards surging towards me, and then as they got closer, hoping they wouldn't in case I let a goal through, which was pretty certain to be the case. Win or lose, the best part of any match was the tea after we had bathed and changed into our normal clothes. Schools vied with each other to lay on scrumptious teas, and even Walton

Lodge did not lag behind. There were sandwiches made of Shippams 'Chicken and Ham Paste', sardines, meringues, currant cake, cream buns, and tea that really tasted of it, instead of the disgusting hogwash we usually had to drink. In the summer we often got strawberries and cream as well. On one occasion, Pat Mortimer, our wicketkeeper, ate so many of them that we had to keep stopping the charabanc all the way home to let him off at various judiciously chosen suitable places. There was much conjecture as to how many marks he would be able to make on Matron's Daily Constipation Checklist – for constipated he certainly was not.

The currency at the school was based upon the one shilling and threepenny block of Cadbury's milk chocolate. These were originally introduced by Mr Simpkins, who would buy a block and distribute it among those he considered worthy. Each block was divided into eight large squares stamped with the Cadbury's tree trademark. As he probably earned only about ten bob a day plus his keep, this was a considerable gesture on his part. It was the era of pounds, shillings and pence. No-one ever imagined it could be different. We knew that foreigners used something called metric, but it did not bother us. There were three types of copper coin: the farthing, four to a penny, a halfpenny called a 'haypenny', and the penny itself. This was an inch across and could also be used as a measure of length. The farthing was about the same size as a 1998 penny. On the front was the Monarch's head, and the back was stamped with a wren. It had considerable purchasing power. For instance you could buy four candles with a farthing, and many goods, especially in haberdashers and milliners, were marked up in farthings, such as 2/11¾, to make the price appear less than three shillings.

There were twelve pence to a shilling, which for some time after metrication, did duty as a 5p piece. In the 1920s it was made of silver and would buy you a gallon of petrol (4.5 litres). It was popularly known as a 'bob'. There were two other coins to go with it: the very attractive little 'threepenny bit', often put into Christmas puddings along with other trinkets, and the equally fetching sixpence, known as a 'tanner'. All coins above a penny were of silver and beautiful to look at. There were two others, the 'two bob bit' and the half-crown, which was 2/6d. The smallest note was for ten shillings, the next being for £1. A £5 note was a huge square of crinkly white paper, and the writing on it was in copperplate. A 'fiver' was a lovely object, rarely seen and the size of a small pocket handkerchief. It had enormous panache and dignity. There were twenty shillings to a pound. The system has been accused of being unwieldy and complicated, but in reality was far more practical than the metric, because it could be divided in so many more ways and give rise to instant calculations. For example if an egg cost four pence, they would be four shillings a dozen or five dozen for £1. However there was one complication. Some prices were quoted in guineas, and a guinea was twenty-one shillings. This was especially the case in the fashion trade, top-grade tailors or anything to do with horses.

The standard tip for a taxi driver or the porter who carried your luggage to the train and found you a corner seat in an empty compartment was a tanner, or a bob if you were travelling first class and had a lot of luggage. For an uncle, tipping his small nephew going back to prep school for a new term, it was half a crown, or in Walton Lodge currency, two blocks of Cadbury's milk chocolate. We were lucky if we went back to school with more than about ten bob. I once managed 13/6d and thought I was Croesus. We were made to hand in all our money to Mr Gwynne at the beginning of term – I imagine in case we bought a railway ticket and ran away. All the time I was there I never heard of anyone stealing anything from another.

Money was only doled out for some specific reason, such as the annual buying, in the winter term, of Gamages Christmas catalogue. These cost a shilling, and everyone had to have one to look at and drool over the model railway section, especially the steam engines. We were allowed to have our trains at the school, but only if they were clockwork. By combining we were able to build up quite a complex network, mostly of Hornby origin and nought guage. John Reynolds, however, a day boy who lived in Clevedon, had a wonderful collection of steam engines. There was a German model costing 28/6d including postage from Gamages, which for me has always remained a measure of good value for money. It went superbly and could outperform far more expensive locomotives made by the famous model makers, Basset Lowke of Northampton. But the apogee was an engine called the Great Bear, painted in the green London and NE Railway livery, Pacific class with four bogie and six driving wheels. This paragon cost a whole five guineas; untold wealth.

In the summer we all took photographs. The cameras were invariably Kodak Box Brownies. Our films were developed by the local chemist for sixpence, but the printing we did ourselves. There were two types of printing, gaslight and daylight. Gaslight needed a darkroom and was a matter for professionals. Daylight was easy. All you needed was a printing frame and a small dish for dissolving 'hypo' crystals to 'fix' your results. Because the negative size was large, there was no need of enlargement. Especially clear pictures, however, were often enlarged, but this again was a matter for the chemist who would 'send it away to get done for you'. Sometimes you would be shown a picture that was apparently so good that you would be asked to look at it with the accompanying standard remark of 'I'm thinking of sending this one up'. I never discovered this mysterious 'up' to which they were about to be sent. For daylight printing you placed negative and paper together sandwiched in a wooden frame with a glass front, and left it in the sun. You could open half the back to see how well it was being cooked. This usually took five or six minutes. You then took the print out and dropped it into the hypo solution to fix it. Here it had to remain for ten minutes before being washed for half an hour or so in a basin of running water. Finally you stuck the print onto a clean window pane to prevent it curling and to improve the gloss.

One summer term, Mr Simpkins tried to stimulate our interest in aircraft by buying a model aeroplane kit of parts, which, when assembled, actually flew. The frame was made of balsa wood, and the wings, tailplane and rudder were of thin fabric, fastened to it by the same kind of 'dope' used by aircraft of the day. Propulsion was by thick catapult elastic connected to the propeller and running the entire length of the frame. This had laboriously to be wound up by the forefinger and held. The machine was then placed on smooth ground and let go, whereupon it would race away on its wheels and take off. The trouble was getting it to land safely again. One took off and was last seen heading for Lady Bay. Another crashed in a hedge nearby and wrote itself off. As no more were available, interest waned, and what remained of the elastic was used for catapults.

Mr Simpkins also introduced us to H.G. Wells' book 'Little Wars', in which toy soldiers and cannon could be moved around like chessmen, after a battle area, consisting of hills, roads, forests, rivers, houses and villages, had been constructed out of paper, cardboard and greenery. I can never understand why such games were not adopted by the Army, instead of the stupendously boring and soporific 'Sandtable Exercises' in which it indulges.

We all had model lead soldiers. They were made by a firm called Britains, and were sold in long cardboard boxes costing half a crown (2/6d). Each consisted of some eight soldiers and an officer. Most of the regiments of the British Army were available, both infantry and cavalry, dressed in the full dress parade uniforms prior to 1914. They were accurate in every detail, and some of the cavalry officers were especially resplendent. Most popular at Walton Lodge were the Coldstream Guards, the officer marching with drawn sword at the salute, the men at the 'slope' with fixed bayonets as if taking part in the King's Birthday Parade on Horse Guards. Their rivals were the Royal Welsh Fusiliers, whose box also contained a minature white goat, the mascot of that Regiment. In fact in practically no time at all, there was such a herd of these goats wandering around the school that they seemed to outnumber the soldiers. Other popular regiments were the Buffs, which had men kneeling with bayonets fixed ready to receive cavalry. The only Scottish regiment available was the Gordon Highlanders, its men running very fast, someone unkindly said 'both ways', with bayonets fixed and one leg cocked up behind in a rather ridiculous manner.

There were two main artillery pieces, the first being the 4.7-inch naval gun mounted on wheels. This fired a wooden bullet about an inch long propelled by a spring and could knock over a soldier from about five feet. The other was a highly sophisticated exact model of the 18-inch howitzer used on the Western Front. It fired a large lead shell projected by a spring in the base of the shell itself.

94

As with the actual howitzer, the charge could be varied by changing this spring to alter the range. Such a shell landing on a bunch of lead soldiers would wreak havoc, but unlike the real thing, heads could be stuck on again with matchsticks.

However, by far my strongest memory of my time at Clevedon was the incessant bullying and fighting which took place at the school, and which, if the staff were aware of it, they took absolutely no steps to check. Matron must have known from treating black eyes and bleeding noses. Such was the schoolboy code of conduct that no-one among us would ever have dreamt of 'sneaking'. People were judged entirely by whether they were 'good fighters' or not, and fighting broke out on the slightest provocation. Pat Mortimer was by far the best fighter, followed by John Reynolds, but both were day boys and did not really count. I was about third and the best of the boarders. One boy called John Read, about a year older than myself, with protruding front teeth, in some mysterious way had managed to seize power over a number of other boys whom he collected around him and directed at anyone who displeased him, usually against me, whom he considered a rival. He never took part in any of the fracas himself, merely, like Stalin or Hitler, standing aside and watching.

I look back on it as a kind of martyrdom. Day after day, term after term I would find myself attacked by a gang of other boys who had hitherto been my friends, but were too frightened to do otherwise. I even found myself at his behest, attacking real friends such as Pat Mortimer or John Reynolds, for which I still feel deeply ashamed. It has, however, left me with an insight into the methods of gangster bosses and dictators, who exert not only a moral but a physical fear, and of the two, the moral is by far the worse. These 'feuds' went on for days until John Read considered you had learnt your lesson. They would then suddenly stop and one's friends would come creeping back to treat you as if nothing had happened. Feuds would start on the slightest pretext or no pretext at all. For instance on one occasion, in a trial of strength my clockwork engine had pulled 14 trucks to the 13 which was the best his could manage. I knew from the way he looked at me afterwards that there was going to be trouble.

I always knew when a feud was about to start. My friend

95

'Stinker' Stack would begin behaving in a funny manner, going out of his way to avoid me, but at the same time pretending all was normal. Stinker's real name was Talbot Bagot-Stack, and he was called Stinker because he smelt terrible at all times. Furthermore when it came to stinking he could give a polecat points and win hands down. Despite this he was a great friend and except for the smelling, we shared a lot in common. We used to keep glass jars full of the little red meadow ants together, and watch them making their tunnels and moving about underground. He knew all about heraldry, archery, Guy Mannering and the White Company, model railways, lead soldiers, especially the Royal Welsh Fusiliers, of which he had a large enough herd of white goat mascots, to gladden the heart of any Landi-Kotal Pathan. His chief attraction was his vivid imagination, and he used to organise the most plausible mutinies of his soldiers against their officers, in his desk. Each boy had a desk at which he sat for lessons. Every desk had a sloping lid hinged to a flat piece at the top, which contained a white china inkwell and a small hollow for pens and pencils. Generations of boys had grooved tramlines on these lids with lead pencil, carved or written their names and the dates they were at school. When he opened it, a few short years before, R.F. Gwynne had obviously procured a job lot of these desks from a school that had no further use for them. Most were on their last legs. Inside the desks, exercise books, Latin Primers, English and history books could be arranged in the form of a fort, with sliding doors to partition off a section for the officer's mess. Thus directly a mutiny began, the officers could shut themselves off until help arrived. It always did, and the officers always won. Stinker replaced me as the school goalkeeper when I was promoted to right back. Perhaps it was thought that the all-pervading stench would act as a deterrent to the opposing forwards, but he let through even more goals than I had done.

Thus it can be seen that once you got used to the smell, Stinker Stack was a most likeable character. Many claimed that he had a weak bladder and wet himself all the time. This was probably the case, for instead of sleeping in the dormitory with the rest of us, he had a room to himself. Most days he and I would play chess, or ping-pong on the big table in the bow window of the upper

96

classroom. A sure sign that something was brewing up was a polite refusal to play on some trivial pretext or other. He never took part in any of the attacks upon me himself and was usually the first to come creeping back after the period of the feud, probably a week, was over. Whilst they lasted, they were day and night-long misery; especially as I knew that except for John Read, all were hating themselves for doing it, but were too scared to behave otherwise. It was not only physical attacks that made these feuds so unpleasant. Almost worse was being ostracised, ink 'accidentally' spilt over your work, favourite lead soldiers trodden on 'by mistake'. It was general persecution and made life unbearable.

The main targets of these episodes were Pat Mortimer, John Reynolds and myself, all of whom John Read regarded as a threat. On one occasion when Pat arrived as a boarder, a feud was immediately organised against him in which I joined. He must have told his parents what was happening, for he was taken away and sent to another school. We lost our best cricketer. The trouble was that once a feud began you had nobody to turn to. The school-boy code forbade any complaint to the staff, and in any case, I doubt they would have listened. Both my parents were in India, and my grandmother would not have understood. As for my Aunt Gertie and Uncle Jimmy, they would merely have thought me a wretched little sneak, unable to stand up for myself. Later on, during the great public trials in the Soviet Union in the 1930s, I was able to understand, how from sheer terror, Ministers under Stalin would come forward to denounce or testify against those who had been their friends and former comrades in arms. In many ways the similarities were striking. In his own little pond, John Read was as much a dictator.

In many ways too, however, I was able to look after myself. I was too good a fighter for anyone to take on single-handed. It was always a case of battling against three or four, sometimes even up to ten. One particular small red-headed boy, called Speyer, would cling onto one's arm like a leech and refuse to let go. During the winter months, most of the action took place in the gym, which was pitch dark. A corridor through it connected the two class-rooms. All our tuck boxes were piled into one corner, and these I

97

built up into a kind of hiding place in which I would lurk from after supper until it was time to go to bed. Those seeking to attack me were at a grave disadvantage. In the dark, I knew that all were foes. I would sally forth from my lair, bash one or two, and be back before they scarcely knew what had hit them, leaving them shouting and accusing each other. On many such occasions too, I would get a soft word of encouragement, 'Sorry, I don't mean it,' whispered through the blackness.

All this had a disastrous effect upon my general conduct. Funnily enough my work did not suffer, nor did my games and I got good end of term reports for both. But I assumed a general air of bravado in flouting as many school rules as I could, an attitude which won me a kind of spurious awe and popularity. I was continually being awarded Stripes, doing detention or getting beaten. At times I felt as though the entire world was against me and I can trace many of the flaws in my character to those days.

To make matters worse, one winter term I had terrible earache. It was the most fearful pain I have ever experienced, and no-one would believe me when I complained of it. Eventually Matron took me away and poured hot oil into my ear, which I imagine was just about the stupidest and most dangerous thing she could possibly have done. I then started having large boils on the back of my neck, which she delighted in squeezing, after hot bread poultices had been applied to 'draw them to a head'. In between the feuds and the earache and the boils, life at Walton Lodge went on placidly enough. Mr Simpkins continued to wield his Skeeter, we were always freezing cold and the food was terrible. From an academic point of view I imagine the tuition was adequate, and when I went to another prep school, I was well up to standard for my age. But as each term began and we arrived back at its grim portal, I always thought, written above the door in bold letters, should have been 'Abandon hope all ye who enter here'.

9

Sometime in 1924 my grandmother, Aunt Gertie and Uncle
Jimmy left Barry y va and rented a house at Taplow, before buying
one in Maidenhead. Uncle Jimmy had taken a job with Metal Box
in London and had to commute every day. That Christmas my
mother returned from India for good, with a strange man in tow
called Leslie Brown. I had just turned eleven, and here was this
curious woman, whom I had not seen for nearly three years and
more or less forgotten, with an odd man in tow, saying, 'I'm your
mother, you have got to love me.' She was then 33 and at the
height of her beauty, though to me she seemed awfully old. Leslie
Brown was some six years younger, and I suppose nowadays
she could have been accused of collecting a toy-boy, for that he
certainly was, being one of the handsomest men I have ever seen,
He had the looks of Ronald Colman, an ex-Coldstream Guards
officer turned Hollywood star of the silent film era, who caused
many a female to swoon at the mere thought of him.

My mother had met Leslie Brown in Peshawar, where he was
serving as a Captain in an Indian Army infantry regiment. The
instant attraction was mutual and after a wild affair, the scandal of
the cantonment, he resigned his commission and returned to
England with her. They were together through lean times, mostly
they were very lean, and good, until she died over 53 years later.
After her death, he sat in an armchair and over weeks and months,
deliberately drank himself to death. In 1924 my grandmother,
uncle and aunt were deeply shocked by their 'living together',
although the latter had done exactly the same themselves. But in
those days such conduct was something only to be spoken about in
whispers. To my aunt his very name was anathema, her sister

99

living openly with a man called Brown without even an e at the end of it. Furthermore she accused him of being a 'half caste', and 'you could tell he was one by the blue half moons at the base of his nails'. She was probably right, for in his last days, he forgot to shave, grew a white beard and looked just like any other old Punjabi from the bazaar. He was always very nice, kind and generous towards me, but an ever-continual source of embarrassment. My mother would bring him down to see me at the various schools I was at, and people would ask, 'Is that your father'? and I would have to produce long explanations why he wasn't. To make matters worse, she would often appear in the most outrageous clothes, such as long tiger skin or leopard coats, which she had shot herself and had made up. Fundamental rules for all visiting parents then were, 'Never be seen kissing or displaying any form of affection', and above all, 'never wear or do anything likely to draw attention to yourself'. My mother failed on both counts. I looked forward to their visits with dread and trepidation. No amount of hints or downright requests could make her change her ways.

After that Christmas, which we spent in Taplow, my mother and Leslie took me to London for a few days. We stayed in a small and rather sleazy hotel near Victoria Station. I was taken to see Bertram Mills famous circus, which played every Christmas time at Olympia. They also bought me, after much entreaty, a pair of piebald mice called Adam and Eve, and another pair, Samson and Delilah, to take back as a present for Awdry. It was a great mistake to buy mice of different sexes, for in no time at all we were completely overrun by piebald mice. Taking Adam and Eve back to Walton Lodge next term presented a problem. I had no idea how they would be received. Everyone told me I would not be allowed to keep them, because they smelt so horrible. This I indignantly denied, and anyway however bad they smelt, it could not be worse than old Stinker Stack.

The essential was to get Mr Simpkins on my side. Fortunately he boarded my train at Twyford. I broke the news to him gradually, with talk of animals in general. Having warmed him up and obtained his interest. I asked him point blank, 'Do you like animals Sir?'. Having admitted that he loved them, I introduced him to Adam and Eve, who was by this time heavily pregnant. Other than by throwing them out of the train window, he could not now refuse me permission to bring them back to school. I was allowed to keep them in a remote corner of the gym. In the end they bred so fast we had to make a large cage for them outside the lower classroom window on a piece of waste ground. Here, over a period, they tunnelled their way out by gnawing through the floor-boards and escaped. For all I know, there may be generations of piebald mice still around Walton Lodge to this day. It was an escape story worthy of any wartime exploit from a German POW Offlag, and as carefully planned. All the naked babies, every single mouse, disappeared, and the exodus must have been spread over many nights, normal 'mouse activity' being kept up during the day by the rear party. I was not all that sorry to see them go. I admit that they did smell a bit, and even Stinker Stack complained.

The thousands of men who had been demobilised at the end of the Great War, expected, as they had been promised, to come back to 'a land fit for heroes'. Instead there were few jobs for them, and most were unemployed. In London you saw them on every street corner with all their medals up, their war gratuity gone, trying to scratch out a living selling matches, shoelaces or trinkets. Many ex-officers were in a similar plight. Now it is the long-cherished belief of all regular officers in the British Army, dating back for hundreds of years, that military training automatically provides the necessary knowledge and expertise to become a farmer. They were as convinced of this as their belief that the only form of military training necessary for a serving officer's education was fox-hunting, shooting and fishing, with a spot of polo and pig-sticking thrown in for good measure. Thus a spate of small farms sprang up all over the country. For some reason, many of these were poultry farms, it being considered that chickens were, on the whole, more amenable to good order and military discipline than other forms of livestock. One officer I knew, had brought with him a large supply of Army forms, in the shape of 'Company Conduct Sheets'. Each hen was allocated her own sheet, on which was entered her egg-laying performance and general record. Any misdemeanours were also noted, and if necessary the hen was 'put on a charge', and brought up next day on 'Farmers Daily Orders'. Too many entries meant that the unfortunate bird inevitably ended up in the cook pot.

Leslie Brown and my mother decided they would go into farming. Using his war gratuity, they bought some seven acres of land near Wokingham in Berkshire, built a small house on it and started up. At first they kept a few pigs, Large Whites and Berkshires, and grew vegetables, all of which they sold at the weekly market in Bracknell. My mother grew very fond of the pigs and they became friends. The fate which awaited them after being sold became too much for her. Every friendly grunt of every pig brought its fate more closely home, so they switched to chickens, of which already there was a glut. It was hard work and most distasteful, especially after the near-halcyon existence of garrison life in Peshawar, with the Peshawar Vale Hunt, tennis courts, balls at The Club in white tie and tails every Saturday evening, polo, duck and quail shooting, servants for every whim, horses and all the wonderful aspects of life, taken completely for granted by British officers in India; not to mention the delightful dilly-dallying and general poodle-faking in Kashmir during the hot weather. Even with the switch, they were not making a worthwhile living, and it was only the allowance of £40 per month, now about £2000, which my father was obliged to pay her, that kept the wolf from the door. For him the situation was wel-nigh intolerable. He was desperately anxious to divorce her, but circumstances were such that he was unable to do so. As for Leslie and my mother, he was their food ticket. The last thing either wanted was a divorce from him.

The divorce laws at that time were both complicated and crazy. If both parties wanted a divorce, they could not get one. If they arranged the evidence to obtain one, it was known as 'collusion' which made it impossible to obtain. There were really only a few reasons for divorce, the most general being insanity, adultery and non-consumation. If either side trotted out a middling-sized child as evidence, the last was hard to prove. Insanity was left as a last resort, even harder to prove. That left adultery, and a complete industry developed around it. On the whole men were chivalrous and willing to provide 'evidence', so that the the wife could

102

appear as the injured party and be awarded alimony and other benefits. There were many agencies which provided women who were willing to help. All that was needed was proof that the couple had booked into a hotel, shared a bedroom and be seen in bed together the following morning. Thus they would spend the night, usually fully dressed and the man probably sitting up in an arm-chair. Sex was not usually included in the price, though it could probably be provided as an optional extra. When the time arrived for the maid to bring in early morning tea, an essential element of the scenario, he would leap into the bed. The maid would come in, shriek with horror and throw the tray in the air. In the meantime a hired photographer would rush into the room with a large half-plate Press camera, and take a picture by igniting a magnesium flash of the couple in bed together. The fact that they were fully dressed was immaterial. It could be claimed that they liked it that way. In some cases, the wife would agree to provide the evidence, and the agencies also produced men for this purpose who could be relied upon to act in a professional, non-physical fashion, unless given due encouragement. These were the 'Co-respondents' in nearly all such cases, and the men invariably wore brown and white shoes, known as co-respondent shoes.

With the evidence complete, the case could be brought to court and a decree nisi obtained. But the trouble was by no means over. The King's Proctor was now let loose, who watched the couple like a hawk. If they met or corresponded in any way, they could be accused of collusion which would nullify the entire proceedings. The nisi period lasted for six months, and during this time both sides were secretely and most carefully watched for any sign of such collusion, or on the side of the plaintiff, any hint of an illicit liaison with a third party. Naturally a man's visits to a brothel or prostitute did not count in this respect, but only a proper liaison which might lead to a future marriage. Nobody could accuse the King's Proctor of not being broad-minded, and many stories were around, probably apochryphal, that his officials were often to be seen in the best brothels, mingling with the clientele. If the couple managed to clear the nisi period, a decree absolute was given and they were home and dry; parted until death.

Despite my father's anxiety to obtain a divorce, he was caught between the short hairs of collusion and the naivete of his own character. '*Incidis in Scyllam cupiens vitare Charybdim*' as he would remark, always ready to throw in a Latin tag, a habit he had picked up from his brother Robin. On hearing of her affair with Leslie Brown, he had foolishly written her a letter suggesting that if she wanted a divorce, he would be willing to provide her with the necessary evidence, including the hysterical maid throwing the early morning tea tray in the air and the photographer with the magnesium flash. She turned this very generous offer into a weapon. Furthermore, when he came home on leave from India during the summer of 1925, he added idiocy to error, by actually visiting them in their house at Wokingham and staying the night. He was trusting and gullible enough to believe what they told him, that their joint occupation of the house was just a 'business arrangement' to make the running of the chicken farm easier. Thus not only was he guilty of collusion by writing the letter, but by staying with them, he was also condoning the situation, even approving of it. On every occasion in the future when he even made mention of divorce, my mother's solicitors, a firm named Vesey with offices at Bush House in Aldwych, would refer to the letter and kill all progress stone dead. In the end my father got his divorce, but only after a mysterious fire had burnt all the documents in Vesey's office.

On the social scale, I suppose, his solicitors could be described as one up on Vesey, for their offices were in Lincoln's Inn, and they came from a very eminent family in Westmoreland. They rarely gave up trying, and kept my mother and Leslie under constant observation by relays of little men with binoculars, dressed in cloth caps and long greasy macintoshes. My mother never discovered what they were hoping to find, for the couple had made no secret of the fact that they were sharing a house. Perhaps the little men hoped to discover they were also sharing the same bedroom. Even that was insufficient evidence for a divorce, for they could claim that they occupied it in turn, one having to be on permanent duty looking after the farm animals. They had actually to be found in bed together. Every now and again, my mother would see one peering at the house from the bushes, looking cold, wet and miserable. Taking pity, she would ask him in for a cup of

104

tea and a biscuit. Leslie Brown would appear, fresh from cleaning out a hen house, ply him with whisky and send him reeling tipsily back to his vigil. It was the very heyday of the matrimonial detective and divorce industry, and as one of the little men remarked, 'a far better job than standing about in a muddy trench in the Salient outside Ypres, being shot at by Germans.'

There was now open war between my Aunt Gertie and Uncle Jimmy and my mother and Leslie Brown, whom I was obliged to call Uncle Leslie. My aunt, although a beautiful woman herself, had always been bitterly jealous of her sister, resenting her being much younger and attracting more attention. Whilst my mother was able to provide tiger shoots on elephants, she kept this to herself, but back in England under changed circumstances, all the old jealousies flared up once more. My grandmother also cut herself off from her daughter, for with her strict Victorian upbringing she regarded the situation as highly immoral and sinful. She added her own disapproval to that of my aunt. She moved to Tenby in Wales, and took the two top floors at No 7 the Esplanade. Here I would spend the halves of my school holidays that I was not compelled to stay with my mother.

My cousin Twig also spent his holidays with our mutual grandmother, whilst his parents were in India, their marriage already past breaking point. We became great friends, made bows and arrows and shot them among the sand dunes off South Beach. We constructed model yachts called Sea Hawk and Sea Dragon and sailed them in rock pools at low tide. We both had bicycles and pretended we were knights of old on chargers, riding at each other with long poles as lances, the object being to knock the other off his bike. Why either of us was not badly hurt, I cannot understand. On one occasion, wishing to make an artificial pond on which to try out a new design of yacht, we shot a hole with an airgun in the ballcock of the water tank just outside our bedroom window. This was contained in a kind of bricked-up enclosure on the roof of the downstairs lavatory. We felt that if we could flood this we would have our model yacht marina. The idea worked like a charm. The enclosure was flooded; we tied up the ballcock to shut off more water and tried out our boats. All went well for at least a week, our grandmother unaware of what we had done.

Her brother, Joseph Leeds, had been sent to Canada by old Sir Reginald, at an early age as a 'remittance man', with £100 in gold sovereigns in his purse and a tearful farewell. He was now an old man retired to the land of his birth and fearfully critical of it. 'Not the way we do things in Canada,' was his verdict on practically everything. It was his habit to visit the lavatory just beneath our water tank, every morning after breakfast, and let forth a crescendo of farts, grunts and other noises reminiscent of an opening barrage of shellfire on the Western Front. We knew them as 'Uncle Joe's thunderstorms'. On this particular morning he had played an especially noisy overture. Perhaps the extra volume of it had caused the roof to crack and split, for just as he was reaching out for the paper, half a ton of water cascaded upon him through the roof, washed him off the seat, burst open the door and carried him halfway down the stairs. It certainly was not the way 'they did things in Canada'. It was also sometime before either of us got much pocket money, though I detected a slight, barely concealed smirk on my grandmother's face each time she spoke of what had happened. As for my mother, she yelled with laughter at the news. My father in India was less overjoyed when he got the bill for the damage.

Our time in Tenby was the happiest in my childhood. Twig was an ideal companion, and we enjoyed doing everything together. In the winter we had our steam trains, in the summer our yachts, our airguns, our bows and arrows and the freedom of the sand dunes and golf course. We ran wild. A favourite occupation was 'fighting the tide'. A little below high water we would dig a sand castle with its walls and ramparts around us. As the tide came in, we would frantically try to shore up our defences. The idea was to see how long we could defend our fortress before being overwhelmed by the sea. On occasion when the walls finally crumbled, we had to swim for it. Such events were regarded in triumph. In a way one cannot help comparing it with old age, when time instead of the tide becomes a far more insidious enemy, and one's body the fortress. Prop it up as you may, with a new hip joint here and a new eye or a pacemaker there, the end result will always be the same. You are going to be overwhelmed, but the struggle is just as worthwhile.

No 7 the Esplanade was an imposing house of some five storeys, built when Tenby was at its zenith as a Victorian seaside resort. Besides the two top apartments, my grandmother also had the use of the attics, which at one time must have served as servants' bedrooms. In fact one was occupied by her cook-cum-housemaid, a greying middle-aged spinster called Huns. I never found out whether this was her real name or merely what she was called because the actual one was unpronounceable. Huns was highly neurotic, allergic to any criticism, and regularly gave notice at the drop of a hat. On one occasion at lunch, she brought in a rhubarb tart that had not really risen properly and whose pastry seemed to have caved in upon itself. When my grandmother mildy asked what had happened, Huns stormed out, shouting 'I ain't sat on the rhubub Mum, I ain't sat on the rhubub, and 'eres' me thirty days notice.' She was back again with the evening meal as if nothing had happened.

In another of these attic rooms, its floor laid with linoleum, we were allowed to lay out our rail tracks and play with our 28/6d methylated-fired steam engines. One day whilst our trains were tearing round the tracks, there occurred an event for which I can offer no explanation. At one end of the room was a curious hole in the wall leading to a ventilation shaft. The hole was covered by a large wooden board, securely fastened into it. Suddenly and at the same moment, Twig and I both felt that something or somebody was watching us. We simultaneously remarked on it, wondering why? Then with a loud bang, the board was pushed out of the hole and fell with a crash to the floor. This was too much for us. Only staying long enough to blow out the flame in our engines, we tore downstairs in panic. Our grandmother was a firm believer in ghosts, so collecting our bows and arrows – it was surprising the comfort they gave – we took her back upstairs with us. There was nothing. All was peaceful and serene. The engines stood where they had stopped, the rails gleamed in the electric light; but as proof of our fears, the board lay where it had fallen. She stayed with us whilst we packed everything up and took it away. We never played there again; and she told us that whilst we were away at school, there were constant bangs and other curious sounds coming from that room.

107

The opposing solicitors had agreed that whilst my father remained serving in India, things were to remain as they were. Part of the agreement was that I should spend half my holidays with my mother in Wokingham, and the other half with my grandmother. It was an arrangement I utterly deplored. For a start I was cut off from both Awdry and Twig and had no companions to play with. Unfortunately I had also become rather snobbish and proper in my outlook, and living conditions at Wokingham were lamentable. My mother seemed to have no ability to distinguish between extravagance and squalor. She would spend large sums on some perfectly useless object and yet live in what appeared to be abject poverty. There was no furniture of any kind save a sofa and two very expensive armchairs. All the rest was contrived from old orange boxes and tea chests. Even the beds were made out of them and there were no sheets. We slept between blankets. We used upturned boxes instead of a dining room table; shelves and cupboards were also made from them, stacked one upon another.

I am convinced that all children like order and routine, their meals and bedtime worked out and laid down. Life at Wokingham was chaos. Meals were at no set times, sometimes we ate lunch for breakfast and sometimes breakfast for lunch. Sometimes we just ate when someone felt hungry. My mother had never had to cook in her life, and at this time her culinary ceiling was scrambled eggs, which she did very well. She tried to make ridiculous savings, such as using margarine instead of butter. In those days you could certainly taste the difference – it was harder to be certain that the margarine wasn't axle grease.

Bedtime was rarely before midnight. This I thought splendid at first, but soon became bored and fidgety with it. Leslie would smoke his pipe and drink whisky, my mother, who did not smoke, just drank whisky. They interlarded their speech constantly with Hindustani, and called the drinks '*chota-pegs*'. We would listen to the wireless, a large contraption with light-up valves and a huge, bakelite horn of a loudspeaker, or read. But mostly they would sit up, hour after hour, telling me what a frightful fellow my father was, and how I must say that I wished to live with my mother when the case came to court. All the time I knew him, my father never said a word against either of them, and his very silence predisposed me more in his favour than anything else he could have done.

It also amazed me to see my mother, usually so wild and independent, now completely subjugated and under the thumb of Leslie Brown, whom she adored and seemed to regard as some kind of demi-god. She who had been surrounded by servants and comfort, had ridden horses, hunted, shot tigers and mingled with the highest in India, seemed content and happy to be little more than an unpaid servant and live in squalor. I found over the years that wherever they went and whatever they did, the place where they lived soon became a dreadful slum. He appeared to have the most extraordinary hold over her. If she ever did anything to annoy him, or of which he disapproved, he would punish her by sulking, and would not speak to her for days, but be overly friendly towards me. At such times the atmosphere in the house was miserable. Then suddenly for some reason his mood would pass, and all would be sunshine and smiles again. Being by myself like this for half of all my school holidays was dreary in the extreme. I had all my train sets, but playing alone soon got monotonous, and there was a limit to the variety of track layouts. They encouraged me to make things. I was a good carpenter and model maker, something I have kept up all my life. The yachts Twig and I made were almost professional. He was a better carpenter even than I was. One day Leslie drove their beat-up Model T Ford into Reading and brought me back from Heelas, the big store there, a treadle fretsaw, which gave me endless pleasure making useless and dust-collecting objects for various relatives and friends.

One such was a mad great-aunt called Mabel, my grandmother's youngest sister, who lived with a faded, greying female companion, Miss Charlotte Jellie, in a small house in Frimley near Aldershot named Croxton after her father's estate. I adored Miss Jellie. She laughed at my stupid jokes and we used to play chess together. She seemed to like me and enjoyed my company. Aunt Mabel was the only member of the family who would accept my mother's situation without disapproval, but always regarded me with rather a jaundiced eye. She was inclined to throw tantrums. On one occasion she remarked that my hair was much

109

too long and I should get it cut. On being told that it did not really matter, she fled shrieking from the house, shouting, 'Let him die then! Let him die! Hanging by his hair like Absalom, from a tree!'!

Like so many Victorian youngest daughters of a large family, she had been kept behind to look after her parents in their old age. She had been beautiful, well-read and highly intelligent. She had not been allowed to marry, and suitors had been discouraged or sent away with fleas in their ears. She had been constantly told that it was her duty to remain with her parents and repay them for 'all they had sacrificed for her', whatever that was. The process had to some extent unhinged her mind and made her highly excitable. Many years later when I was at Sandhurst, I was called urgently to the Guardroom, where I found her, hat askew, beating a cowering Sergeant of the Guard over the head with an umbrella. Apparently she had heard I was to have my appendix removed as a precautionary measure, before going to India. It had been what the medics called 'rumbling'. Clutching a box of Beecham's pills, she rushed to the Military College, insisting that I be dosed with them at once. The Sergeant had refused to let her see me, so she had set about him.

On the chicken farm all the birds were housed in four huge prefabricated barns. They roosted on shelves placed along the sides and scratched about in the deep litter in the middle. Every day Leslie or my mother would feed and water them, collect the eggs and pick out those to be taken to the weekly sale at the market in Bracknell. The hen houses were on the land beyond the house, but could be smelt from afar off. The smell of chickens en masse is especially revolting. Besides the poultry, there were four dogs; a splendid white bull terrier called Garm, two of mixed and uncertain breeding rescued from the Battersea Dogs' Home, by name Chowkidar and Dua (Watch and Pray in Urdu), and my mother's little smooth-haired white fox terrier, Rouge, called for her pink nose. She had been brought from India and gone through the six months anti-rabies quarantine from which her health and her mind, never really recovered. Dua was a sweet bitch and instantly made herself my dog, following me everywhere and sleeping on my bed. I loved her dearly, and she did much to make life tolerable during the halves of all my holidays I had to spend at Wokingham. She had the sweetest face and gentlest eyes of any dog I have ever known.

Besides the dogs, there were cats, some 18 altogether, each with its own name and character, who lived in the house. On one occasion they entered the living room by a door that was only sufficiently open to allow one animal through at a time. In they came, nose to tail, keeping formation, a 30-foot long snake of cats winding its way sinuously around the room. In theory the cats were supposed to make their messes out of doors, but in practice they all seemed to do so on trays lined with old newspapers in the hall just inside the front door. The way they looked at it was, why go out in the cold and scratch around in the garden when everything you need is close at hand? The whole place reeked of cat in its most virulent form, and this was also the characteristic smell of every house that Leslie Brown and my mother ever lived in. They collected cats. Getting back to Walton Lodge was almost a relief. Even the pungent odour of old Stinker Stack seemed like roses.

10

During the summer of 1925, my father came home on leave from India. Things at Walton Lodge had being going from bad to worse. I was very unhappy, often ill, my work had gone to pieces, and my conduct reported as being 'generally bad'. I believe that in these days it is difficult for a school teacher to give an adverse report from fear of personal blame for the condition, and subsequent legal action. I have even heard of a rich parent's retort to being asked to remove his obstreperous son, of buying the school and immediately sacking the headmaster. Nobody at Walton Lodge suffered such fears. My reports were atrocious. Just as my father arrived home, I was again in trouble, being involved in the sinking of a large and very expensive model ocean liner in the boating pool at Weston super Mare.

A number of us had been invited to a friend's birthday party there, and among the presents, was this huge, two-foot-long, clockwork driven, four-funnel, four-propeller, German-made model of an ocean-going liner, the *Aquitania*. Everybody admired it, wished it was his and wanted to see it sail. The trouble was that it was a typical West Country summer's day, blowing half a gale and pouring with rain. Nothing daunted, after an enormous tea of jellies, meringues, potted shrimp sandwiches, swiss rolls and all the other essential ingredients of a children's birthday party, we set forth for the boating pool to sail the ship. The fact that the wind was whipping the surface of the water into quite high waves merely added spice to the maiden voyage. All went well for a time, but about halfway across it was obvious she was in trouble. We gazed in horror as she began to take on water and sink by the head, until finally, propellers spinning wildly, just like the *Titanic*, she slid below the surface. For some reason I was unable to understand at the time, and still cannot, I was held directly responsible for the disaster. Apparently I had egged the birthday boy on to go and sail his wretched boat. Nor was any great harm done, for it was fished up a couple of days later with a shrimping net, and after a few drops of oil to its clockwork motor, was as good as new. But I was in disgrace for weeks.

My father decided that the sooner I was taken away from Walton Lodge the better, and gave them notice that I would be leaving at the end of the Christmas term, and a week before it ended at that. Funnily enough, now that I was leaving, it was one of my better terms. The feuds had ended by most of those who had been under John Read's thumb at last having the courage to come over to my side. It only took a couple at first, and then the whole lot came over. John Read merely relapsed into the protruding toothed nonentity he had always been, and probably would remain for the rest of his life.

The new school which had been chosen for me was Windlesham House, then in large grounds at Portslade near Brighton. It had been founded by the Malden family in 1837 in Brighton, and remained in that family until about 1990, when it was handed over to a governing body by the then headmaster and his wife, Charles and Elizabeth Ann. It was and still is, one of the very best preparatory schools in the country. My son was there from 1959 to 1964, and my granddaughter went there in 1998. It is now situated at Highden, near Washington in East Sussex.

When I arrived for that Easter term in 1926, old Mrs Charles was in the process of handing over to her son Christopher, 'Mr Chris', as we had to call him. She had been running the school since her husband died early in the century, soon after the move from Brighton to Portslade. Although nominally headmaster, Mr Chris still had to leave most of the day-to-day direction of the school to his powerful mother. She was intensely religious, and everything centred around the beautiful little chapel with its stained glass windows, oak pews donated by Old Boys, and the shields bearing the coat of arms of the various public schools to which they went. Below the coat of arms on each shield was a scroll proclaiming the motto of the particular school, '*Stet*

Fortuna Domus' for Harrow, Eton's '*Floreat Etona*', and '*Sursum Corda*' for Haileybury, to which I was destined. The whole building had been brought over brick by brick from Brighton when the school moved, the same thing happening for the move to Washington, where it now stands. Its interior smelt of furniture polish and beeswax from years of loving care and polishing. Whenever I smell either, I am immediately carried back to the chapel at Windlesham.

As far as Mrs Charles was concerned, I was quite convinced that she conducted a daily two-way conversation, with God. On one occasion when I was discovered growing mustard and cress in my face flannel, a popular agricultural pastime, she asked me, 'What would Jesus think!' Frankly I could not see why He should object, but I was equally certain she was away to get on her celestial blower to inform Him that 'young Willoughby was growing mustard and cress on his face flannel'. If I was convinced she was in daily communication with God, she was just as sure that all children spent most of their time fiddling with themselves or with each other. She had actually written a whole chapter on the subject in her book on how to run a preparatory school and the management of children. Either after our Confirmation or just before leaving the school, she gave us all a long talk on sex generally, with very carefully worded pseudonyms for the various organs. These were solely to be employed after marriage, for the purpose of procreation only, and even then, very sparingly. Being grown up sounded no fun at all. The main emphasis however of these talks was on the dangers of 'fiddling', either with ourselves or each other. Dire consequences would follow. For a start, we would never grow up strong and healthy, and our children, if we could have them, which was doubtful, would be puny and deformed. Furthermore and worst of all, we would never manage to get into our public school rugger XV or cricket XI when the time eventually came. To most of us, all this talk of 'fiddling', merely opened up new vistas of which we had never even dreamt.

After Walton Lodge my new school seemed like paradise. The food was delicious. There was no fighting, no bullying, all was order and calm. I arrived one Sunday evening as a new boy, to find old Mrs Charles reading to a circle of boys in the drawing room. In

1959, on a Sunday evening, when I took my son there, new Mrs Charles was reading to a circle of seemingly identical boys in the drawing room. There was a product which both old Mrs Charles and Mr Chris called 'the Windlesham boy': a combination of good manners, athletic prowess, scholastic achievement, to which I could never aspire, and, dare I add, a touch of self-righteous priggishness. Nearly everyone had been there from the age of about 8, whilst I had already turned 12. For me to become a true Windlesham boy after the rough-and-tumble of the near penal conditions at Walton Lodge was, I felt, nigh impossible. There were many things about the place which astonished me. For a start, apart from teaching, the assistant masters had little to do with us. Out of school hours, everything was run by the senior boys. Windlesham was organised on the public school prefectorial system, except that prefects were called monitors.

There were some 80 of us in the school at this time, varying in age from 8 to 14. We were divided into four dormitories of about 20 each, named after a public school, such as Haileybury, Marlborough, Rugby and Oundle. The main assembly room was called Harrow. Each dormitory or 'House', had two monitors, one of whom was 'Head of House', the other his deputy. They slept on each side of the door, I imagine in case anyone wished to slip out for a midnight feast. At the other end of the dormitory were two sub-monitors. These were always more officious than the monitors themselves. There was also a 'Head of the School' and a Captain of whatever particular game was being played, cricket in the summer, soccer in the Christmas term and rugby during the Easter. Under the direction of Mr Chris, the monitors ran the school with amazing efficiency, tact, discretion and firmness. I never ceased to marvel at the sheer ability of these 13- and early 14-year-olds. For instance we used to have prayers lasting some 20 minutes twice a day in the chapel, morning and evening, always taken by the duty monitor, who read the lesson, conducted the prayers and controlled the hymn singing. Another boy, who was learning music and later became a bishop, called Waddy, played the organ. No church could have put on anything more professional. Every Sunday morning we had a proper hour-and-a-quarter long service taken by Mr Chris, in surplice and cassock, with often a visiting Old Boy to preach the sermon and give a general boost to the proceedings.

Besides such duties, the monitors controlled every aspect of school life. They had no powers of punishment themselves, such as were then in the hands of prefects at public schools, of beating small boys for misdemeanours. The monitor's only weapon was to tell you to 'go and report yourself to Mr Chris'. Failure to do so would double the offence, and the monitor would always check to see if his order had been obeyed. Reporting was not easy. You would go to Mr Chris's study door, screw up your courage and knock. On being told to come in, you would enter and stammer out your confession of whatever school rule you had broken and by whom you had been sent to report it. Punishment varied from deprivation of the twice-weekly fourpenny grub ration, to walking around the playing fields a specified number of times, overseen by the monitor on duty. There was usually a procession of rather miserable small boys walking round the fields most afternoons, their hands, like the popular song about Felix the Cat at the time, 'kept firmly behind them'. If the crime was bad enough, you got 'spatted'. Instead of a cane, Mr Chris used a leather strap, divided into a number of fingers at the end. The spat was used on the hand and was extremely painful. For a really serious offence it was used on the bare bottom. In either case it was employed very rarely, and someone being spatted was practically a school event.

The day began with a half-mile or so run down to the school gates. Mr Chris and his pack of monitors would bring up the rear, sweeping up the laggards. We would then have breakfast followed by chapel. Hours of work and holidays were much the same as at Walton Lodge. The top form was 1A, followed by 1B. These two forms, especially 1B were almost entirely for cramming boys for scholarships and Common Entrance to public schools. The real education took place from forms 6 to 2, each one of 12 to 15 pupils. In 1B there were usually 16 to 18, and in 1A, only four or five. I managed to get into 1A my last term and reached a standard of learning that I never attained again. I began to learn Greek and was proficient in trigonometry, thanks to the wonderful tuition of Mr Drummond, the maths master. At Windlesham, mathematics was my best subject. After two terms at Haileybury it became by

116

far my worst, which only goes to show that whether a child learns or not depends entirely on the teacher. 1A was more or less a university. There was no obligation to work, or even attend certain lessons. We worked with, rather than learnt from, our teachers. Or that is how we felt.

During ten years education at two prep schools and one public school, I became convinced that all schoolteachers were to a lesser or greater extent mad or they would not contemplate becoming school teachers in the first place. They were miserably paid, but in return, like Army officers, lived a comparatively genial and sheltered existence under pleasant conditions, with plenty of holidays, cocooned from the outside world. It was a job for life, and if they behaved themselves and did not rock the boat, they might even fetch up as headmaster somewhere. Schoolmastering also put them in a position of considerable power, of being able to work out their frustrations from time to time, by giving some reptilian small boy a sound beating. Nearly all, through the passage of time, developed curious habits and eccentricities, which were faithfully mimicked by school wags. It was only they who got older, the boys always remained the same age. Mr Drummond, for instance, developed the habit of absentmindedly knocking his pipe out on your head. The aroma of singeing hair would often waft under the door of 1A's classroom, and the smell of a wet dottle took days to wash out. Mr Long, form master of 1B, on the other hand, would catch you a stinging slap across the face for any inattention or silly mistake. Another had the curious desire of suddenly raising the lid of his desk and bringing it down with an enormous bang, frightening us all out of our skins, and certainly waking up those dozing gently at the back.

When I arrived I was given a test and put into form 1B, enjoying the full extent of Mr Long's wrath over my pronunciation of Latin. At Walton Lodge we had pronounced it exactly like English. At Windlesham they used the 'New Pronunciation'. Cs were pronounced as Ks. Thus Caesar would be called Kaiser. Vs were pronounced as Ws, and there were a lot of other differences. It was too much for me altogether and I was put down to form 2 until I could learn to speak it properly. The master here was a Mr Mills, who had a terrible stutter which did not help. My desire to obtain

117

cheap notoriety and a spurious popularity among my peers by defying authority, which has always been my chief weakness, once again came to the fore. I was continually in trouble, endlessly being ordered by some monitor to report myself to Mr Chris, perpetually without my grub ration and walking round and round the fields with my hands behind my back. Every week on Monday mornings, the class results for the whole school were given out in Harrow, the assembly room. I was usually bottom of the form.

At some time during that first Easter term, I must have decided that enough was enough and that I was going to pull myself together. The next Monday, my name was read out as top of form 2. The surprise was such that a kind of gasp ran through the assembly. And there I remained for the rest of the term. The next one I was promoted back to 1B, to face the perils of Mr Long's bony hand once again. He was a very tall, thin man, with a big nose and a mop of thick, unruly, black hair. Among other subjects, he took us for Latin, French and Scripture. Much of the work was concentration on old Common Entrance exam papers. Year after year the questions were similar, if not identical. After all, the public schools' bread and butter depended upon a steady supply of boys from prep schools. If you were lucky you would often get questions in the exam which you had already answered. Mr Long's classes were somewhat like a game of snakes and ladders. He would fire a question at the top boy and, if he could not answer, to the next and so on down the line until he got the correct one. That boy then went to the top and everyone moved down one. It was a wonderful way of keeping everybody on their toes. Sometimes a simple question could take you from the bottom of the class to the top, but if you missed two consecutive questions, you automatically went to the bottom. At the end of each period, you got the marks of your final position and these were added to your weekly total. Mr Long's Scripture teaching was purely factual and historical, dealing exclusively with the Old Testament at the time of the Prophets and the Kings. They were fascinating in their detail. All religious content he left to our attendance in chapel. No-one bore him a grudge for his frequent slappings. There was always complete order and attention during the periods he took us, and he taught so well that the time never seemed to drag. Boys like and admire a strict master. It is the lenient ones, usually who cannot teach or keep order, who are despised and unpopular.

As for the new Latin pronunciation, I soon mastered it, but it might just as well be spoken like English as any other way. No-one knows or can know or even guess how Latin was pronounced, and it would obviously have been spoken differently in the various parts of an empire stretching from Scotland to the Middle East. There would be regional differences, according to the local language, the passing of the centuries and other conditions. Greek would have had a strong influence on how it was pronounced, for every educated Roman prided himself on his knowledge of Greek. Wealthy, aristocratic young Romans were sent to Athens to be 'finished' and learn good manners, though the Greeks were despised for their homosexuality and considered effeminate. There was probably a correct Latin, spoken by the Emperor and the upper classes, with its emphasis on syntax, proper case endings to the nouns and other grammatical niceties of which the common people would be quite ignorant. However, in court circles it would be wise, if you were in contact with such characters as Caligula for instance, to try and speak much the same way as he did, in case he took offence and considered you might be better employed amusing the lions, along with the Christians, at the next set of Games.

Games too, were taken very seriously at Windlesham, though not with the semi-religious fervour I was to meet later. Work was always the more important, and really clever boys such as Asher, Waddy and the Davies brothers, all in 1A and all of whom got scholarships, one even to Winchester, the most difficult of all, were admired and respected. We played the usual triumvirate of British school games; cricket in the summer, soccer in the winter, and rugby in the spring. rugby was by far the favourite. I had never yet played it. We also had a Sports Day during the summer term. At Walton Lodge I had been a prominent player in all the teams, and expected to walk into those at my new school. How wrong I was! With 80 boys to chose from, a place in the first team was far harder to achieve than when there were only 20, and where if you were over about ten and not actually semi-paralytic, you were certain to make the team. Windlesham too was going through a period of invincibility. For a year it had not lost a match against any other school at any game. Its Second XI could have beaten most. The soccer XI especially was a well-drilled goal-scoring machine. The ball would be kicked out to Gibson on the wing, who would pass it in to the centre forward, Nigel Bennett, to score. Hero of the defence was a tireless right back, called Hankin-Turvin, who became a great friend.

There did not seem to be much going on in the way of games that first Easter term, but after the Easter holidays when we returned to school, where by now I had established myself as bad boy turned 'goody-two-shoes' under the influence of Windlesham, which was probably true, I was asked if I was any good at cricket, and did I bat or did I bowl? I modestly admitted that I was probably regarded as the Demon Bowler of North-West Somerset, and had once taken six wickets in a match against Darcy's. It cut no ice. I was given a trial and put firmly in my place, which was the 2nd XI. We also had a Sports Day and I surprisingly did much better, winning the 100 and 220 yards races and the high jump. At the prize-giving afterwards Mr Chris made a little speech congratulating us on our running, and hoping we we would 'always do as well in the face of the enemy'. The Boy Scout troop gave us all a strong military flavour.

Everyone in the school had to be a Wolf Cub until he was ten, and then a Boy Scout. There were some six Scout Patrols of ten boys each, with a leader and a deputy leader, who wore white stripes on their shirt pockets to show their rank. Each Patrol was called after some animal, Lion, Tiger, Bear and so on. A member of staff acted as a kind of Colonel-in-Chief of each. I was allotted to the Hawk Patrol, Mrs Charles' Own. It was quite the worst, and I imagine I was put there in the hope of giving it a boost. I failed miserably and the Patrol was later disbanded. I found myself in the Lions, headed by Miss Euphie, the headmaster's sister, who took us for Art classes. I dearly loved Miss Euphie and eventually became Patrol Leader. When I left she gave me a copy of P.C. Wren's *Beau Geste*, with words of thanks inside the front cover, which I still have.

Scouts wore the traditional uniform devised by Lord Baden-

Powell. It consisted of khaki shirt with rolled-up sleeves, and dark blue serge shorts. A scarf had to be immaculately folded and knotted around our neck. These scarves were of different colours, denoting the name of your patrol. For instance the colour of any Hawk Patrol was always pink. Around one shoulder was a lanyard with a whistle at the end of it, kept in the shirt pocket. Around our waist was a leather belt with a buckle showing the Scout badge of a fleur de lis. Also attached to the belt was a huge knife, consisting of an enormous blade, a marlinspike and a thing for getting stones out of a horse's hoof, without which no self-respecting boy's knife was complete. Nowadays it would instantly be confiscated by the Police as an offensive weapon. On our head we wore a wide-brimmed khaki felt hat with four indentations in the crown and the Scout badge in front. Stout brogue shoes and woollen stockings completed a very smart outfit. In our hands we carried the traditional Boy Scout pole. There were numerous proficiency badges you could earn, and these were sewn onto the sleeves below the shoulder. By far the most popular in the summer was the Cook's badge. There were many parts to it, and it meant cooking over an open fire which you had to make and light yourself with only two matches every Sunday morning, instead of going to chapel. With luck and judicious management, you could spin out earning your Cook's badge the whole term.

Another outdoor activity during the summer months was 'bugging'. Anyone taking part in it was described by old Mrs Charles as a 'bugger'. I cannot believe that she so naive as to be unaware of the true meaning of the word, and more probably used it as a kind of innocent joke. I remember her introducing one small boy to a visiting parent, 'This is MacAnally, one of our keenest buggers'. In fact, bugging was the keeping and raising from the egg of different varieties of moths and butterflies. They were usually moths, because the caterpillars are far more striking. At the start of every summer term people would write to Newmans, a butterfly farm in Bexley, Kent, for eggs or newly hatched caterpillars, and special breeding boxes or cages to keep them in. The most popular choices were Puss and Poplar Hawk moths. Both lived on poplar leaves, of which there were plenty in the grounds. Puss moths are indigenous to Sussex and are only found in the county. The caterpillars, or larvae, are wonderful to behold, with two long whiplash tails at the back. During their growth period of about six weeks, they moult their skin six times, the last moult leaving them with a huge kind of armour-plated head. There was tremendous competition among us 'buggers' to produce the first armour-plate. They then entomb themselves in the bark of the poplar tree, chewing off tiny pieces and cementing them with saliva. The result is a tomb so strong that it can be stood upon with impunity. Inside it, they turn into a chrysalis, biting their way out and emerging as an 'imago', or fully fledged Puss moth, the following summer.

My chief joy at Windlesham was the swimming pool. This was indoors and heated. We used it all the year round. It was here that I learnt to swim and dive really well. The aim was to become a 'Dolphin' and to wear the coveted round silver brooch with the dolphin emblem in the centre. That it was so hard to achieve made it all the more desirable. The examination consisted of a series of difficult tests in swimming, diving, swimming underwater and life-saving. My mother wore my dolphin badge for many years afterwards, until it got lost in the general mess in which she lived. Possibly one of the cats mistook it for a goldfish. Besides the swimming pool, we had an excellent nine-hole golf course around the grounds. By the time I left, I had learnt to play quite well, but, to my great regret now, never played again. Every time I thought of taking up golf once more, it was rather like the idea of going to Ireland for a holiday. There always seemed something better to do at the time, such as maybe ski-ing, riding, swimming, mountain climbing, tennis, or merely just lying in the sun. Golf has the immeasurable advantage that it can be played to a great age, long after all the others have become impossible. It is also a highly social game and can considerably add to your chances of rapid promotion. This is especially the case in any profession where being agreeable to your boss and letting him win often enough counts most, such as any of the services, barristers, solicitors, politicians and many of the business conglomerates. Here it can mean the quickest way to the boardroom. A young assistant who plays a good round of golf after a conference is always an asset and a credit to his employer. Anyone with a sufficiently low handicap may be sure of swift advancement, irrespective of all other merit.

Until the outbreak of war in 1939, and probably for some years after it had finished, nearly all boys in Britain under the age of 14 wore shorts. In fact, 'going into long trousers' was an event in life not unlike that experienced by girls early in the century, when at the age of about 17, they 'put their hair up and came out'. At Windlesham we wore grey corduroy shorts, shirt and the black-and-white tie of the school colours. Over it was worn a vee-neck pullover trimmed with black and white, as were the tops of our woollen stockings. For lessons and general use we wore elastic-sided leather house shoes. The whole outfit was smart and eminently practical. On Sundays, however, it was a grey flannel jacket instead of the jerey, Scots boys often being in Highland dress.

Having seen me settled at my new school, my father returned to his last posting in India, that of commanding the Jhansi Brigade of one British and three Indian battalions. I spent my holidays as before, half at Wokingham, counting the minutes until I was able to leave for Tenby, to spend the other half with Twig and my grandmother. My only consolation was my dog, Dua, whom I loved dearly and was inseparable from. It was not that my mother or Leslie were unkind or mistreated me; far from it, they both went out of their way to make life as agreeable as possible, to such an extent that it made me feel guilty that I did not appreciate it more. They were always buying me toys I knew they could not afford, such as new trucks for my railway or boxes of model soldiers. It was just the general set-up that I loathed being part of, and the social opprobium in which they were held. Above all, I loathed the general discomfort and the stench of cats amidst which they lived.

Furthermore my mother continued to cause me great embarrassment at school by coming down with Leslie and taking me out almost every weekend. For a start I did not want to go out, but would have preferred to stay at school with my friends and take part in some of the many activities that were available. Then she would usually appear dressed in the skin of some unfortunate animal she had shot, causing considerable comment, and if there is one thing a boy at prep school loathes at all times, it is visitors who cause comment. I was sick of explaining why Leslie Brown was not my father, and I knew his presence caused concern to the Maldens, who had been told by my father that he had obtained a court order that Leslie was not to be brought down to the school. Matters came to a head during my last term, the summer of 1927. There was to be a total eclipse of the sun which could only be seen in North Wales. My mother told the Maldens that as there would not be another over Britain until 1999, she proposed to take me away for a few days to see it. They replied that it would interfere with my work for the Common Entrance exam, and unsettle me. They could not agree to me going. She insisted that she would take me anyway, to which Mr Chris wrote her an answer, which he showed me: 'By all means take him if you wish, but if you do, please do not bring him back here'. I cannot ever remember being overcome with more shame. I did not go, but she and Leslie went off to Wales for the eclipse. I do not think they saw much, for it poured with rain. It often does, that being an old Welsh custom.

Of all the places of education which I attended, I was happiest at Windlesham. In its general attitude and enlightment it was much nearer my idea of a university than a school. People learnt and worked because they wished to, rather than because they were made to. This was especially the case for the five of us in Form 1A. I managed to get into the cricket XI and rugby XV, and that last summer won the school sports and became Victor Ludorum. I was even made a monitor, running with Mr Chris every morning down to the school gates, sweeping up the laggards. Mrs Charles liked me, Mr Drummond would affectionately knock his pipe out on my head, even Mr Long's slappings seemed to have lost their sting. I really felt I had become a 'Windlesham boy'. Perhaps the only person I failed to convince was Mr Chris, but then with him you always had to walk like Agag, very delicately.

11

When it came to my mother's turn to have me for her half of that summer holidays, she took me down to Llanstephan near Carmarthen in South Wales. My Aunt Mabel, madder than ever, had a little house there, and my mother with Leslie Brown and the three dogs lived nearby. The dogs had a habit of running off and not returning for hours. When they did, he used to beat them as a punishment. On my pointing out that they merely considered this an unwelcome reward for coming back, he told me that the dogs were fully aware of what they were being beaten for. Whether they were or not, I do not know, but I found the sound of their beatings most distressing, for the two who were not actually being punished set up as loud a yelping and a whimpering as the one which was. Nor could I see that it achieved anything. Why Leslie did this I cannot understand, because he loved the dogs and they loved him. He was usually kindness itself, but justified his action by saying, 'They must learn discipline'. It seemed a daft way of teaching it.

Whilst in Llanstephan, I fell victim to the then current medical fad of the time, that of 'poisoned tonsils'. But before this I was involved in a curious incident, almost of second sight, with a gypsy. My mother had taken me to a local fair, where I spent much time on the merry-go-round of wooden horses, rising and dipping as they circled the steam engine in the centre which drove them, and also operated an organ. I remember the tune it was blaring out from Bizet's *L'Arlesienne*, and every time I hear it now I can see myself astride that horse at the Llanstephan fair. As I dismounted, a gypsy woman approached and asked to read my fortune. My mother refused to let her, so instead, she tapped my chest with a bony finger, saying, 'Too big! It's too big!' and walked away.

Doctors seem to follow fashionable trends. In my early days it was appendicitis and bad tonsils, which they whipped out at the drop of a hat, and maybe sooner. In Llanstephan I caught a cold, ran a temperature and an elderly doctor was called in. He gave one look at my tonsils, sucked his teeth, shook his head, murmured 'Oh dear! Oh dear!' and said, 'These will have to come out in Carmarthen, they have probably poisoned his heart as well.' This he found to be the case. My heart had become what he described as 'enlarged'. All in all I gathered I was only just about one jump ahead of the undertaker, who was hot on my heels. He confined me to bed for an indefinite period, until an operation for my tonsils could be arranged. There was no question of my going to Haileybury, into which I had passed, for my first term. I pointed out that if my heart was in such a bad state, how was it then that I had managed to become Victor Ludorum at the school sports only a few weeks earlier at Windlesham? He talked sagely of 'tremendous compensation'.

Tremendous compensation there may have been, there was also a tremendous family row. My father was in India and relayed instructions by telegram. My grandmother came down with Mr Hobhouse, the family solicitor from Pennington and Sons, who could but rarely be lured away from the fleshpots of Lincoln's Inn. He was a dear old buffer and I could hear him arguing with my mother downstairs. Every now and again he would exclaim, 'Come! Come! Mrs Willoughby, Come! Come! This will not do at all.' I was not allowed to see either of them. My mother had possession, and that was nine points of the law. She refused to let them take me away to London for a second medical opinion or for any other reason, as they were very worried at my having to miss a whole term's education at Haileybury. Furthermore my father had already paid for it, and this riled him not a little. I felt that with me in her hands, my mother had the perfect stick with which to beat him and make herself as awkward as possible. In the meantime I was incarcerated in bed until my heart was thought strong enough to take the concoction of ether and chloroform used in those days as an anaesthetic. My dog Dua slept on my bed and kept me company. I whittled model yachts out of pieces of wood, and Miss Jellie used to come up and play chess with me. After a few weeks I was admitted to Carmarthen hospital and had my tonsils removed. It was excruciatingly painful.

When I recovered, I was taken back to Wokingham, where I spent the whole of that winter term. I can remember little about it, other than listening to the BBC Armistice remembrance broadcast from the Albert Hall on 11 November 1927. It was the first time it had been done, and the Hall was full of men who had been in the trenches only nine years previously. I had no doubt that Mr Simpkins from Walton Lodge would be there, singing his head off. From the noise, all had forgotten the horrors, but only remembered the fantastic comradeship and the better things. We listened to it through a large bakelite loudspeaker, the valves of the wireless set glowing in the lamplight. Unlike World War Two, the Great War produced some wonderful tunes and songs, such as 'Tipperary', 'Pack up your Troubles', 'Carry Me Back to Blighty', 'Goodbyee, Don't Cryee' and many others. The thousands of men packed into the Albert Hall roared them out. I envied them and I envied their experience of war. At that time, the general opinion was that 'The War to end all Wars had been fought and won'. There would never be another.

Each month I was taken to a consultant heart specialist at 86 Brook Street in London. He would stand me up in front of a large X-ray screen and trace out the outlines of my heart on a piece of transparent paper. These were then compared with each other, and it was found to be indeed getting smaller and back to its proper size, which he indicated with a dotted line. In the meantime, the legal eagles had not been idle. I had been made a 'Ward of Court', under the jurisdiction of Mr Justice Romer, and taken from the control of either of my parents. He ordered that as I had been so long with my mother, I was to spend the Christmas holidays with my father, who had managed to get 'compassionate leave' from the Army to come home from India, and sort matters out. Justice Romer gave instructions that on no account was Leslie to accompany my mother to see me at Haileybury, an instruction which was totally ignored. I spent those holidays with my father and grandmother, who had now left Tenby and set up home with her daughter and Uncle Jimmy at Norfolk Lodge, a mock-Tudor house in the Oldfield Road at Bray, near Maidenhead. I lived in a kind of attic on the third floor, with a dormer window, from which I could watch all the Great Western Railway expresses, pulled by the superb 4-6-0 Castle Class locomotives, as they roared their way up from the West Country to Paddington. I loved it. The place must have originally been a maid's bedroom, and with its linoleum floor suited me well, for I could run my network of steam trains over it without risk of setting fire to a carpet.

I was also fitted with the standard dress for Haileybury. During weekdays we wore either a blue or dark grey double-breasted serge jacket over grey flannel trousers; the more near-silver in colour, the more fashionable they were. On Sundays we wore a dark suit and a straw hat with a band of the house colours around it. During the week we sported a house cap, which for the first year had to be worn right down over the ears, especially if you were a 'New Guvnor', as new boys were called. My father warned me that from his own experience my first term would be as near an approach to hell as I would ever know in my life, but never mind, I could make someone else's hell even worse, my second. What he told me was a complete understatement, and I was so disgusted by our treatment that I made no attempt to pass it on the next term.

Haileybury had been built in the early part of the 19th century by the East India Company to train cadets as officers to serve in India, in much the same way as the Royal Military College at Sandhurst and the Royal Military Academy at Woolwich produced officers for the Army. The East India Company came to an end after the suppression of the Indian Mutiny in 1858, when India became part of the British Empire. Haileybury then became a normal public school. It quickly gained a reputation for being rough and tough, a hard place to be. This lasted certainly past my time; perhaps only Sedburgh was considered tougher. The Governors of the Company had thought to build something very grand and had chosen a site on Hertford Heath, a small village between Hertford and Hoddesdon, some 20 miles north of London. It was built around an enormous quadrangle. There was a clockhouse in the centre of the northern side with rooms for the staff. A long drive led up to an imposing, classic pillared entrance from the west. The Romans had built a road nearby, and in fact the school song began with the words, 'The Romans were a knowing race, they built a road unto this place'. As Jeeves might have remarked to Bertie Wooster, 'Doubtless to be able to get away from it the faster, Sir.' The southern side of the quadrangle was dominated by the chapel, a huge building with a vast copper-covered dome, not unlike that of St Pauls. From the outside this was part of a wonderful terrace, overlooking the 1st XV rugby ground. The left-hand side of the terrace contained the headmaster's quarters, and the right hand, the dining hall. In my time the headmaster was a kindly old man called Talbot, popularly known as 'Botty'. The very fact that the school buildings were close together and structurally tight knit gave it a very special sense of esprit de corps different from many public schools, where houses and classrooms were scattered throughout a town.

I had been posted to my father's old house, Batten. In fact the 'houses' were not houses at all, but very long dormitories, six of which were built around the main grass-covered 'quad' in pairs, one above the other. Batten however, was the middle of a group of three, with Le Bas above and Melville, below, in what was known as 'little quad', approached through an arch in the side of the main one. It was surprising how little boys from different houses had to do with one another. Members of each house very much kept to themselves. Although every dormitory was theoretically identical, there was a subtle difference. It was strictly forbidden to enter another house without permission, but one occasionally poked one's nose through the door into what appeared a foreign country. It was not unlike the British Army, where every regiment is absolutely identical, yet completely different. In addition to the houses grouped around the main school, there were two others a little distance away, Hailey and Highfield. The latter was where the 'rich boys' went. Each had a room to himself, like Eton or Harrow, and the food was much better than the horrible swill the rest of us had to eat. People from Highfield were despised as cissies, and all the time I was at school, they never put any kind of team worthy of the name into the field.

The authorities had very wisely given instructions that new boys arrived a day early so that they could get their bearings. My father took me down and introduced me to my housemaster, Bill Adams, who taught maths and was in the way of being a

129

mathematical genius, but who struck me as being completely mad. He was an enormously tall gangling man, with a shock of greying hair and a wild look in his eye. He never wore other than dark grey drainpipe trousers which only came down to well above his ankles, showing about three inches of sock above huge army boots. These invariably had their labels hanging out. He was a kind-hearted man and always gave prior warning of any punishment. 'I'm going to beat you boy,' he would say of a Saturday morning, 'come and see me in my study on Monday.' I was also taken to see the medical officer, Dr L.R. Lempriere, to whom my consultant had written about the condition of my heart. He told me that I was not to play any games, or run when 'fagged', and that he would make sure that Bill Adams was made aware of this. He also made unkind remarks about the physical standards of boys entering the school at the time.

My father left me, saying he would be back as soon as possible to take me out for the weekend. I found myself with the two other 'New Guvnors', all of us as forlorn as each other. One was called Pillitz, an unfortunate name, I thought, with which to start a school career, and the other Fennell, who lived with an aunt nearby, and a couple of terms later disappeared in mysterious circumstances, never to be spoken of again. The following day the rest of the boys returned, and our tribulations began. For the first year at Haileybury, one spent the time out of school hours in the dormitory classroom, on the landing just outside the house, which contained 12 or 13 boys. From here you moved across the quad into one of two houserooms, where you spent another two years until you became eligible for a study for four. Usually only college prefects or members of the rugby XV or cricket XI were eventually awarded a study to themselves. During the day, the dormitory was strictly out of bounds to all but college and house prefects.

The Batten dormitory classroom, known as the DC, was a large, high-ceilinged room with a window looking out over the cricket pavilion and the playing fields. There was a big radiator below a window which had to be kept open at all times or there would be a 'fug', which British schoolboys were trained to loathe and despise. The head of the DC was a small boy with a limp, called

130

Meyer, who could not play games. As I recall, he was still head of it a year later when I had gone to a houseroom and was wearing 'side'. For the first year, school caps in their distinguishing house colours – Batten's was brown with a yellow cross on it like a hot cross bun – had to be kept pulled well forward, over forehead and ears. After a year you were allowed to 'put on side'. This meant a new and much smaller cap altogether, perched at a rakish angle on the back of the head. Members of the rugby XV wore the school crest of a winged heart on the peak, and there were other emblems for other games. The cricket XI wore a magenta ribbon, that being the school colour, around their straw boaters on Sundays. Such people were known as 'bloods', and were regarded as little removed from gods.

There was not very much furniture in the DC: two large kitchen tables, some benches and wooden chairs, with a bank of lockers along one side in which to keep our school books. The floor was bare boards, scuffed uneven by the feet of scores of small boys over the years. Meyer drew a line in chalk down the middle of the room. 'That is your side,' he told us, 'you will not cross over unless you are called to fag.' In theory only prefects were allowed to fag small boys. They did so by shouting 'Fagable' from the dormitory, whereupon all the occupants of the DC had to rush to the call, the last one to arrive being given the duty, which was usually to run down to the grubber, as the tuck shop was known, to bring back something for the prefect's tea, such as maybe a loaf of bread, half a pound of Anchor butter, or perhaps a Lyons swiss roll. In practice of course, it was made sure that one of the New Guvnors arrived last, and woe betide if it were not so. New boys too were mercilessly fagged by the other members of the DC, which was strictly illegal, being sent on endless errands to the grubber for food, and having to run both ways. You would be watched from the window. No sooner had you brought one his order than you were sent off on another task. Any misdemeanour or laziness was rewarded by being beaten on the bottom with a gym shoe. Usually all three of us were beaten at least four times a day.

To be beaten you had to kneel on the seat of a wooden chair, lift your coat tails and hold the back of it with both hands. Ten or so boys would take a run and wallop your backside as hard as they knew how with the gym shoe. It hurt, particularly the third or fourth application, and was utterly humiliating, which was the main idea of it. The weekends especially were a dreadful experience. Not only was it painful and humiliating, but it made one feel ashamed and unworthy. At first I was spared the horror of the weekends, as my father used to come down and take me out, but later in the term, Mr Justice Romer, in his wisdom, decided it would upset my studies and forbade it. I was in class when I was told the news, and I'm afraid I broke down and cried, which made me feel even more miserable and ashamed than ever. It would be safe to say that for a New Guvnor at Haileybury in 1928, there was not a single moment of the day when he was not actually in class that he was not being tormented in some way by the other small boys of the DC. What is perhaps even more amazing was our acceptance of it without question, as if it were right and proper, something to be undergone, an inevitable part of the fabric of life, like mumps, measles or chicken pox.

Perhaps it was worse for me. I was classed as 'having a weak heart', excused all games and any form of running. I walked on 'fagables' and paid the inevitable penalty, so, weak heart or no, I ran. It was easier than useless explanation. Nor did I puff or pant or show any other symptoms, so I really wonder if there was actually anything wrong with me at all? It is, however, difficult to explain the scorn you were exposed to from one and all, to whom games were little short of a religion, at being labelled as 'having a weak heart'. To have been classed 'mentally deficient', as many of the better games players undoubtedly were, would have been infinitely preferable. From top to bottom, every boy knew what was going on and how New Guvnors were treated. They had been through it themselves. The masters, known as beaks, could not have failed to know either. Far from attempting to stop it, they approved. It was the right treatment for new boys, and knocked the cockiness of their prep schools out of them. The only ones who were spared this misery were the lucky small boys who had rooms to themselves in Highfield. 'If you wanted proof that the rest of the school was right, just take a look at them, no bloody good at anything!' What was even more amazing was that directly your first term was over, all bullying ceased, and I never came across another instance of it all the four years I was at Haileybury.

My tribulations came to an end a fortnight before the finish of that Easter term. I woke up one morning with swellings under my jaws like a bullfrog. I reported to the 'Sick House' at the top end of little quad. 'Please Sir,' I said to Dr Lempriere, 'I've got mumps.' 'Bend over,' he replied and promptly gave me six of the best with a cane. 'That,' he went on, 'is for venturing a medical opinion about which you know nothing. Now go and tell Sister to give you a large dose of castor oil and admit you.' Everybody who was admitted to the Sick House for whatever reason was automatically given a large dose of castor oil mixed with lemon juice. 'Oh blessed mumps! Oh blessed castor oil!' I had escaped my tormentors at last. The term would be over before I left my sickbed. As for the beating from Dr Lempriere, it had not been hard. I bore him no grudge. He was a fine fellow, besides he had been in the school rugby XV in 1908. His name was up on the board in the Dining Hall for all to see. There was talk of him having been a Cambridge Blue. Furthermore life in the Sick House, under the care of the delectable red-haired Thelma Townsend, was very pleasant. However, never again have I volunteered a medical opinion to a doctor. As Virgil used to say, *'Medici quamquam intellegunt nunquam tamen aegris de morbo semper dicunt'*, 'Doctors prefer their patients to remain ignorant of what is the matter with them. Then they cannot really complain if they die of it.' As for the delectable Thelma Townsend, I heard later that she had married a beak called Groizy Matthews, 'groize' being school slang for grease, such as a concoction called Anzora, used by the fashion-conscious to slick down their hair, the prototype of the Brylcreem used later by fighter pilots of the RAF. As for Groizy Matthews, I cannot remember him having a lot of hair to slick down, but he had a generally rather sallow and greasy appearance.

During that first term too, you had to learn the rather complicated etiquette of Haileybury life. The DC held an oral exam on this after a fortnight, and each failed question meant a beating on the spot. The school had its own special slang, most of which I have now forgotten, but a 'toby' was a school servant and the word 'nervy' was used instead of 'cheeky'. When applied to a New Guvnor, it had much the same connotation as an 'uppity nigger' in the Deep South at the time of the American Civil War. Being called a 'nervy New Guvnor' meant instant physical retribution as well. Then you had to know the names of all the heads of houses, and of all the beaks' nicknames, and which form they took. The oldest beak was Charles Atherton, Charlie A. He had been at the school when my father was there. Others were Johnny Bower, thin-necked with a large Adam's apple which bobbed up and down as he spoke, Cheesy Champion, Bill Adams, my housemaster, and Daddy Dawes, who was reputed to be an ex-RN Admiral. He was a splendid fellow who went around with a large bulldog and taught Scripture. In fact he usually read his class thrilling stories of escapes from German POW camps, or offered half a crown to any boy who could write the longest essay, irrespective of any merit. All was then peace except for the frantic scratching of pens, whilst Daddy Dawes got on with something he wished to do, such as reading the daily paper. I think his highest actual rank had been a Lieutenant in the Royal Navy Volunteer Reserve, but I only discovered this many years later.

The 'houses', really dormitories, were long high rooms containing about 60 boys, 30 on each side. Each bed was contained in a cubicle with wooden sides three feet high, holding a curtain rail and curtain, but this was never drawn The narrow iron bed, covered with a red-and-black-striped blanket, had a strip of theadbare carpet beside it. There was also a chest of drawers for clothes. Every garment had to be marked with your name and school number – mine was 612 – and everything was checked by the House Matron. As all queueing or waiting was done in alphabetical order, bearing a surname beginning with W was a great disadvantage. At the far end of the dormitory slept the head of house and his deputy. Then came the New Guvnors, followed in strict seniority by the rest. Thus everyone slept among his own contemporaries. At the other end, by the entrance door were the cubicles of the house prefects. Along the entire length of the dormitory ran two large hot water pipes for central heating, one on each side. Each cubicle had a small window, which had to be kept wide open at all times, whatever the weather. The floor of the house was bare boards, worn rough by the passage of many feet.

In the middle of the dormitory was a wide entrance to the washroom annexe. There was a big wooden table here, reserved for the prefects, plus notice boards on which were pinned house events, such as teams, colour awards, and other items of general interest. The washroom consisted of two banks of basins, a number of footbaths or 'toe-pans' with a low bench on which you sat, and two large enamel baths. The floor was a kind of Roman mosaic which sloped away all round into drains, allowing the water to run off. When the washroom was in use there was always an inch or two of water sloshing over the floor. Beyond the washroom was the drying room, where clothes were hung up after rugby. With so many unwashed clothes in close proximity like this, skin diseases were inevitable. The most common were scrumpox, impetigo of the face, and *taenia cruris*, a form of ringworm on each side of the crutch, which Dr Lempriere treated with large quantities of Gentian Violet ointment. The impetigo looked particularly disgusting, and I am glad to say I contracted neither. There was no flush lavatory at all, and in fact none was available nearer than those not far from the dining hall, some hundreds of yards away. These were in long rows with no doors, and the bowls had no seats, only two little cork strips, one to a side. People were utterly uninhibited, and daily after breakfast, groups could be seen at the entrance to each cubicle, chattering to a friend as he sat on the throne. The bigger the 'blood' the greater the retinue. It was a fine assessment of his social standing. Although there was no loo in the dormitory, I never heard of anyone being taken short. If they were, it was a quarter of a mile gallop to the college 'bogs'. Each bed, however, was equipped with a chamber pot, and it was the duty of the unfortunate house toby to empty these every morning when he made our beds.

The day began at 7 a.m. with the house toby opening the door, switching on the lights in winter, and ringing a large bell to wake us up. Everyone then took off their pyjamas, seized the towel hanging on the side of their cubicle and rushed to the washroom. Here all the taps were turned on at full volume. We each had a large sponge, the smaller boys splashed themselves all over at the basins, the middle school at the toe-pans and the prefects lolled, three at a time, in one of the baths, their legs hanging over the side. The other bath was kept full of cold water, with the tap running. Everyone had to plunge in and out of it before drying and racing back to their cubicle to dress. For half an hour every morning, the washroom was a cloud of steam in which some 60 naked boys, big and small, flitted mistily, shouting, splashing and singing.

Besides all this washing every morning, those junior boys not entitled to a toe-pan, where they could soap themselves properly, had to have a weekly bath at bedtime. The ritual was so bizarre that it even struck me as odd at the time, used as I had become to the seemingly incomprehensible. The two baths were filled to the brim by the House Matron, with absolutely scalding water, and four boys to each were allowed a quarter of an hour in the bath in relays. The first pair found the water so impossibly hot that it was all they could do to dip a hasty finger or toe in it. The second pair roasted, the third had a pleasant bath and the fourth froze. Except for the final pair, soap was forbidden in case it dirtied the water.

It might be thought that all this contact of naked bodies was a kind of homosexuals' charter, but it was by no means the case. During my four years at Haileybury I never encountered a single incident of homosexual behaviour. True, there were romantic friendships, but certainly no buggery. For a start, such an act would have been difficult, if not impossible, due to the almost total lack of all privacy. Besides, buggery and all forms of homosexuality were highly frowned upon, and if found out, meant that ultimate disgrace, being expelled. Even suspicion of it could seriously affect your chances of getting into the rugby XV. True, there were small boys in their first year who were known as 'College tarts', girlish figures with big eyes and long lashes. But they were more of a joke than anything else, and I never heard of anybody having an affair with one. Nor were romantic friendships confined to the pupils Some of the beaks had them with senior boys, notably Bobby Blunt, the arts master, brother of the notorious Soviet spy, curator of the Queen's art collection.

Time goes much more slowly when one is young. Half an hour is a long time, three-quarters never ending. Chapel was at

7.30 a.m. every day. The chapel was some 200 yards from Batten, and in the last few seconds before this time, streams of boys could be seen sprinting across the quad to get a foot in the cloisters before the clock struck and they were 'late for chapel'. As they progressed through the school, boys got blasé about getting up, especially in winter, leaving it until the last minute. I remember on many occasions, remaining in bed until 7.20 before seizing my towel, rushing down the house, washing in the toepan, having a cold bath, drying, dressing and running as fast as I could go to chapel. The dining hall was next door to it, so everyone went straight in to breakfast after the quarter of an hour morning service. Breakfast was eaten by houses. Each one had its own long wooden table. Prefects and seniors sat at one end, the rest in strict order of seniority down each side. Large trays of food, eggs and bacon, eggs and sausages, fish and so on, depending on the day, were brought from the kitchen by the dining room tobys, and put on the table, to be served onto hot plates by the prefects and passed down. Toast was an extra, paid for by one's parents, as was jam or marmalade. The jars had to be carefully labelled and were put out ready each day by the tobys.

Work began at 9 a.m. The classrooms were all together in a block, just inside the imposing main entrance to the school, whilst the science laboratories were at the other end in the Bradby Hall, near the house called Hailey. Lesson periods were of 40 minutes each with a five minute break in between and lasted until noon, when a feature of Haileybury life, 'the hour', began, lasting until lunch at 1 p.m. It was free time for us all, seemed like eternity, and I usually went down to the very well-equipped carpentry and engineering shop. This was equipped with a variety of wood and metal lathes, in addition to all the tools and materials to make most things. Whenever I could, I spent the 'hour' there until I left, but was not allowed to do so that first term as I would not be available for fagables. At lunch we sat by forms, with a beak at the head of each table to serve out the food. This was of the 'meat and two veg' variety, and generally very horrible. The meat was normally stringy or tough, overcooked, full of fat which I loathed, and had large blood vessels running through it. Vegetables were over-boiled, and the frequent cabbage often had interesting dead things in it, such as slugs or caterpillars. Puddings were nearly always covered in lumpy, yellow custard.

Games were played every afternoon save Saturday and Sunday, with work from 4 to 6 p.m. in the winter and Easter terms. In the summer, work began immediately after lunch until 4 p.m., leaving the evening free for cricket. Games were compulsory unless medically excused, everyone had to play, however bad they were or however much they disliked them. There was prep every evening followed by supper, more chapel and bed. On Sundays we had two full services complete with sermons. Many of the beaks had been ordained into the Church of England – no other religion was tolerated – before joining the school, so there was no shortage of clergy to take services. A senior boy, studying music under 'Haggerstaggers', Mr Hylton-Stewart the music beak, usually played the organ.

12

I was released from the Sick House on the last day of term, so that I could pack and go home with the rest. The atmosphere of the DC had completely changed. It was the 'end of term', nothing else mattered. We New Guvnors had served our apprenticeship and were now accepted members of Haileybury College. Only one more ordeal lay before us, that of each having to sing from the approved song book before the whole house that evening. I chose the only one I knew, 'Young Lochinvar rode in from the West, in all the wide Border his steed was the best'. As well as New Guvnors having to sing on the last night of term, those who were leaving also had to do so. The ceremony was not only a welcome, but also a farewell. Now singing was never my strong point. Furthermore, Haggerstaggers, the music beak, had tested me for the choir when I arrived. 'I can't sing,' I told him. 'You can certainly tell the truth,' he said after he had heard me. Out of tune, cracked or words forgotten, every song was greeted that evening with rapturous applause, and a chorus bellowed by everybody afterwards.

'For he's a jolly good fellow, (repeated three times)
and so say all of us, and so say all of us.
It's a way we have in the Navy, it's a way we have in the Army,
It's a way we have in the public schools,
for he's a jolly good fellow and so say all of us.'

I had become a Haileyburian.

Like it or not, we felt we were an elite. The whole ethos was unashamedly devised to train and produce an elite; future leaders, administrators and defenders of the British Empire, a strain of fearless, physically hard, incorruptible, self-assured people, used from an early age to taking responsibility over others through the prefectorial hierarchy. But there was another side of the coin. If we were an elite, we also had the duties of an elite, honour, duty and self-sacrifice. We were told that we must be the first to fall in any conflict. School chapels all over the country bore witness to this, of thousands of young men, many aged under 19, and straight from school, who had been killed in the Great War, a far greater proportion than the rest of the population. The average life of a subaltern in the trenches was three weeks. To train its pupils to shoulder such responsibilities and duties was the fundamental purpose of all British public schools. To call them 'public' was a ridiculous misnomer, for the fees that had to be paid to go to them was far beyond the reach of most people. They also sometimes produced a type of person so totally convinced of his own superiority over all who had not been so fortunate, that others found it excessively irksome.

Almost the first question asked about anyone was, 'Where was he at school?' Friends made there lasted through life, resulting in much nepotism through the 'old boy net'. Stanley Baldwin, who was at Harrow, remarked on becoming Prime Minister, that he would 'form a Cabinet of which Harrow could be proud'. In many cases it meant the advancement of the mediocre, if not downright inept, into positions where their incompetence was only equalled by their ignorance, which led to many disasters, especially military. No one who had not been to public school was welcome in the Navy or the Army. The RAF was less particular and its social standing suffered accordingly. Fortunate indeed that it was so, for if the Army had still been in control of flying, we would have entered the war in 1939 still flying 1918 biplanes instead of Hurricanes and Spitfires. Other almost 'closed shop' professions were the diplomatic, the legal, especially the Bar, the medical and the Church of England. Congregations expected their vicar to be a gentleman and to speak like one. As for Stanley Baldwin, after he had been Prime Minister for some years, he was sitting one day in the corner of a first-class railway compartment when another man got in. After gazing at him for some minutes, he remarked, 'Baldwin isn't it, weren't we at Harrow together?' On Baldwin admitting that he had indeed been at the Grove, one of its houses, the man went on, 'Tell me Baldwin, what have you been doing since you left Harrow?'

The Classical tradition was very strong in the nobility and gentry who controlled Britain during the 18th and 19th centuries, when the public school system was being devised. They based it on the Spartans of Greece around 400 BC. The Spartans had a similar problem: they had to hold down an indigenous population of Helots, who outnumbered them some forty to one. The British ruled a third of the population of the entire world. The odds were much the same. Spartan boys were taken away from their mothers at the age of about eight, and put into 'messes', run by men, where they were educated and also had to live under the most rigorous physical conditions, which have become a legend for harshness, and in which they took great pride. Their ethos was '*Etan epitos*', to come 'back on their shield', as the Spartan dead were returned for burial after a battle. 'Why are you shaming me by coming back alive?' a Spartan mother is reported saying to her son. Public school mothers did much the same in the Great War, speaking with pride, steely eyed, without a quiver or a tear, of 'having given two sons', by their fortitude bestowing even greater honour. Whatever its faults, the system worked. Throughout the Empire its peoples lived in a peace, order, justice and prosperity that they had never known before, or have ever known since it ended. As for the public schools, the whole reason for their existence disappeared with the Empire. Perhaps the main argument for their continuation is the fact that their ideals and principles do remain much the same, if often derided. Most also nowadays give a remarkably good education to both girls and boys, plus the somewhat dubious social cachet which they still carry, and which, in many professions, for example politics, is a downright handicap.

I returned for that summer term of 1928 to find W.A.R. Sumner sitting on the table of the dormitory annexe, dangling his feet and whistling 'Mountain Greenery', a song from the latest London show, '*The Girl Friend*'. He was still in holiday clothes, the most silver of silver grey flannel double-breasted suits, with huge, wide, baggy-bottomed trousers, known as Oxford bags, then the very acme of fashion. Bill Sumner was the new head of house, he was a blood of bloods, had been captain of the rugger XV and was now captain of cricket. To us juniors, he was as a god incarnate, the sort of chap who had three or four members of the rugger XV and others from the cricket XI, standing around nodding him yes, as he sat on the bog of a morning. There is no doubt that those who reached such a pinnacle of power and adulation whilst still at school found that if they became Field Marshals or even Prime Minister, nothing could really come close to it. Ever afterwards all they did was but an anti-climax. This is why boys who did abnormally well at their schools so often disappeared into nonentity, never to be heard of again.

The idea of such people being treated as gods was actively fostered at Haileybury. Bloods who were college prefects had their own special room near the school entrance, called Elysium, where the Greek gods lived in ancient times on Mount Olympus. Here it was reputed, that they were actually allowed to drink beer. But then what was the criteria for such prestige? Was it character? Certainly! Was it brains? Certainly not! Mostly it was the ability to play rugby football and to a lesser extent cricket, both adjudged undoubtedly to bestow the necessary character.

After we juniors had gone to bed, the house and college prefects would often skylark around the dormitory. On one such occasion, Sumner decided he would climb out of a window and walk on the ledges from window to window, all 60 of them, around the house and get in where he had climbed out. Halfway round he fell some 40 feet to the ground, which fortunately was of turf. He was badly injured and carried away to the Sick House with bad concussion and a broken arm. He was back playing cricket within a month, and passed into the RMA, 'The Shop' at Woolwich, for a career in the Royal Artillery. Here he won the Sword of Honour on the same day as another OH, P.J. Keen, won it at Sandhurst. We were given a whole holiday in celebration. For Bill Sumner, the consequences of his fall were more serious than realised. He died as a result of damage to his brain soon after leaving The Shop. In Batten he had been the object of intense hero worship. Half of us incorporated his peculiar type of signature into their own, and mine is based upon it to this day.

I found myself in the same form as I had been as a New Guvnor, Upper 4A. This was the top form of the lower school, there were two below, the Lower 4th and the 3rd. From it one passed into LM2, the lowest form of the middle school. As with everything else, the system of form numbering was both archaic and incomprehensible, but once learnt could never be forgotten. However it was realised that boys' abilities for maths and other subjects differed widely, so for mathematics we were divided into sets. A boy from a high form could easily find himself in a low maths set. I was put in one taught by my housemaster, Bill Adams. The number of boys in each form or set was usually about 25. At Windlesham under Mr Drummond, maths had easily been my best subject. With Bill Adams I became abysmal. I could never understand what he was driving at, especially in algebra. He had a deplorable habit of running his fingernail up the blackboard with a terrible shriek that set everyone's teeth on edge; with the shouted exclamation, 'For the sake of the weaker brethren I shall explain that again.' I considered myself very much a weaker brother, and maths was always my worst subject until I went into the Army Class and was able to give them up altogether. I found I was quite unable to learn anything at all from Bill Adams, whom we regarded as eccentric to the point of being slightly mad. But few if any long-standing beaks were otherwise or they could not have survived. Over the years, teaching generation after generation of boys, each one developed pecularities, mannerisms and ways of speech which were widely copied or mimicked. Some gave little jumps as they walked across the grass of the quad – no boys were allowed on its holy turf. Others skipped, or like 'Labby' Lloyd, housemaster of Hailey, spoke with a curious buzzing sound. 'Purple' Pickles of Highfield was once heard exhorting his wife 'wider Phoebe, wider', only to be discovered urging her to open their sitting room window. 'Wider Phoebe, wider' echoed round college for months.

My form master in Upper 4A was Johnnie Bower. Each form had an equal parallel, for instance Upper 4B, which did the same syllabus. Johnnie Bower had come into pedagogy through Holy

Orders, having been ordained. He took us for Latin, English and History. Charles Fair, housemaster of Trevelyan, took us for French. Scripture we were taught by Daddy Dawes, who was probably a heathen. Bower, a small, thin little man with scanty hair, was a good teacher. 'Rickman,' he would order one of the class, who afterwards became a distinguished racing correspondent, 'get up on your hind legs and translate from the Latin.' The reference to 'hind legs' was heavy humour at Rickman's well-known interest and propensity for horse racing. Latin seemed to make Johnnie Bower's adam's apple bob up and down faster than any other subject.

If the boys wore a standard form of dress, then so did the beaks. It consisted of a tweed jacket, usually threadbare and much patched with leather, sober dark grey drainpipe flannel trousers – no silver grey Oxford bags even for the young ones – shirt, collar and tie. Older ones like Bill Adams wore a stand-up stiff collar, with tie awry and halfway round his neck. During school hours they wore a mortar board and flowing gown. When boys met a beak they greeted him with a half-raised hand and a flick of the fingers, to receive a similar greeting in return. Many of the beaks had been ex-college bloods, like LR. Lempriere. They had gone through school to Oxford or Cambridge University, obtained a degree and hastened back to an assured place where they had felt godlike, safe and happy. And there they would stay for the rest of their life, which had consisted of prep school, public school, university, and public school once again. It would be an ill-paid if pleasant enough existence, getting slowly more and more idiosyncratic as they grew older and a never-ending stream of seemingly identical boys slipped past and disappeared into the future. To some of the beaks, young enough to be able to take part, the Great War must have come almost as a welcome diversion. Along with the boys who fell, their sacrifice was recorded by their names on the War Memorial on the chapel walls. At the end of the war many had returned, decorated for their service and gallantry. Although we boys in college did not realise it, there was much friction, cliques and discord among the beaks, who were roughly divided into three groups, so well described by Bobby Blunt, the Arts beak, in his book about his time at Haileybury: those who had been too old or unable to fight, those who had done so, and those who now, ten years later, had been too young. The last were able to relieve their military ardour by becoming officers in the college Officers Training Corps, or OTC.

Although destined for the Army, I loathed and detested everything to do with the Corps parades. They were dull, repetitive and seemed an utter waste of time. Perhaps the Army would be better. Later, to my chagrin, I found it to be much the same. Corps parades took place every Wednesday afternoon. Mostly they were in plain clothes, with just the green Army webbing belt in which to carry our bayonets, worn around our jackets. The rifles were the standard short magazine Lee Enfield (SMLE), a wonderful all-purpose weapon which was standard throughout the British Army from the Boer War until the Second World War in 1939. The Home Guard continued to use it. Once a month we had a uniform Corps parade, which was considered the most dreadful bore, because we had to polish all our buttons and also the fiddly little pieces of brass on our webbing equipment, 'green it' with blanco, and polish our boots. Our uniforms were the same rough khaki serge as worn by the Other Ranks of the Army. Jackets were done up to the neck and puttees bound tightly round our legs to the knee, with the tops of the trousers turned neatly over them. We were affiliated to the Bedfordshire and Hertfordshire Regiment – the Bedfs & Herts, with their training depot in Hertford. Our Commanding Officer was Major Denny, who had had a distinguished career during the war. Company and Platoon officers were junior beaks and bloods formed the senior Non Commissioned Officers – NCOs.

Nobody enjoyed Corps parades or thought much of a career in the Army. The Army Class, for those destined for it, was generally regarded as the last refuge of the congenitally stupid, unable to do anything else. When my father commented to my later house-master, Groizy Matthews, that he was pleased I had got into the sixth form, Groizy replied with a curl of his lip, 'yes, but only in the Army Class.' This at a time when over half the Generals in the Army were OHs. Perhaps the regard for generals among those who had taken part in the war was not very high. It was passed on and shared by the boys. As for Groizy, it is unlikely that he had

145

ever been near a trench. Corps parades were unimaginative, mind-numbing and deadly boring. We did endless foot and arms drill, or had demonstrations with rifle or the Lewis light machine gun, which rarely went beyond 'naming the parts'. The college ran a good shooting 'eight' which competed annually at Bisley for something called the Ashburton Shield, but most of us never fired a shot. One event keenly enjoyed was our day's autumn manoeuvres. We were issued with ten rounds of blank ammunition and marched the few miles out to Hertford Heath. Part of the Corps had been selected to act as enemy, and we ran about shooting blanks at each other whilst confusion and pandemonium reigned.

We also had to take an exam in Military Proficiency called Certificate A. For this a board of examiners came up from the Regimental depot in Hertford. We were inspected for turnout, asked questions on minor tactics, and had to drill a small squad of about ten others also taking the exam. All commands on the move have to be given on the 'correct foot'. This is not easy, because it seems continually to be the wrong one by the time the command reaches the squad. Desperately trying to turn my marching men about on the correct foot, I saw them disappearing into the distance, across the quad, past the bogs and out of sight down the road. 'You better run after them and bring them back,' my examiner said. I doubled away and, panting, caught up with them. 'For God's sake, chaps,' I pleaded, 'turn round and go back.' I must have finished on the right foot. Round they went in a perfect 'about turn', and my day was saved. As a result I was promoted Lance-Corporal. To my astonishment when I entered Sandhurst, I found I had been awarded high marks for 'Previous Military Proficiency'.

It might be assumed that boys at Haileybury were flogged almost on a daily basis, but except for one's first term, this was far from being the case. Apart from the beating I got from the good Dr Lempriere for informing him that I had mumps, I was only beaten one other time, and that was by Bill Adams, my housemaster. Nor can I recall Lempriere beating anyone else, so it probably had something to do with the way I told him I had mumps, such as being cocky and dogmatic. All beating was performed with a thin,

146

very flexible cane, a store of which was kept at the bookshop, which also handled all our exercise books, instruction manuals, pens, ink, pencils, geometrical instruments and so on. Beating was done on the clothed bottom, and rarely consisted of more than six strokes. Some people padded out their trousers with blotting paper, also bought from the bookshop. But if you were caught, it meant removing it on the spot and the beating starting again from scratch. It was rumoured that the bookshop had a secret arrangement to inform the beaks if anyone bought an unusually large quantity of blotting paper.

College prefects were allowed to beat, but had to get special permission from the headmaster before doing so, and it could never be done solo, but two or three prefects would be chosen to carry it out. Next to being beaten by the headmaster himself. a prefects' beating was the penultimate disgrace, usually coupled with expulsion and reserved for sexual exploits with other boys, such as buggery, or for theft. I cannot recall a single prefects' beating during my four years, nor a case of theft; unlike Sandhurst, where stealing was so common that it was endemic. There were no written school rules, the only rule being 'no breach of obvious common sense'. This could be interpreted any way a beak or prefect liked. All beaks could beat and were entitled to do so without permission, prior warning or witnesses. In fact they rarely did, but preferred to send a boy to his housemaster with the recommendation that he be beaten. Canings were humiliating as well as painful and were designed to be both. They were few in number and at no time were taken lightly, either by the boy concerned or the cane wielder. The ultimate disgrace was to be beaten by the headmaster, normally also a prelude to expulsion. In the most extreme case, for instance, disgracing the school, the headmaster's beating could be carried out publicly on the stage in Big School, the assembly hall at one end of the quad. There were no headmaster's beatings during my time, and by 1928 accounts of them were lost in the mists of legend and antiquity. From my own experience, caning did nothing either for the beater or the beaten other than stir up feelings of guilt and animosity which would never fade. However, a sound thrashing, in addition to any other sentence imposed, for those who commit crimes against the aged or the helpless, would be a just and most effective deterrent.

Our usual punishment for misdemeanours was to be ordered to write out, five, ten, fifteen or twenty times, 'dates'. These were devised to replace the usual repetitive 'lines' done in most schools, and had a threefold object: instruction in history, improve handwriting and instil a habit of neat, clear, unblotted work. When awarded dates you had to go to the bookshop and buy a date card, which varied from term to term, together with sufficient date paper, at a penny a sheet, for the number you were set. Each date card consisted of 12 sentences, sometimes long, sometimes short, with a date at the end depicting some famous historical event, such as 'The Hegira, the flight of Muhammad from Mecca to Medina, AD 622', or 'Cavour's diplomacy and Garibaldi's sword led to the unification of Italy, AD 1860'. Date paper was double lined with a wide gap between each set of lines. Small letters had to fit precisely between these lines, with capitals clearly defined. All i's had to be dotted and all t's crossed. There could be no ink blots, nor could the work be written in pencil. The completed dates had to be handed in by a set time, and inaccurate or shoddy presentation, meant doing them all over again. When completed, the contents of the date card exactly fitted a sheet of date paper. Thus ten times dates, the usual amount, would cost you a couple of bob (10p), a not inconsiderable sum. For instance, a Lyons French Cream sandwich, a large and delicious cake enough for several days' tea, cost one and threepence (6½p), from the Grubber.

For the Easter term of 1929 I was allowed to 'put on side', having been at college for a year, and wore my now very small housecap perched at a rakish angle on the back of my head. It had not been a bad year. My heart had apparently shrunk to its proper size and function, and I was allowed to play games again. I had played reasonable cricket and done well at rugby, having played in 'firsts' the whole Winter term and even managed to get into the house team, before wearing side, as wing three-quarter, but only because we were undoubtedly the worst team in College. Although wearing side for a further year I would have to walk around with my jacket buttons done up. After two years I could then leave them open. After three, I could not only leave my coat

148

open, but keep the ends back by putting my hands in my pockets. Disregard of such etiquette could get you into serious trouble with your seniors. It was an unwritten code of conduct few would either dare or care to break. I remember doing so with glee in the safety of the holidays, saying to myself, 'Look at me, coat open, hands in pockets after only a year! I'm no end of a blood!'

Public school customs die hard. Even directly after World War Two, when skiing was still very much the domain of their Old Boys, there was the famous Round Table in the Eiger bar at Wengen in Switzerland, reserved by unspoken and unwritten law for members of the Downhill Only Club – DHO – who had spent at least five seasons at the resort. To break such a rule and sit at it, especially for a non-club member, meant being frozen out far more quickly and effectively than falling into a crevasse on the Guggi glacier. From the earliest days of skiing, Wengen had been so public school British that the native inhabitants were thinking of getting up an independence movement, prevalent at the time. But the possible loss of revenue so terrified them out of their wits that they desisted. Besides sitting at the Round Table, it was also fashionable for the better skiers, ski-bloods and bloodesses as it were, to walk around with their boots undone, the laces trailing behind, and their anorak zips unfastened. To reach such a pinnacle, you had to have been there for seven seasons at least and be a SCGB Gold.

At the same time as putting on side, I was moved from the DC to a house room. There were two of them on the other side of the quad, one on each side of a narrow stairway leading to the house rooms of Bartle Frere above us. Each house room contained some 14 boys, aged between 15 and 16. As in the DC there was a bank of lockers for our school books, a wooden sofa with a padded seat, four or five wooden chairs, two of them with their legs broken. Like the DC, the floor was of scuffed bare boards. In winter there was always a roaring fire in the grate. During the 1950s when I was at Fontainebleau with NATO, I took a Dutch colleague, who was thinking of sending his son to Haileybury, around the school. I showed him my old house room. It was exactly the same as I remembered it, even down to the two broken chairs. 'Do you mean to say that parents actually have to pay to send their boys here?' he asked me. When I assured him that this was the case, he went on, 'If we put our soldiers in such a place we would have a mutiny on our hands.' Out of school hours, the house room was to be my home for the next two years.

At Haileybury the only criterion which mattered was games, and games meant rugby football and cricket. Both were regarded with a fervour that was more than semi-religious in its intensity and in its awe and worship of those who formed its transient pantheon of demi-gods representing the school at either. At Windlesham, clever boys who were not good at games were regarded with the same respect as those who were, and I had become used to doing so, but quickly changed my attitude to match that of those who regarded such people as 'nothing but swots'. Work in the lower and middle schools was directed at taking the national education exam, known as School Certificate, and if you did well in any given subject you were awarded a 'credit'. It was essential to obtain at least four or five credits. If things had gone according to plan, a boy should have passed his School Certificate by his third year when he would enter the upper school in the fifth form, and spend his fourth, and in some cases his fifth year in the sixth, which, if he was any good at games, would also be his glory years. I took my School Certificate during my third year and then joined the Army class. In addition to games and school work, we had to do Physical Training once a week in the gym, under the instruction of Old Groizy Whiskers, an ex-Army PT instructor with all the standard patter, such as 'One apple jump, jump!', meaning 'one upward jump'. I used to wonder how you could perform 'one downward jump'. Like all Army PT instructors, Old Groizy Whiskers appeared to be made entirely of india-rubber. He had acquired his name through the grease, then known as pomade, and to us as groize, which he used to twirl his moustache into sharp points on either side of his face. PT was not popular. We did free-standing exercises, climbed ropes, performed on the vaulting horse and parallel bars. Though largely hugely disliked, it had its devotees, and there was a flourishing 'Gym Six' which competed successfully with other schools.

I was happy at Haileybury. I was good enough at games not to

150

be worried about it. I played wing three-quarter for Batten, and my last term was playing for the XXX, as the 2nd XV was known. I did not get my colours but on occasion even played for the XV itself. Instead I was awarded my house stars, three stars to wear on the peak of my side cap. I was also a useful opening bat for the house cricket team. We all felt that life began and ended with the college, and those who had left lived in a kind of nether world, without aim or even existence. Old Boys who had left the previous few terms used to flock back at weekends, trying to recapture their former kudos and glory, to find their places had been taken by others. They flitted about like ghosts, insubstantial and unreal and after a while faded away, to be seen no more.

13

Sometime during 1929 my father managed to get his long-sought-after decree absolute, and immediately entered into hot pursuit of a war widow called Mrs Parsons, who lived with her mother in a large house on the outskirts of Guildford. Gladys Parsons was a slim, attractive woman in early middle age, who seemed very old to me, but then so did my father, who was 47. She had two children, Lionel, a year younger than myself, and Joyce, two years older. Lionel was at his father's old school, Shrewsbury, and Joyce was at Bedford Physical Training College, being a large and busty girl with whom I promptly became, for at least a year, completely enamoured. How far the affair between my father and Gladys Parsons continued I cannot say, or even if it was an affair, but he certainly hung around and about, staying at their house for months on end, until I imagine she gave up out of sheer desperation or boredom. In return for the hospitality, he took them all, plus my cousin Twig and myself, for a fortnight's winter holiday at Grindelwald in the Swiss Bernese Oberland, where we stayed at the Park Hotel Schoenegg. At this time Switzerland was very cheap for the British. With the exchange rate at 25 Swiss francs to the pound, full board was about £3 per week per head. Twig had just gone to Wellington and a friend of his, Desmond Wakely, came along too. My father was an experienced skier who had been to Lenzerheide and other Swiss resorts prior to the Great War. He was anxious to introduce me to the sport. Little did he know that it would become my abiding passion, eclipsing all else. Some fifty years later, whilst working as a ski journalist for the *Daily Mail*, I found an old photograph in the ski museum at Chateau d'Oex of him and my cousin Beatrice Pennington at the New Year's Eve fancy dress ball of 1908 at the Palace Hotel there.

In those days, nobody but the British skied in Switzerland. The only Swiss ever to be seen on the slopes were the professional mountain guides who took parties climbing during the summer, which was the main season, and gave ski lessons during the winter. Each hotel had its own resident ski instructor, who taught whatever method suited himself best and which he had thought out and perfected over the years. Whichever way the guides skied, their skis were always kept tightly together and they were able to travel with speed, ease and elegance over any kind of snow, from deep powder to breakable crust. The object of skiing was to be able to cross snowy mountains. There were no pistes, and those skiing usually had the entire mountain to themselves. There were no ski lifts either, but some resorts, such as Wengen, Grindelwald and Villars, used the mountain railways built for summer tourists for skiers in the winter. Such places were highly popular. Otherwise you climbed by fastening seal skins to the bottom of your skis, which prevented them slipping backwards. Such climbs usually lasted two or three hours, when you found a sheltered or a sunny spot for a picnic lunch, took off the skins, looped them around your waist and skied home for an enormous tea in front of a roaring log fire.

At the Park Hotel the resident instructor was Emil Steuri, a tall, athletic young man who always dressed in conventional dark blue ski clothes. These consisted of baggy trousers folded over low-cut, square-toed leather ski boots, a long belted jacket, and a peaked dark blue ski cap. His English was usually a direct translation from Swiss German; 'Now go vee zee hill down, bend more forvaerts zee kneez pliss'. Another favourite was, 'Feel pliss more zee toey', but this always left us in doubt as to which 'toey' we should be feeling. Emil was hired to give us ski lessons and took us out onto a small snowy hollow behind the hotel, with gentle sloping sides. I was agog to begin skiing downhill, but he would not allow this until we had perfected walking and doing kick turns on the flat and on the slope itself, a movement which could only be carried out by a practiced contortionist and is now no longer taught or even recognised.

153

As well as kick turns we learnt elementary climbing by stepping endlessly up and down. The result was that I got bored with the whole procedure and lost interest. Later, when I became a qualified ski instructor, I realised that all pupils, especially teenagers, want to start going downhill as soon as possible and are not willing to listen to explanations until they have had a go and found it rather harder to do than they expected. Tumbling in a heap from a gentle slope concentrates the mind most wonderfully, and afterwards can be included in 'how to get up from a fall' part of the lesson. This principle should be the base of any form of physical instruction. The Army bored everyone with hours of teaching on how to fire a rifle before anyone was allowed a shot. How much better to take recruits onto a range, explain the fundamental safety rules and let them fire off a few rounds at the target? Only then are they prepared to listen with interest to long explanations; for explanation without experience is worthless, whatever it may be. As for Emil, once we had vaguely mastered the basics, he took us up the mountain and we found him a first-class guide and instructor.

Our skis, apart from bearing the same name, had little to do with those used today. They were carved out of a single piece of hickory, though the cheaper ones were of ash. People would use the same skis for 20 or 30 years. They were whippy and thin at the top, the easier to slice through deep snow when turning, and stiff behind the heel for stability. In the centre was a flat platform for the binding, with long tapering ribs pointing each way down the middle for added strength. The bottom, of unvarnished wood, had a deep groove running its entire length and had to be carefully waxed before every run, or the snow would stick in heaps. There were no steel edges, as icy pistes were unknown, but reinforcement of the edges was just appearing in the shape of plastic or brass screwed-on edges. The correct length of a ski was measured by standing with one arm raised with fingers extended, when the ski tip should reach the ends of the fingers. Most towns and villages had their own ski factory, where you could actually choose the piece of wood of which you wished your skis to be made, in the same way as choosing a piece of cloth at your tailor. Halfway through manufacture there would be a 'fitting', when

154

you could decide if they were coming along as you liked, 'perhaps a little more off here please, to make them more whippy', or 'no more off here, I want them stiff behind the heel'.

Each resort too had its own cobbler shop, where for about £5 they would run you up a pair of made-to-measure ski boots overnight. These were of leather, low-cut to the ankle and laced. They were square-soled in front and held to the skis by a kind of metal stirrup with an adjustable strap across the toes, or 'toey', which Emil was so keen on our feeling. Around the back, fitting into a deep groove in the heel, was another strap fastened by a quick release. This strap kept the boot firmly in the stirrup, but allowed the heel to be fully raised, an essential part of one of the ski turns being taught, the Telemark, in which you actually knelt on the ski with one leg.

There were no such boot niceties for us. We wore our Corps Army boots with some large hobnails driven into the heel to prevent the straps slipping off, which they did continually. Although women and girls usually wore proper ski clothes, this was far from the case with men. We wore riding breeches with puttees or thick woollen stockings, shirt with collar and tie, a jersey and an old tweed or Norfolk jacket belted around the middle. On our heads we wore the conventional dark, peaked ski cap or a woolly balaclava helmet. It was in fact, exactly the gear worn by Everest climbers of the period, and in which Finch had recently reached the record height of over 28,000 feet

Skiing was not the only part of a winter sports holiday, although by this time it was beginning to assume its later major role. People would get up a party for winter sports in Switzerland. There they might ski one day, skate the next, or go lugeing. A luge was a small Swiss toboggan on which you sat or, if very daring, lay to go downhill, and pretended you were riding the Cresta at St Moritz, which is how the Cresta began in the first place, as a mild relaxation for British consumptives, as those suffering from tuberculosis were then called. In addition to our party, the hotel was full of other British guests, most of whom we knew, had met or heard of, or were at similar schools. One such party consisted of young people in their early twenties, men and women, who spent the entire time at meals laughing and joking, chaffing each other or pulling their legs, in a way that would now be termed highly 'sexist'. To my indignation and jealousy, they took Joyce Parsons away most evenings to dance or go to the local night club, the Spotted Cow. She would appear the next morning at breakfast, bleary eyed, hung-over and half-awake. We boys were considered much too young for night clubs and packed off to bed. What Gladys Parsons and my father got up to, is anybody's guess, but knowing my father, probably not very much. But then where women are concerned, it never does to underestimate men.

There was also the inevitable fancy-dress ball in our hotel, and another at Grindelwald's biggest, the Bear. Otherwise everybody changed for dinner every night, the men into dinner jacket with boiled shirt, stand-up collar and black tie, the women into long evening dresses, and this is how they would go later to the Spotted Cow, having danced probably until midnight to the small hotel band. Such customs continued certainly up to 1950, when the whole tempo of skiing in the Alps changed, as package tours for all took over. Another popular evening amusement, which we did a couple of times, was 'tailing'. This consisted of sitting on one of a long line of luges, generally in couples, and being pulled behind a sleigh up to an ice cave at the base of of the glacier, where we drank hot spiced wine, called *glühwein*, hopped on our luges and went racing all the way home, falling, flirting, laughing.

It was not until the winter of 1932 that I was able to ski again, when I went to Chateau d'Oex, with Twig and his mother. She who had ensnared his unfortunate father by jumping into his bed during a thunderstorm in India. This was considered highly compromising, especially as he was in the bed at the time. After he had died, undoubtedly thankful to escape, she had married a Major Corner in the Indian Cavalry. They had retired to a house in Shiplake, where he soon after died as well, probably as grateful for this ultimate release as poor Colvin Birch had been. She was a small woman, not much higher than maybe knee-high to a grasshopper, and at Chateau d'Oex, in her mid-thirties. She was convinced that every man she met, had met, or was likely to meet, was as she herself described it, 'madly in love with her'. Marjorie Corner was perhaps the most horrendous woman I have ever known, and I am far from being a raw hand when it comes to meet-

156

ing horrendous women. She did not ski, and spent most of her time demanding that the unfortunate Twig dance constant attention upon her, which he did with surprising forbearance. The holiday was not a success. Furthermore, I was suffering from a most virulent phase of adolescent spots on my face, to which she continually made reference, and of which I was highly self-conscious.

At the end of 1930 I had broken my ankle in a rugger house match, and spent ten days in the Sick House, making love-lorne eyes at the Matron, the delectable red-headed Thelma Townsend, and being generally treated by my fellows as some kind of hero who had been wounded in battle facing fearful odds. The rest of the party had gone to Grindelwald again and sent postcards telling of the wonderful time they were having. Then just before the winter season of 1931, Britain went through the first of those periods of economic crisis, which were later to become so familiar. We went off the Gold Standard. The value of the pound dropped to about 17 Swiss francs. Even so, the cost of living in Switzerland was still considerably less than in England, and those who had retired there for this reason were not too dismayed. However, the British Government let it be known that in order to save foreign currency, it was the patriotic duty of everyone not to go abroad. There were no regulations as later, on the subject. We were simply asked 'not to go', and you would be considered a stinker if you did. The response was immediate. Nobody went skiing that year. Efforts were made to attract people to the then very rudimentary facilities for skiing in the Highlands, but it turned out to be that rare occurrence, a completely green winter. For the hotels which opened it was a flop. Nor were the hoteliers themselves too keen on the idea. As one proprietor told me later, 'Who wants skiers in here, with their wet boots and general mess?'

My father was very keen on my learning languages, and during the summer holidays of 1930 he sent me to stay with a French family, where I spent perhaps the happiest six weeks of my life up until then. The place he chose was the Chateau de la Matholière at Tigy, some 20 miles from Orleans. He took me there himself, and we travelled by boat and train to Orleans and then boarded 'le petit train' to Tigy. At this time there was a network of these little narrow-gauge trains connecting almost every large French town or

157

city to its outlying villages. They were almost the only way of general transport, for there were no buses and few cars, the roads being mostly deserted. La Matholière was owned by Monsieur le Baron and Madame la Baronne de Moncuit de Boiscuille, whose family had been ennobled either by Napoleon Bonaparte or during the Second Empire. He was a small man in his mid-sixties, a Norman, with bright blue eyes, sparse sandy hair, great charm and perfect manners. Unfortunately he had contracted Parkinson's disease and spent most of his time sitting in an armchair in the drawing room, able to do but little for himself as his right arm and hand were semi-paralysed and shaking terribly. La Baronne was his second wife, small, dark and sharp as a sparrow, she darted hither and thither, nothing escaping her observation. Le Baron had several children by his first marriage, most of them blue-eyed and blonde like himself, all in their late teens or early twenties. There were Yves, Jacques, Robert, Cilette and Françoise. With the exception of Yves, who worked in Paris, all were living at home. By his second wife, he had a single daughter, Friquette, who was ten.

The family lived by taking in foreign guests who wished to improve their conversational French, for there was no actual instruction and we all had to have a fair knowledge before being accepted. Discipline was strict, with much emphasis upon good manners. Furthermore anyone overheard speaking any language other than French was required to leave by the next train home. My knowledge of it was elementary English schoolboy, but to my surprise and delight I found that in a very few days I was able to speak quite well, and at the end of the six weeks I was really fluent. I discovered that I had an aptitude for learning languages quickly, provided I was not tied down to grammatical niceties. Many years later, with reasonable Spanish conversation at my command, I spent a month doing a concentrated language course in Spain. It consisted almost entirely of correcting my grammar, and while admitting my pronunciation was good, it left me quite tongue-tied. Although my reading and writing had greatly improved, I was so afraid of grammatical errors that I could not utter a word. Now all I can remember of it, is the undoubtedly useful phrase, 'Said the Matador to his Cuadrilla, that bull is much too dangerous to catch by the balls'.

158

There were some 15 of us guests at La Matholière that summer. At 16, I was the youngest, but most were between 18 and 25. There were two English students besides myself, a boy from Eton and David Renton, who was up at Oxford and destined for the Bar. There were two or three from America, but the rest were mainly from Scandinavia, Norwegians or Swedes. The sexes were about equally divided, and never were girls more carefully guarded and chaperoned than these, who were not allowed to be alone with a man for a single minute. It must have given Madame la Baronne many a sleepless night, imagining that some girl might be returned home not in the same pristine condition in which she had arrived. Besides Madame, the whole family joined in the task. The Chateau was surrounded by a large estate, used for 'la chasse' in the autumn. The soil was sandy, with silver birch trees and much heather. It was also infested with the fiercest horse flies I have ever known – Scottish clegs have nothing on them. Whilst at Tigy, I also learnt a secret, exclusive to French horse flies. They only bite the person in front, the one behind goes unscathed. During the 1950s whilst at Fontainebleau with NATO, I used to go riding in the forest with General Jim Martin, the British commander there. As a dutiful Major, I always let him ride first down the narrow paths between the trees, respectfully remaining behind and watching with sardonic glee as the horse flies bit him half to death.

However hard they tried, all the family could not watch all the people all the time. Couples would go down to the courts for tennis and wander away for a walk, not to be seen again until *déjeuner*, the midday meal, when they would arrive separately from different directions. However, in those far-off days of sexual self-restraint, it is unlikely that anything really serious happened. The family were fervent Catholics, much under the influence of the village priest. He came up daily to say prayers in their private chapel attached to the house. He decreed that one of the girls would have to be a nun. Françoise was chosen. Whether she decided this for herself I never discovered. She went off to the seaside for a final holiday and returned fit and tanned. Then most of her hair was cut off and she disappeared into some convent as a novice. To my amazement, many family decisions, especially over food, were made by the priest holding a small lead weight, possibly a holy relic, at the end of a string, and giving a judgement depending on whether it swung in circles or up and down.

La Matholière was a typical French 18th century *chateau*, complete with moat and wooden shuttered windows. There was a small lake in front of it, and the house was connected by a long drive with poplars on either side, to the main road going down to the village of Tigy. This consisted of a few shops, a garage, some wine bars, a small hotel, and the church. We would walk down there of a morning for a drink and to buy cigarettes. Everybody smoked, it was the thing to do, part of being grown up. Besides, smoking was the best defence against the horse flies which flew by day, and the ravages of the mosquitoes by night. To me, the only cigarettes which ever had any taste were those made from black French tobacco. We smoked Gauloise Caporal, in a blue paper packet, the cigarette of the French Army and Frenchmen generally. The girls usually preferred Gitanes, which did not contain so much of the loosely packed tobacco of the Gauloises. Nearly all the men in France, workmen or artisans, wore a kind of standard uniform of blue denim overalls and two or three days growth of beard. They were normally big and burly and all invariably had a half-smoked, unlit cigarette stuck firmly to one corner of their mouth. It fascinated me to watch them working, talking, eating, drinking, whilst keeping it wholly in place. They probably slept with it in position as well. I used to wonder if they actually bought them like that, half-smoked and ready to stick to their lip.

Our day began at about 8 a.m., when *petit déjeuner* would be brought to our room, a bowl of coffee and milk, delicious and smelling as only coffee made in France can smell. With it came cuts of fresh white bread, butter and jam. I usually read until about ten. I had found a number of books in the library and discovered I could read them quite well. In particular, one was called *Nach Paris*, a lurid account of rape, pillage and mayhem by the Germans during their advance into France in 1914. At Haileybury, French, like Latin, was totally unreal. You could not imagine anybody actually speaking it. Now to my joy, it had suddenly become alive. I found that reading helped me to speak, and speaking helped me to read, in an almost geometrical progression. I would

160

then get up and dress, wander down to the tennis courts for a game, or stroll into the village with someone for a Dubonnet or a *pastis* before returning for *déjeuner* or lunch, which took place at midday. The butler would throw open the doors into the salon, and announce '*Madame la Baronne est servie*', when we would all troop into the dining room. We sat round one long polished table, using the same knife and fork for all courses, and placing them upon little rests between each. The food, always delicious, was passed down on large dishes, which we held for each other whilst they helped themselves. The meal invariably ended with a large dish of sour cream, I suppose it might be called yoghurt, which I did not care for at all, and took tiny helpings out of politeness. We drank a local wine, a sort of Vouvray, from the family's vineyards.

After *déjeuner* we would generally play tennis or swim in a pond at the bottom of the drive. The small lake in front of the Chateau was too shallow and too muddy. Around five o'clock we would all assemble in the *salon*, the drawing room, '*pour le five o'clock*'. This was a ritual, with weak tea and lemon in small cups, and spiced buttered slices of bread, which the girls handed round. Etiquette was strict. For instance, it was grossly ill-mannered for anyone to sit on the sofa, which is reserved for the mistress of the house. The same rule applied in Germany. My first day, I offered to hand round the tea and spiced bread. It was explained that solely women were allowed to do such things in the house, and only men were allowed similar tasks outside it, such as maybe dealing with a punctured car tyre. The evening meal was at eight o'clock, and we had to change for it, men into a dinner jacket, '*le smoking*' as the French called it, and the girls into long dresses. After dinner we played cards, sat outside on the terrace, smoking to ward off the mosquitoes, or strolled around the garden in groups; carefully herded by one of the family.

Every now and again we were taken on small cultural excursions in the two family cars, one an ancient, capacious and classic Panhard et Levasseur. We visited famous Loire *chateaux*, such as Azay le Rideau, or the cathedral at Chartres or Orleans, with their wonderful architecture and stained glass windows. I loved it at La Matholière. For the first time in my life I could do as I more or less liked, wear what I liked, say what I liked, and everybody liked me. I suddenly became aware of the great sense of freedom that I always feel whenever I arrive in France. I got on very well with the family, and Jacques the eldest boy told me, '*Tu fais partie de la famille*' (you are now a part of the family). I felt that I belonged, and will always so feel, to La Matholière. When I got back to Haileybury the next term, I was agog to try out my French on Charles Fair, our French beak, who always insisted on pronouncing the language exactly as if it were English. He was unimpressed. 'We don't want any of your fancy French accents here,' he told me, 'this is an English school and you will speak French like a gentleman', implying that speaking it correctly was somehow an affectation of cads and bounders. He certainly was not alone in this belief, for the British have always been intensely suspicious of anyone who can speak a foreign language fluently, considering that there is obviously something wrong with them or they would not be doing it. Later that term, a French touring theatre company paid us a visit to play Molière's '*Le Bourgeois Gentilhomme*' in the Big School. As senior French beak, Charles Fair was told off to take care of the actors. Neither he nor they could understand a single word of what the other was saying.

A revolution had taken place at Haileybury. Suddenly everybody began to call each other by their Christian names. Hitherto it had been almost a deadly insult, an offence even to know another's name. It had been all surnames, and brothers were known as Major or Minor, such for instance as Payne Major. He was a college boxer, very tall and thin with long arms. Thus he was able to box some two weights below his capacity and his arms were so long nobody could reach far enough to hit him. Suddenly everything had changed. We all began to call each other by our Christian names, it was the thing to do. However you had to earn the right, especially from a senior. New Guvnors were obviously still called by their surnames, making the poor creatures feel even the more inferior.

I had taken and passed my School Certificate, not very well, but I had passed, and was now in the fifth form in the upper school. Up until now my school reports had been utterly consistent, 'He could do a lot better if he tried'. My father despaired. There was talk of my becoming a doctor and going to St Mary's Hospital in London, where apparently they had a good rugger team. Instead I joined the Army Class, which was more of a set than a form. There were some 15 of us in it, from both the fifth and sixth forms. Our beak was L.A. Speakman, who took us in History, English and French. He encouraged me to speak French correctly, and reinforced my love of history which Mr Simpkins had started at Walton Lodge. Speakman was undoubtedly the best beak I encountered at Haileybury, or perhaps throughout my education. He was not a man to be trifled with. My first day, for some inattention he hurled an entire box of pen nibs at me with unerring accuracy. No-one dare fool around during his lessons. He was then in his late fifties, of medium height, and a red complexion from perhaps a spot or two of port in the beaks' common room. A scratch golfer and a confirmed bachelor, he was ultra-Conservative by nature, describing himself as 'the last real Tory'. We gave up maths altogether. I imagine it was thought simple addition and subtraction was all that was ever required in the Army or RAF, for which there were also candidates, including Peter Townsend of Princess Margaret fame. We also did science under 'Cheesy' Champion. The labs were all in the Bradby Hall, at the opposite end of the school to the classrooms. Each term we did a different science subject, heat, light, electricity and magnetism, along with chemistry every term. The popular Daddy Dawes continued to read to us about escapes from German POW camps during scripture lessons. Scripture was not part of the Army entrance exam; cramming for which the entire syllabus was designed. We did an old entrance exam paper at least once a week.

As well as the Christian-name revolution, another had also taken place. We were allowed to play gramophones. At first this concession was confined to Sunday afternoons, when we were permitted to take them to the squash and fives courts, which bordered the 20-acre playing fields, and listen to them there. Our gramophones were of the portable clockwork wind-up variety, which played hard, black wax records at 78 rpm. These were 10 or 12 inches in diameter, came in a paper cover with a large circle cut out in the centre, so that you could read the label. They cost three and five shillings respectively. The 12-inch were mainly for classical music. They scratched and broke very easily. At exactly two p.m. every Sunday, groups of boys could be found clustered round each machine, oblivious to the general cacophony, intent on listening to their own instrument. Every now and again one of the beaks would drop accidentally by, I imagine to ensure there was no hanky panky going on. It was the era of the big bands, such as Roy Fox, Paul Whiteman, the Savoy Orpheans, Billy Cotton and so on, playing tunes from the Hollywood musicals and the London shows. Noel Coward's music from *Bitter Sweet* was very popular, as were the songs of the dashing young Frenchman, Maurice Chevalier.

The Rolls-Royce of gramophones was the HMV portable, which cost £6. It was covered in black grained leatherette, had a small container at the side for needles and a space inside the lid which held six 10-inch records. As well as having to be wound up each time, the needle also had to be changed to prevent excessive wear. Running the HMV very close at £4/15s (£4.75), was the Columbia portable, whose sound arm had fluted elbow joints, claiming that sound reflected like this, in parallel waves, retained its purity. To get some idea of the relative value by 1999 prices, in those days, a Savile Row suit cost around £6 made to measure, which today would be at least £600. I eventually saved up and bought an HMV, which was the apple of my eye and travelled with me everywhere until it eventually disappeared, stolen from a friend's flat in London around 1948.

Every Saturday afternoon when there were no school matches on, we would get permission from Groizy Matthews, our house beak, and walk the few miles into Hertford to spend the time listening to the latest hits in the gramophone shop, which had several little fitted booths where you could sit and listen. The unfortunate girl assistants must have got heartily sick of us, for hundreds were heard but few bought. Having given us our gramophone concession, the college authorities must have admitted to themselves that listening to such music was not the first step down the slippery path to iniquity and degeneracy, as they had imagined. Unbelievably, those of us in studies were allowed to play wireless sets for an hour, on Saturday afternoons, when Jack Payne and the BBC dance band came on the air, and a sudden blare of dance music would echo all round the school. I had left my house room

164

and was now sharing a study overlooking the Little Quad, with three others, Nicholls, Bond and Davidson. Nicholls had become a very great blood, being vice-captain of the rugby XV.

Most of us had made our own wireless sets. Mine I had bought from an advertised kit of parts, called a Cossar Melody Maker, which cost £10. It had four valves, a screened grid, a detector, a low frequency and an output stage. Later I incorporated it in a highly sophisticated portable in a mahogany case which I made in the workshops. I called it the Moon Pig, because I had cut out a wooden silhouette of a pig standing in a crescent moon, and glued it inside the door. Looking back, I think the combination would have had great commercial possibilities. Wireless sets in those days, now called radios, were large and bulky. Instead of transistors, they had valves the size of electric light bulbs, which lit up. They were powered by a 2-volt accumulator which had to be charged once a week. This was done mostly by the local garage, where rows of them could be seen being charged. A dry 120-volt high-tension battery was also required as well as a smaller one called a grid bias. The sound most coveted from the loud-speaker was a really booming bass, nothing else really counted, 'Just listen to that bass!' was the cry. Pillitz had run himself up a set the size of a ship's cabin trunk, which even incorporated an early version of a radio-gramophone. He got a concession from Hagggers-Taggers, the music beak, to play it during 'the hour', in one of the piano rooms in Big School, which were reputedly soundproof. He kept the volume so loud that if you opened the door it would practically knock you down. He enjoyed demonstrating that if you held a lighted candle to the loudspeaker, a good bass note would blow it out.

The winter term of 1931, I went up to London to take the entrance examination to Sandhurst, sang my farewell song on the last night, and found I was very sad to be leaving Haileybury. I had enjoyed my time there, especially my last year. Due to the national financial crisis there was no skiing for anybody that year. I spent the Christmas holidays with my father in Guildford. I even knocked up a small Moon Pig portable for Joyce out of bits and pieces of other wireless sets I had collected. It was here that the results of my examination were sent. Some 180 of us had passed,

165

and my father read through the last 50 names. Flinging the paper onto the breakfast table with a snort, he said 'You've failed'. It was not until later that morning when somebody rang up to congratulate me on passing, that we discovered the truth. Even more to my amazement than his, my name was among the top ten, and in addition I had won a small scholarship.

14

'Where's Fucker Fairlie?' a voice rang out from a couple of bicycles ahead of me, to be greeted by a roar from the darkness behind; 'Here's Fucker Fairlie and you're under arrest.' The junior term of 1932 at the Royal Military College, Sandhurst, was out for a night map-reading exercise on the Hertford Bridge Flats near Camberley. Fucker Fairlie was an amiable enough officer in the 11th Sikhs, spending 18 months on attachment to the RMC, as we called it, to vet officer candidates for the Indian Army. The only reason he was known as 'Fucker' was because his name began with an F, for generally he was well liked and popular, as well as being in charge of map-reading training. It had not taken us long to learn the four-letter 'F word' and its various derivatives, without the use of which the British Army would undoubtedly be struck completely dumb. It had been rarely used at Haileybury, though dirty and vaguely humorous smutty jokes had been commonplace. Nor was the word used much by officers, but we were not yet officers and it seemed smart and grown-up to use such expressions.

The 180 of us Juniors who had passed the entrance examination were told to report at the College on 11 January. With some 44 others I had been posted to No 5 Company, 'Cushy Five', 'Idle Five', or 'Lovely Five', depending upon which way you looked at it, the most easy-going of the four Companies, each about 150 strong. There was no No 2 Company, it having been disbanded in the recent Army cuts. The words that 'Speakers' Speakman had dinned into me at Haileybury came to mind. They were a quote from the last line of Fortescue's *'History of the Army'*, and read 'The vengeance of the British Public upon the British Army is insatiate and insatiable'. Thus it has always been and always will remain. The aim of every Government has been to destroy it, but somehow it manages to linger on. Nos 1 and 3 Companies were housed in the New Building, a red-brick rather garish Victorian edifice, whilst Lovely Five, along with No 4, shared the Old Building, gracefully Georgian, with two Waterloo cannons guarding its main entrance.

When I use the term 'slacker and more easy-going' as applied to No 5 Company, the terms are purely relative, for nothing at the RMC was either slack or easy-going. It was run on the Brigade of Guards principle that only the highest possible standard was acceptable, except that the standard required of us was infinitely higher than anything expected of the Guards. The Commandant, at that time Major General Sir Reginald May, was always a Guardsman, as was the Adjutant, Captain Norman Gwatkin of the Coldstream, whose riding boots were so highly polished you could have shaved in them, and whose eagle eye could spot a cadet wearing a belt instead of braces at a hundred yards. This was a heinous crime, for it made your trousers stick out at the back and spoil the line of the tunic. Nor can trousers ever hang properly from a belt.

In 1932 there were a number of ways of getting into the Army. Most took the Sandhurst entrance examination from their Public schools, and had to be over 18 and under 19 at the time of joining. They were known as 'Gentleman Cadets' or GCs. However moves to make entry more egalitarian were already afoot, and it was possible to enter by serving in the ranks. However, calling such people Gentlemen Cadets was really stretching equality a bit too far, and they were known as 'Army Cadets' or A Cadets. On arrival they lost the NCO rank they had held, usually Corporal or Sergeant, but continued to be paid at that rate. Their board, lodging and tuition was free, whilst the parents of GCs had to continue to pay as if their sons were still at school or university. The Indian Army was also going through a democratic phase, known as Indianisation, accepting officers of Indian as well as British origin. There were also, therefore, a number of Indian GCs, who had taken the normal entrance examination. Many had been educated at British public schools and had even forgotten their own language. One called Nair, ex-Cheltenham College, failed the lower standard Urdu exam three times and nearly had to leave the Army when he got to India. One of these Indian cadets, by name Majumdar, became a close friend, sharing with me a love of jazz music. They were usually the sons of rich potentates, destined for cavalry regiments. Added to these was an assortment of princes and kings from countries affiliated or friendly to the British Empire. In 5 Company we had King Chalambol of Siam, a diminutive figure, often the butt of our Company Sergeant Major's lighter-hearted jokes.

There were two other ways of becoming an officer in the British Army. The first was through the Supplementary Reserve, the SR, doing an attachment to a regiment for about a year as a 2nd Lieutenant, and then taking the final Sandhurst passing-out examination. We cadets loathed and despised these people who were invariably known as 'SR bastards'. We considered they were getting into the Army by the back door, and to make matters worse, when they came down to the RMC to take the same passing-out exam for which we were sitting, we had to salute them and stand to attention when addressing them. However the real back door was through a University Commission, of which we were ignorant. Candidates passed direct into the Army with 18 months seniority after obtaining a degree and serving in the university OTC. The War Office was very much in favour of such entry and did all it could to encourage it. The system worked and most of those who used it did very well subsequently, avoiding the strait-jacketing of the mind which was to some extent the inevitable consquence of 18 months at the RMC.

No 5 Coy was commanded by Major Wilson of the 60th Rifles. I met him many years later in connection with the Duke of Edinburgh's playing fields scheme, and he told me that our Junior entry was the only one that had given him misgivings during the entire three years he had been in command. There were certainly some very odd characters in it. Under him was Company Sergeant Major (CSM) Giddings of the Grenadier Guards, tall, straight as a ramrod, hair shaved up the back of his head to his cap, the peak of which was pulled down so low over his eyes that one wondered how he could see out. However, just as at public school, the

169

day-to-day running and discipline of each Company was conducted on the prefectorial system. Instead of prefects, they were called Under Officers (UOs); one Senior Under Officer (SUO) and four Junior Under Officers, (JUOs). They were all taken from the senior term, and one of the SUOs would always be awarded the 'Sword of Honour' during his final passing-out parade. All UOs carried swords instead of rifles on parade and marched in front of the Company, just as they later would in their regiments. They also wore an officer's blue blazer with brass buttons instead of the red-and-white striped ones which we used. UOs wielded considerable power, but were in no way regarded with the semi-mystical awe and reverence of bloods at Haileybury.

Our SUO was a charming GC, Desmond Fitzpatrick, who went into an Irish Cavalry regiment and rose to high rank as a general. In his later years he would often be seen hobnobbing with HM the Queen on the dais, as she took the salute during her annual birthday parade on Horse Guards. Under him were the four JUOs, each commanding a platoon of some forty cadets. One of them was Tom Walls, son of the well-known comedy actor of the same name, whose horse April the Fifth was to win the Derby later that summer. I found myself in No 20 platoon, under Bobby Combe, a dead spit of the then Prince of Wales. Each platoon had a Platoon Sergeant and four Corporals, all GCs, each in charge of a Section of about ten cadets. These were called Cadet NCOs (Non-Commissioned Officers).

The evening of our arrival, we Juniors assembled in the Mess anteroom, dressed for the evening meal in dinner jackets, which is what we would have to wear until our blue patrol uniforms, in which the Intermediates and Seniors were dressed, became ready. These consisted of dark blue serge trousers with a red stripe down the side, worn over calf-height, soft leather Wellington boots, and a high-necked dark blue jacket with brass buttons. Fitzpatrick welcomed us to 'Lovely Five' and told us how lucky we were to belong to such an easy-going establishment, which no longer treated Juniors as lepers in the same way as the rest of the RMC, informed us we would be 'on the square', doing drill for two months under CSM Giddings, and relied upon us to win the

170

Junior's Drill Competition for the Company. How misplaced was his trust! He warned us of the wiles of a certain Edna, who was reputed to roam the college grounds at dusk, seeking whom she might devour, and who carried a particularly virulent form of clap, likely to be detrimental to one's military future. I never knew anyone who had met or seen the mysterious Edna, though everyone knew someone who knew somebody who had done so. The general ethos, philosophy and outlook of not only the RMC, but also the entire British Army in the 1930s, was still that of the previous century, and when I told my father about Edna, he laughed and said, 'Oh yes, we knew all about her when I arrived, back in 99.'

Our SUO also explained to us how correctly to address members of the College Staff. Officers were to be regarded as little removed from God, always saluted, and could only be spoken to whilst standing rigidly to attention. Such was the awe engendered in me by an officer, that whilst coming back from Switzerland the following winter, I found by accident that the man to whom I had been nonchalantly chatting, sitting opposite me in the train dining car, was an officer in the Royal Scots. To his astonishment and that of my fellow diners, I leapt to my feet and stood rigidly to attention before him, until he told me not to be a fool and to sit down. Fitzpatrick continued that all Staff NCO instructors were to be invariably addressed as 'Staff', except for the BSM, the Battalion Sergeant Major, or 'Bosom' as he was nicknamed, who was to be called 'Sir' at all times, as he would explain to you himself if you accidentally addressed him as Staff. 'You says Sir to me Sir, and I says Sir to you Sir.' Sir he might say to you Sir, but Mr Dobson, the Bosom, had been a Regimental Sergeant Major in the Coldstream Guards, and such was the power and majesty that he conveyed whilst stalking around the parade ground, that most of us were quaking too much at the knees to be able to call him anything.

After our talk we all trooped into the dining room, a huge hall with eight long polished tables each laid with 40 places, gleaming with regimental silver and spotless glass. At the head of each platoon table sat the JUO with his cadet NCOs ranged on either side. In the centre of the room, against the wall, were displayed the

171

uncased Royal Military College Colours, whilst in the middle, on a raised dais, under Bandmaster Mr Jarman, the college band, known as 'Jarman and his Discordia Boys', played soft music from light opera. We sat down to eat to the traditional tune of the 'Roast Beef of Old England'. The entire walls of the hall were decorated with rosettes made up of ancient weapons, muskets, bayonets, swords and sabres. Soft-footed waiters in livery passed down the tables, taking orders for drinks, or serving dishes of food. The five-course meal was delicious, as was invariably all the food. All the time I was at Sandhurst, administration, drill, discipline, turnout, pride, nothing could be faulted, except perhaps the one thing it sought most to instil, common sense. That first evening I sat next to our own future SUO, Kenneth Bols, who went into an Indian Cavalry regiment and was very badly beaten up on the ship going out to India by former fellow GCs of No 5 Company who bore him a grudge. No wonder Major Wilson had misgivings over our intake!

For me the greatest and most disturbing difference between Haileybury and the RMC was that at the latter, no-one it appeared could ever be trusted to go anywhere on their own. They had to be marched there. Instead of the leisurely walk, chatting to friends from one classroom to another, we were subjected to the endless parade rigmarole that I had detested so much at school. The calling out of 'Right marker', the forming up beside him, the repeated right-dressing, forming fours, right-turning and quick-marching. Left on one's own, you could be halfway to where you had to be before the others had even started. The bogwheel – RMC slang for a bicycle – parades were worst of all in this respect. Every cadet had to bring a bicycle with him, the A cadets being supplied with GS (General Service) models, each weighing about a ton. Bogwheel drill was modelled entirely on the Cavalry Manual. The NCO in charge would call out 'Right marker', who would march out and come to attention with both hands on the handle bars. On the command 'Fall in', we would form into line, stand to attention and right dress, when all front wheels had to be in line within a millimetre of each other. This usually took five minutes or so. Then there would be repeated commands of 'Attention' or 'Stand at ease', because the movement had not been smart enough, or the cadet NCO wished to impress a member of Staff nearby. The order then would be given, ' Move to the right in half sections, half section right.' We would all turn our front wheels smartly to the right, often having to repeat it two or three times to reach the required standard of perfection.

Next came 'Walk march', and we would set off, two by two, 'half sections' in cavalry parlance, followed by 'Prepare to mount', and then 'Mount', when we would pedal off in a long and often wobbly line. Sometimes we would meet an officer and give 'eyes right'. Many of the Indian and Colonial cadets could hardly ride a bicycle anyway, and this was too much for them altogether. Down one would come with a crash, everyone behind, eyes and head turned rigidly to the right, piling in on top. On arrival at our destination, the whole agonising process had to be reversed. Thus a journey which would normally take five minutes would be stretched to 25. Bogwheel parades were held to go to the gym for PT, for classes across at the New Building, to the riding school for equitation, and for map-reading exercises. Many years later, when I was a ski instructor at the Cedars of Lebanon, in the same way valuable hours of instruction were lost, teaching soldiers to 'slope', 'order' and 'present' skis properly and smartly.

The morning after our welcome by Desmond Fitzpatrick, we fell in on the Company parade ground at the right-hand end of the Old Building for our first drill parade under CSM Giddings. He was a tall, athletically built man in his early thirties, with a beaky nose and the quirky sense of humour shared by all drill instructors. We were fallen in, sized, 'tallest on the right, shortest on the left', which ended up in some strange way in two ranks with the shortest in the middle. This was followed by the order, 'Fall out on the left, RCs, Parsees and other 'eathen.' Their names were duly noted to be excused the weekly Sunday Church parade. Having ordered them to rejoin the squad, Giddings then made acid comment on the length of our hair. His own he said, 'was much too long' and he was getting it cut that very afternoon. Turning round, he showed us the back of his head which appeared to have been close shaved. 'Most of us', he went on, 'had hair practically down to our waists and looked like girls.' Anyone appearing like that, or with 'goatee beards', indicating the odd whisker some had on their chins,

173

'would be on a charge in future'. We were then marched briskly into Camberley to the tailors to be measured for our uniforms, and to the bootmaker, Stallwoods, for the finest boots I have ever known, one pair for marching, one worn with gaiters for riding, and one for ceremonial parades. I was still using them, ten years and hundreds of miles later.

Until our uniforms were ready we would wear a kind of civilian uniform, dark suits, all buttons always done up, and a cloth cap, known as a 'Gor blimey', pulled down straight over the ears. Our new uniforms would consist of Blue Patrol, two Service Dress khaki rough serge jackets, worn with Sam Browne leather belt over baggy plus-fours and puttees. Being marched around Camberley like this, with people staring at us, made me feel as if for some reason I had gone to prison.

We had all been in our school OTCs; the A cadets had done their initial squad drill in the Army. We considered we were pretty smart. Nothing had prepared us for the onslaught from Giddings. Every day for two hours, we marched and counter-marched, turned about, formed fours, saluted, quick-marched, slow-marched, double-marched, sloped arms, ordered arms, presented arms, until the whole squad appeared to be pulled by a single piece of string. At the end of the two hours, we would go back to our rooms, take our shirt off and wring the sweat out of it into the basin. We also reached a peak of physical fitness never attained before or since. Ours was a standard infinitely higher than than that of the Guards. On a visit to London that Junior term, I watched the Changing of the Guard at Buckingham Palace, and considered the standard of drill and turn-out ineffably 'dozy and idle', in Giddings-speak. It had taken him sometime to learn all our names. An unfortunate GC called Moule, next to me in the rear rank, was early on his list. It was continually 'Mr Mole Sir, you're dozy and idle Sir, next time you'll be doubled under arrest to the Guard Room. Sgt Baird, take 'is name '! 'Gottim Sir,' Staff Sgt Baird would shout from the back of the squad. This was known as 'losing your name', and usually entailed being put 'on a charge' and a visit to the Company Office for condign punishment from Major Wilson.

I knew it would be my turn next, but although shouted at I never lost my name, and in fact managed to avoid any kind of punishment all the time I was at the RMC. King Chalambol of Siam quickly became the target of our CSM's humour. 'Mr King Shambol Sir,' he would thunder, 'you're an 'orrible, dozy, idle little king Sir, what are you Sir?' King Chalambol, whose rs were never his strong point, would stammer back, 'I'm an 'ollible dozy, idle little king, Staff.' As the day of the inter-Company Junior Drill Competition approached, Giddings got more and more fired up. A General was coming down from the War Office to do the judging. In all seriousness he told us, 'I want you all to be real smart, this 'ere General is the greatest livin' ortority on the abart-turn.' It was probably, too, the sum total of his military knowledge, I thought.

We did not win the Drill Competition, but achieved a creditable second. Four of us GCs were chosen to get a 'stripe off the square', promoted to Cadet Lance Corporal for excellence at drill, turn-out, general keeness and application. I missed it by one, my fault being 'hunching my shoulders whilst standing at attention'. This came from stress and trying too hard Funnily enough, the same criticism was made when I took my Austrian ski instructor's examination 30 years later. A friend, Geoffrey Worsdell, who became a Brigadier, a mad keen soldier, was made up, as was Kenneth Bols, could it be that his father was a senior General in the War Office have had anything to do with it? Perish the thought! The other two were Parker and Deedes. These L/Cpls would henceforth march us about from place to place, instead of the A cadet NCOs who had been i/c Juniors until then. Our future SUO and JUOs for our Senior term would also be chosen from them.

If our drill had to be exemplary, so did the cleanliness of our equipment. Parade boots had to be polished all over to a mirror-like shine, especially the toe caps. Instead of shoe polish, I thought of the french polish I had used on woodwork in the workshop at Haileybury, tried it out, and my boots shone even brighter. Fearing the surface might crack, I kept them for room inspections only, and used the slightly less highly polished 'equitation' pair for parades. Nobody noticed. We had been issued with our rifles and bayonets. I never fired my rifle all the time I was at the RMC. It was not meant for firing, only for drill, and I hate to think what

175

might have happened if it had been used for its original purpose. The rifle was the Short Magazine Lee Enfield (SMLE), .303 calibre, that wonderful workhorse of the Great War, complete with 18-inch long sword bayonet. Both rifle and bayonet had come from the College Armoury smothered in preservative grease. Every speck of this had to be removed with petrol, every screw had to be undone as far as possible, so that the rifle would make the maximum noise during arms drill. The bolt had to be burnished, and the stock with other woodwork polished to a high gloss with a waxy substance called heelball. At the twice-weekly evening kit inspections, Bobby Combe, our Platoon JUO, would wipe the inside of the rifle and the bolt with a white silk handkerchief. Any suspicion of dirt or oil would mean a 'puttee parade', an hour's drill in full battle order, five minutes after the evening meal.

Our bayonets and their scabbards also had to be burnished and polished to a mirror-like quality. The scabbard was of black leather which had to shine as glass, the steel bayonet to be burnished so that the JUO could use it to shave in, should he wish to. This burnishing was done with a small leather pad some 6 inches square, with a number of steel rings sewn to it. Thousands must have been produced, to lie redundant when a new rifle replaced the SMLE. This had a short, unburnishable, needle-type bayonet. In 1958 when I was Military Attaché in the Sudan, whilst on a journey far up the Nile I saw to my astonishment, that some enterprising Greek trader had bought up the remaining stock, and the statuesque, otherwise completely naked Dinka girls were using them on a string around their middle as a kind of cache-sexe. I was glad the little squares had found a good home, and a far pleasanter form of existence than polishing bayonets at the RMC.

Each cadet was given a room of his own. The furniture consisted of a narrow iron bed, table and chair, a cupboard and a chest of drawers. There was also a washhand stand with china basin and large water jug. In the bedside cupboard was the usual jerry, classified on the Quartermaster's barrack room list as 'Pots chamber china, officers'. At the Army mental asylum in Netley, the issued jerries for officers were noted as 'Pots chamber rubber, officers lunatic'. Other ranks (ORs), sane or lunatic, were provided with a much less deluxe type of both, catalogued as, 'Pots chamber rubber, ORs lunatic'. The floor of our rooms was of bare boards, as at Haileybury. Mine was in a remote part of the building with little heating, known as Siberia, and I loved it. I installed my Moon Pig portable wireless beside the bed, listened to the late-night dance music from Roy Fox or the Savoy Hotel Orpheans, did my homework or polished my equipment and was completely happy. Each room was also equipped with a small metal box screwed to the chest of drawers, in which we were told to keep valuables or money. It was advisable as well to keep the key with you at all times, or everything in it would be stolen. I never ceased to be appalled at the attitude towards theft at Sandhurst. It was, the then current one in the Army, that anything lying around loose was fair game no matter to whom it belonged, and the owner's fault if it disappeared. During my Senior term, after undergoing an operation for appendicitis I returned to find that nearly all my clothes had been stolen in my absence. Each Company seemed to have a GC who would actually be introduced as the 'Company thief' and appeared proud of the fact. Libel laws prevent me from naming No 5 Company thief in my Senior term, but later at a dance I found him actually wearing my tails, with the name label still inside the pocket. When challenged he passed it off with a laugh, saying that he had 'bought them secondhand in Camberley, and they fitted him to a T.'

In 1932 it was of course anathema that an officer should not have a servant, and one such, usually a retired Army NCO or Private. was allotted to each ten cadets. Their labours were cunningly restricted to what they would have to do if the cadets were officers. They had to make the beds, empty the chamber pots and generally keep the room clean and tidy. Their duties also including polishing our Sam Browne belts and cleaning our buttons, in fact the tasks a batman would normally do. They were not required to clean anything else, but naturally if paid enough, would take care of one's entire kit, including boots, rifle and bayonet. The joining instructions which the College had sent out to parents requested that 'in the interests of discipline, it was hoped parents would not allow GCs more than £4 per month in pocket money'. Most ignored this ruling altogether and gave two or three times the amount. My father greeted it with a whoop of delight, as full justification for giving me as little as possible in accordance with the request. Such an opportunity to save money, and at the same time uphold good order and military discipline, occurred but rarely. The £4 was, I imagine, based on the average pay of an A cadet's weekly wage as a Corporal, which he would continue to receive, of about £1 a week, everything else being found.

My servant, whose name I am ashamed to say I do not recall, was an ex-soldier, a small man with a wall eye. He cleaned everything he was supposed to clean and generally did me very well, despite the fact that I was unable to pay him more than the basic ten bob a month. The rest of my kit I had to do myself, and very hard work it was. Bobby Combe was an assiduous taskmaster. One of the servants in 5 Company, a fat and jovial man with a big belly, was a magician when it came to cleaning leather. He was generally known as 'Uncle'. He had been there for many years, and was actually Leslie Brown's servant when he was at Sandhurst in 1916. The criteria of money was very much a part of life at the RMC. At Haileybury boys who seemed to have money to throw around were usually looked down upon and despised. At Sandhurst it became rather a measure of their popularity, attracting a tail of admirers, sycophants and hangers on. We were not allowed to drive cars, but some GCs, especially minor Princes or Kings, in their Senior term would live in a very grand style, with not only motor cars, but chauffeurs to drive them. You would see them every afternoon being driven off somewhere to play polo. Such people attracted a very long tail indeed; not only from their fellows, but from the Staff as well.

For PT parades we wore a uniform dating back to the 1890s. It consisted of white flannel trousers, white gym shoes and a red-and-white striped blazer, the four buttons of which had to be kept done up at all times. With it we wore a red-and-white silk square, and a little red-and-white pillbox hat, kept in place with an elastic band. Red and white were the College colours. Arrayed thus, we mounted our bogwheels after the usual parade rigmarole, and hied away to the gymnasium to strip down to a white T-shirt and flannel trousers. We did PT for an hour, three times a week. The object of physical training in the Army at that time was not to build muscle, but to increase physical fitness, balance, alertness and general well being. Any exercise actually to build muscle, such as the use of dumbells or weight training, was discouraged or forbidden. Lord of the gym was Army Physical Training Corps Sergeant Major 'Jock' White, formerly of the Highland Light Infantry. He was a small man, like most of his Regiment, his forearms covered with tattoos from serving in every corner of the British Empire. Like his groizy-whiskered counterpart at Haileybury, he appeared to be made entirely out of india-rubber, but Jock White's PT standards were infinitely higher than anything old Groizy Whiskers could have dreamed of. Under Jock were seven or eight APTC instructors in blue trousers and the red-and-black striped jerseys of that Corps, its working uniform.

For me the most striking feature of the RMC was the outstanding quality of our instructors at every level, especially the NCOs. Every single one was outstanding in his job, a picked man from thousands, whether it be on the drill square, the riding school or in the gymnasium. They were simply better than anyone else. It was of course a high and much sought-after honour, for anyone of whatever rank, to be chosen to be an instructor either at the RMC Sandhurst, or the RMA Woolwich (The Shop). It was a system which suited my psychology perfectly, which needs a constant goad, and there is no better goad than that of fear and knowledge that nothing but the best is good enough, that only by figuratively running as fast as you could all the time could you remain in the same place. In such a system, no excuse could be accepted for failure to reach the standard, whether for a speck of oil on your uniform, a missed whisker on your chin, or the train being derailed, making you late returning from leave. 'You should have caught an earlier one.' Not only did I enjoy it, but I was exalted that I was allowed to be part of it and hold my own. Funnily enough, after a month or two, such standards became a habit and a matter of routine.

15

When we came off the square, we were given a fortnight's Easter break. I joined my father, who was staying with the Parsons in Guildford. Directly I had become 17, he had taught me to drive his old Hillman 14 HP car. The gears were difficult, as there was no such thing as synchromesh in those days. To change down you had to master an action known as double declutching, in order to adjust to the increased engine speed. With no driving test required, anyone could buy a driving licence which I believe cost five shillings (25p), and drive off. It was advisable however, to get a relative or friend to teach you the rudimentary skills, such as steering, braking and gear changing. The roads, especially in the country, were almost empty, and it could be five or six minutes before you met another vehicle.

Directly I could drive, I bought an old Ariel motorcycle for £10 from a garage in Aldershot. It had the new, rather bulbous type streamlined petrol tank and four gears, worked by a lever on the tank side, instead of the modern foot change. I set off on it with Lionel Parsons, who had a similar but much better machine, for Lands End, where we stayed at a B&B owned by Tom Pender, the coxswain of the lifeboat at Sennen, with its lovely, sandy cove. I should have realised on the way down that my bike was not very reliable, as it had kept breaking down. A friendly AA patrol man had replaced the chain, even though I could not afford to become a member. For riding, we wore breeches with puttees or grey flannel trousers, tweed coats and collar and tie, with a silk scarf and a macintosh if it were wet or cold. On our heads were Great War Biggles-type flying helmets and goggles, our hands protected by leather gauntlets. It had poured with rain most of the way from

Guildford, and we were soaked to the skin by the time we arrived in Sennen Cove.

When I got back to the RMC for the rest of that Junior term, things seemed to have become easier. Perhaps it was because we were no longer on the square, perhaps because we had become adjusted to the routine. An attempt was being made to turn the College into more of a Military University. Thus we were not taught the use of our weapons, this being left to the time we joined our regiments. Instead we studied higher tactics and Army organisation, map reading, history, French, economics and book-keeping. The officer who took us for book-keeping was a Captain Newey of the Royal Army Educational Corps, the RAEC, the social standing of which was possibly bottom of the Army ladder, still in the identical position it had occupied since about 1900. Captain Newey had cultivated an ultra-plummy voice to compensate for this, and would talk of 'won thowsand pownds'. The system of book-keeping he taught was known as double-entry, whereby every transaction was entered on both sides of the page, and was almost beyond comprehension. Keeping accounts was a large part of an officer's regimental duties, so the system had to be mastered. Poor Captain Newey also had very sweaty armpits, and great salt-encrusted rings formed below his arms on his Service Dress uniform. One day a large wasp droned its way into our Hall of Study, as classrooms were called, and buzzed around where he was writing, one arm raised, on the blackboard. We watched, fascinated, as it settled on his armpit. After a few seconds it fell off in a stupor, lying on its back on the floor, kicking feebly.

If rugby football had been the way to obtain social kudos at Haileybury, at Sandhurst it was the worship of the horse. This was my first encounter with the strongly held belief that association with this curious animal was the criterion by which, anything and everything, good or bad, was to be judged. If the British Army had a religion, then it was the Horse. At the RMC there were no compulsory games – we got quite enough exercise from the drill, PT and equitation, which continued throughout the 18-month course. However, everyone had to pretend they loved horses; whether they actually did or not was immaterial. The first thing many did was to go off to Flights, the tailors in Camberley High Street, and get themselves measured up for a check tweed 'hacking jacket', cut very long, pinched in at the waist and flared out at the tails with a single slit up the back, known as a 'bugger's delight', as opposed to the slightly more formal two slits, which posed a dilemma. So amazing was this horse fetish, that I once heard a GC ask his servant, 'Please put out my boots and breeches, I'm going to the cinema', hoping to give the impression he'd been out hacking first, and hadn't had time to change.

Riding, or equitation as it was called, was as expertly taught as everything else, by Cavalry NCO instructors. Nearly all the Cavalry was still horsed and every Company Commander in the Infantry, as well as many other of its officers, were mounted, whether on parades, marches, or manoeuvres, and every self-respecting regiment ran a polo team. It was essential that everyone knew how to ride to a high standard. I had not ridden since I was a boy of eight in India, when I had been a good natural rider, taught by my mother, that female Centaur. I had forgotten all I knew and put my name down for the bottom or beginners' ride. We rode three times a week for an hour and a half, mostly without reins or stirrups, going over the jumps with folded arms. We learnt what was known as the 'forward or Cavalry seat', with knees driven into the saddle by toes turned out and heels down. Anyone on the ground should 'be able to see the soles of your boots'. No part of the calf should ever touch the horse, and on evening kit inspection, Bobby Combe would rub our gaiters with a cloth to see if there was any horse sweat on them, and we had been 'hanging on with our heels', a heinous offence. At the end of the Senior term one cadet would be awarded The Saddle, as the best horseman of his entry. It was considered a far higher award than the Sword of Honour.

Round and round the tan track of the riding school we would go in everlasting circles or figures of eight, 'quit your stirrups', 'cross your stirrups', 'loose your reins and fold your arms', 'walk', 'trot', 'canter'. The horses were so used to the routine that they knew what to do even before any order was given. When we began going over the jumps, still without stirrups or reins in case we pulled our horse's mouth, every now and again someone would fall off, the horse waiting patiently beside him. 'Remount Sir! Remount!' the instructor would acidly order, 'Oo gave you permission to dismount?' When we were eventually allowed to use the reins they were of the double bridle variety, with snaffle and curb. The curb was applied by twisting the wrist, not by pulling back as is so prevalent today. By the end of our time we had all become proficient riding school horsemen, but never ventured out into the country. For me it had been similar to relearning to ride a bicycle, something one has never forgotten. During my service I hunted, played polo and claimed to worship the Horse with the best of them, but it could never replace the devotion to my skis.

During that term I also learnt to smoke a pipe, often making myself sick in the process, or sitting on a lavatory seat expecting to be sick, with the world going round in circles about my head. We all smoked a pipe in preference to cigarettes. It was considered a social asset for many years, giving the impression of cosy, honest self-assurance, as Harold Wilson tried to convey when he was Prime Minister during the 1960s. At a shilling an ounce (5p), pipe tobacco was relatively inexpensive, a gallon of petrol costing the same amount. A pipe could be bought for half a crown (12½p). An excellent example made in Scotland, called the Henry Fraser Lovat, cost this amount. But undoubtedly the one which smoked the most sweetly was the guinea (£1.05p) Dunhill black shell briar. It is difficult to explain the pleasures of pipe smoking, and many years since I gave it up. They were continually going out and needed constant relighting, they burnt one's tongue, the stem filled with a kind of black gunge which every now and again erupted into one's mouth and tasted disgusting. Pipe smoking was indeed a filthy, obnoxious habit, yet it was thought the epitome of British manliness to smoke one.

The great social event of the Sandhurst year was undoubtedly the June Ball, which took place on the Saturday evening nearest 18 June, Waterloo day. It was also one of the social events of the London Season, and many of the girls invited were Debs who had been presented at Court to King George and Queen Mary earlier in the year, attired in white dresses with long white ostrich feathers in their hair. The Ball took place in the huge hall in the centre of the Old Building and was a magnificent affair. Joyce Parsons came as my partner, and joined a party we had got up for it, consisting of Geoffrey Worsdell, Dudley Lincoln and Minden Scot, whose father had been in one of the regiments which had fought at Minden under George II, the last British monarch to take part in a battle, and had named his son after it. The King's wig had fallen off halfway through and he had charged the French without it, his head shining like an egg, to originate the expression, 'going for it bald-headed'. The Ball was a wonderful spectacle with everyone in uniform, the officers in their scarlet Mess kit. Many who had just left came back in their new uniforms, whilst Mr Jarman and his Discordia Boys played themselves into a frenzy on the platform. Supper was served between two and three a.m. in a huge marquee in the grounds, and the dancing went on until dawn. Church parade took place the following morning at the usual time, with its usual panache. There was no allowance for a late night. After all, had not the Duke of Wellington given a huge ball in the middle of June, the night before Waterloo, which ours commemorated? Former guests became spectators, and the chapel was crowded.

Early in July our time as Juniors was complete. We had end of term examinations in which I had held my own, even gone up a few places. My report was good, and my father was pleased with me. Moreover I was free until early September, when I would come back as an Intermediate, and have to choose which regiment or arm of the Service I wished to enter. No-one could imagine that after the 'war to end all wars' there would ever be another in Europe. The Army was purely for policing the Empire and keeping unruly members of it, such as the Pathans of Northern India, in order. However, if the unthinkable ever occured and there was another war, then it would be exactly like the last, with trenches, barbed wire, artillery, machine guns, poison gases, plenty of mud, stalemate and many casualties, the Army term for dead and wounded. My father did not believe this. 'The future battle winner,' he said, 'is the tank, whole divisions of them. You go into the Tank Corps and get in on the ground floor.' Now we had studied the use of tanks during our tactical periods, and although considered possibly useful in their own peculiar way, nobody thought very much of them. The official doctrine was to

1929 Le Château de la Matholière

Pagham August 1931,
L.E. Birch (Granny), myself

Pagham August 1931. Left to right: Awdry Stuart, Mary Brown

Batten House team going out to field, summer 1931. Left to right: N.L. Darewski, F.P. Matthews, O.M. Ruck, A.W.D. Nicholls, C.J. Tite, Myself

Wittering August 1931. My father with Joyce Parsons

Left to right:
A.W.D. Nicholls, P.G. Cane,
Haileybury summer 1931

1931. Myself, Garm, Leslie Brown

Left to right: Klaus Joachim, the Freifrau, Henning Von Dobenick. August 1933

August 1932, the ill fated motor-bike at Evreux

La Matholière,
August 1932,
Left to right:
Cilette, Yves and
Françoise de Moncuit

Me as 2/Lt, Dover 1934.
Officer's 'Battle Order'

1st HLI Bugle-Major Bendy

1st HLI King's birthday parade, Dover, June 1934

1st HLI September Manoeuvres 1934

My little Austin Seven which caused such a furore on arrival at the HLI

1934 Highland Light Infantry (HLI) various forms of 'dress'

I had to sell my Austin and buy 'a dark coloured car instead'

Peshawar, my horse General, later Reichsmarshall Goering, with syce

Peshawar 1936, Jerry Beale

Semaphore - heliograph winking to pickets, Landi-Kotal Brigade, Autumn 1936

Vickers machine gun, Landi-Kotal Brigade, Autumn 1936

Sikh section, Kohat Mountain Battery in action. 1st Royal Kohat Mountain Battery RA
(Punjab Frontier Force) on manoeuvres near Khyber, Autumn 1936

Brigadier Molesworth, commander Landi-Kotal Brigade, 1936

June 1937, H.B. Triumph, Nagim Bagh

Our Manji 1937, Amadoo Wagnoo on trek

June 1937, H.B. Triumph moored in Nagim Bagh, Srinagar, Kasmir together with cook boat

June 1937, Rosemary Collin in my Lagonda

1937, Rosemary Collin

June 1937, Rosemary Collin outside Nedous Hotel Srinagar, Kashmir. She is wearing 'Evergreen', my hat

Peshawar 1938, light tank

Peshawar 1938, Rolls Royce armoured cars on patrol, Kajuri Plain

My bearer,
Mohammed Said Khan

spread them as evenly as possible throughout the infantry taking part in the battle, so that everybody got a share. They were nasty, noisy, evil-smelling things which had to be kept well away from the cavalry or they might frighten the horses. Tanks at the time had a top speed of some 14 mph, the infantry advanced at 2½, if it was lucky. When someone asked, why tie the tank down to the speed of the infantry, he was told not to be stupid, as the tanks would start a long way behind and have to catch up.

I agreed, with considerable misgiving, that I would put my name down for the Royal Tank Corps, and read a book on its exploits during the Great War, where it had been born, so that I could impress Pip Crouch, its officer rep at the RMC, how keen and enthusiastic I was to join it. Despite its poor social rating, available places were hotly contested. Captain Pip Crouch was an Army middleweight boxing champion whose nose and face had been battered almost out of any recognisable shape. The reason the social standing of the RTC was so regrettably low, was because of its lack of anything to do with the horse, and the noise its machines made, which actually scared them. Furthermore with all that oil and grease about, people in it were little removed from garage mechanics and petrol pump attendants. My misgivings intensified when Kendrick Hughes, Awdry's Old Etonian boyfriend, asked me which Guards regiment I would be joining; his uncle commanded a battalion of the Grenadiers. When I replied 'The Royal Tank Corps', he merely said 'Oh!' and changed the subject.

With the best part of three months holiday in front of me, I decided I would ride my motorbike all the way round France, improve my French still further – it had stood me well in the examination – and generally see the country. My father's pursuit of Gladys Parsons seemed to be amicably over, and he had moved to a small house at Cranleigh in Surrey. Despite fierce opposition from my mother, mainly because he approved it, I set off around 20 July, all my clothes, including a dinner jacket, for I was going to visit La Matholière as a first stop, carried on the back in a canvas Army kit bag. Immediate necessities were in a small pack across my shoulders. In those days there were no car ferries and my bike was hoisted aboard the normal cross-Channel packet from Newhaven to Dieppe, where it took about an hour to clear the French customs. Mine was the only vehicle aboard, but every item in the '*Carnet de passage en douanes*', or International Vehicle customs book, had to be checked and re-checked, engine no, frame no, type of tyres and so on, in case you imported one bike and came out with another. Failure to re-export what you had brought in entailed heavy customs duties, far in excess of the vehicle's worth. It had to be returned to its country of origin, in this case the UK, 'even if in small pieces'. Prophetic words!

If the roads in England were empty, in France they were practically deserted. Long, rather narrow and endlessly straight, they were often poorly surfaced, full of potholes and humped in the middle to drain off the rain into ditches on each side. One would ride for mile after mile without meeting another vehicle. It was quite eerie. My machine cruised at about 40 mph and achieved about 40 miles in every hour. At Evreux I took a wrong turning and finished up at Lisieux in exactly the opposite direction to that intended. I spent the night there in a small hotel, discussing the use of tanks, *chars d'assaut*, during the Great War and in the future, with the proprietor. He shared the same views as my father. Next morning I set off for Tigy via Chartres and Orleans. Long before you get to Chartres you can see the form of the cathedral emerging above the plain of northern France. I had a great welcome from Le Baron and Madame de Moncuit, who insisted I stay a few days. The chateau was full of the usual student guests, and I immediately fell in love with one of them, a red-headed Norwegian by the name of Ingrid Werthe Johannessen, 'Moussa' by nickname. She was 18 and came from a little village far in the north of Norway, called Levanger. I was truly sorry to set off again on my travels, for it seemed my interest in her was returned.

Just outside Poitiers, however, there was a loud bang in the engine and the bike came to a shuddering halt. There seemed to be a large hole in the sump, and a piston was sticking out of it in a rather forlorn way. I managed to get a lift in a passing truck, both for myself and the bike, to the nearest village, where I spent the night at the rather grotty hotel and wine bar which every French village seemed to possess. I managed to get Jacques de Moncuit on the only telephone in the place, which was on the

186

main road, after interminable wrangling with the exchange, '*Le numero six à Tigy. Oui! Oui! Le Chateau de la Matholière, le nom du proprietaire? Monsieur de Moncuit*, etc. etc.' He agreed to come and collect me the following day, and we left my bike to follow a week later by lorry. At Tigy, the mechanic looked at the remains ruefully, scratched his head, and said that various parts would have to be ordered from England and it might take some time.

Apparently the reason it had blown up was because there had been no oil in it. I had cleaned it with RMC assiduousness until everything shone, but had not realised that oil should also be checked and replenished. Frankly I was delighted that I could stay on at La Matholière whilst the bike was being mended. Moussa and I began the most innocent love affair imaginable. Every morning we would walk into Tigy, have a drink at a wine bar, and see how my motorbike was coming along. The mechanic had completely stripped it down and various bits and pieces were strewn around the floor. Every time he said nothing had arrived from England we felt we had been reprieved, and he became more and more perplexed that I seemed delighted at the lack of progress. Otherwise we would defy the horse flies, meet secretely in the woods among the silver birches and exchange chaste kisses, or sit on the terrace after dinner of an evening, furtively holding hands and smoking Gauloises to drive off the mosquitoes. After six weeks my time was up and I had to leave the bike where it was and return by train. Moussa gave me a book of poems, '*Toi et Moi*' by Paul Geraldy, and my father had a terrible time sorting things out with the French customs. The motorcycle was eventually returned to England, still in small pieces, never to go again. The following winter, on my way back from Chateau d'Oex, I stopped off at La Matholière. Moussa was the only guest, the chateau was cold and damp and the magic had gone.

I returned to Sandhurst the next term as an Intermediate, the least pleasant of my three terms. I found I had been accepted for the Royal Tank Corps and had to join the Mechanical Engineering course. Here Pip Crouch lectured us on the internal combustion engine, and the importance of keeping it supplied with oil as well as petrol. We also made things out of metal on the lathes in the workshop, measured to one thousandth of an inch, called a 'thou'. There was usually a film shown during the evening classes on some aspect of the IC engine. Furthermore if you wish to produce a genuine specific against insomnia, it would be showing a film about the internal combustion engine, its only comparable rival in soporifics being watching someone else's holiday video on their game park safari in Africa. Such was the pace of life at the RMC that we were constantly physically tired; people would even fall asleep at dinner. What with drill, PT, equitation, and some game we had probably played during the afternoon, such as rugby, hockey or athletics, directly the lights went out and the film began, the entire class would fall fast asleep across their desks. I had taken up hockey, and even managed to play for the College. Thus nobody learnt much about the IC engine. The horse ethos was much too strong anyway. Nobody even wanted to.

An important reason for disliking my Intermediate term was that the teenage spots on my face were back with a vengeance. During the summer I had cured them by sunbathing. Not only was it the latest craze, everybody wished to 'look fit and brown', but it was also the latest medical fad that was reputed to cure everything from piles to tuberculosis. Apparently exposure to the sun's UV rays would cause the build up of various vitamins in the skin, that would keep people free from infections throughout the coming winter. It certainly worked in my case. A few hours in the sun and my spots vanished as if by magic, only to return with redoubled vigour after a few sunless weeks. For the next 60 years I was a dedicated sun worshipper, considering, much to the detriment of my career, that the only things really worth doing were skiing or lying in the sun; preferably both at the same time.

Eventually the term ended and I spent most of my Christmas leave skiing with my cousin Twig, who was with his mother at Chateau d'Oex in the Swiss Vaud. In order to save money I travelled third class, a hideously uncomfortable way, as the seats of the railway carriages in France were nothing but hard wood. However, to sleep, I climbed up and stretched out full-length in the luggage rack. Nobody seemed to mind, but were in fact amused by the ingenuity of this French-speaking young *Anglais*. I slept like a baby, the clickety-click of the wheels murmuring through my dreams, 'to the snows, to the snows, to the snows'. Every now and again the train would stop with a sigh in some empty midnight station and I would peep out at the deserted platform, only to fall back and go to sleep again directly we started. Chateau d'Oex is in the French-speaking part of Switzerland. There were no ski lifts of any kind, and the nursery slopes were in a hollow below the church. A large British community lived in the village, retired people with their families, who found life much cheaper and pleasanter than living in England. A few days in the Alpine sunshine had cured my spots and I felt much happier. Twig and I used to put sealskins on our skis and climb the untracked Mont Chreveuils; or we would take the little mountain train to Saanenmoser and climb the Hornberg, lunching at the primitive and smoky hut refuge at the top, where they sold soup, frankfurter sausages and bread. Then ski down and take the train home. An American, a Rhodes Scholar at Oxford, called Roger Black, often came with us, together with his girlfriend, Barbara Beauchamp, an expert skier who lived in Chateau d'Oex with her parents.

Just up the line, beyond Rougemont, the railway passes into German-speaking Switzerland. I never cease to marvel at the sudden changes of language in that country. Within a hundred yards or so, it will change and you will find most people cannot understand what others were saying only a brief moment before. The Swiss Germans speak a dialect among themselves which changes from valley to valley, but the newspapers and books are written in a different language altogether, *Hoch Deutsch*, high, classical or official German, which is taught at school and they can all understand and speak with that inimitable Swiss accent. The otherwise horrendous Marjorie Corner, Twig's mother, impressed me greatly by not only speaking good French but German as well, and I resolved there and then that I would learn it too. Perhaps an even more amazing thing about the Swiss is that they remain so unalterably and inflexibly Swiss, whatever language they may speak.

During our Intermediate term we all began going up to London on Saturdays. There was a special bus called the Dorcas laid on for this, which cost half a crown return. It left at 11 a.m. and got back at 10.30 p.m., in time to sign the Dining Out leave book before it closed at 11 p.m. This was a large sheet on which you had to enter your name before you left, check it to see it had been approved before leaving, and then sign it in front of the Orderly Officer on your return. He sat, in uniform, at a bare table in an otherwise empty room, with the Staff Orderly Sergeant beside him to arrest anyone who appeared drunk or dishevelled, and march him to the Guard Room. Drunkeness was unofficially not considered much of a crime, and mainly looked upon with kindly eyes. People openly boasted of how drunk they had been, when perhaps only slightly tipsy. To sign in, you had to walk across the room, stand to attention and give your name, then find it on the sheet and sign in the opposite blank place. Unless a cadet was actually sick on the floor or fell over, he would normally pass muster. As well as boasting of their drunkeness, many went to London, talking loudly of their intention to 'have a woman'. Whores abounded, especially around Piccadilly tube station, and the going rate was ten bob up to a £1 for something rather deluxe. How many really 'had a woman' is hard to say, but most, probably not. I never claimed to have done so, not for any high moral reason, but merely because I was far too scared of getting a dose of clap or syphilis, and the agonising wait after the event to see if you had caught it, a fortnight for clap, and a whole month for syphilis, either of which would put paid to a cadet's future as an officer. In an age without antibiotics, the cure for both diseases was long, deliberately painful, shaming and inconclusive.

As for everything else, GCs had to be 'properly dressed' to go to London. This consisted of a dark suit with white shirt and hard starched white collar, school, RMC or dark blue with white polka-dot tie, black highly polished shoes, bowler hat from Herbert Johnnie or Locks, and a tightly furled black umbrella. In winter, a long, dark blue overcoat was worn with a dark blue and white polkadot scarf. I would often meet Joyce Parsons in London and we would go skating at one of the many ice rinks, or to a cinema, the whole day costing well under £1. To return late from Dining Out leave was a very serious offence, entailing at least 14 days restrictions, with 28 for a second offence. No excuse was accepted. If the main punishment at Haileybury had been a beating, at the RMC, and throughout the Army, it would be considered 'striking', a court-martial offence. Even too hard a push or shake by an inspecting officer on a parade could be construed as 'striking', for which he would be disciplined. A man's person was inviolate from both physical and verbal abuse. An officer or NCO could call him dozy and idle and place him on a charge for it, but to call him 'fucking dozy and idle' was a serious offence, and to call him a 'bastard' as well would be even worse. It was a direct insult to the semi-sacred morality of the soldier's mother. In those days, being illegitimate was a terrible social slur.

At Sandhurst the punishments were the puttee parades after dinner already described, ordered and carried out by the UOs and cadet NCOs of the Senior term. These were given for minor infringements of the routine running of the Company, such as being late, unshaved, or with dirty equipment on early morning muster parade at 7.30 a.m. If a member of the College Staff were on parade, then you 'lost your name', and were 'put on a charge' to appear before Major Wilson. For this you would be fallen in outside the Company office, and with cap off, marched in, 'left right, left right, left turn, one step forward march'. The charge would be read out, and witnesses called. Major Wilson would then ask the culprit if he had anything to say, and pronounce sentence. This could be anything from 3 to 14 days restrictions. Graver charges were dealt with by the Commandant, Major-General May, himself, with 28 days restrictions, 'dropping a term', or even expulsion. Luckily I managed to escape all punishments during my three terms. Restrictions were no joke, entailing being confined to the College, wearing uniform at all times, attending frequent roll calls, regular as well as surprise, and undergoing back-breaking periods of barrack square drill, mainly double marching. For some extraordinary reason, the same people always seemed to be on restrictions. In our term it was Rem Thackeray, a most gifted GC, a composer of music, and a brilliant piano, saxophone and clarinet player, perpetually at loggerheads with the Staff, who in fact liked him as much as we all did. Why someone with such outstanding musical talents should wish to go into the Army was beyond my comprehension. Personally I would have been hot-footing it to join Roy Fox, Paul Whiteman or maybe the Savoy Hotel Orpheans. I wouldn't even have turned my nose up at Jack Payne and his Band at the BBC.

I shall always look back to my third and Senior term, along with the time I spent learning to fly in 1942, as one of the happiest episodes in my life, when I was perfectly content and felt fulfilled with what I was doing. Sandhurst was all substance and no froth, just solid worth. Kenneth Bols was our SUO, and I was the senior Cadet Corporal, posted to Geoffrey Worsdell's platoon where he had been appointed JUO. I had a section of ten Juniors to look after, all compliant, anxious to please and do my bidding. One of them was the brother of Maureen O'Sullivan, the film star who played 'Me Jane you Tarzan' opposite Johnny Weismuller in the current jungle films. Her brother invited her to the June Ball, where she created a sensation. Being his Section commander, I even managed to get a dance with her. As well as the June Ball, dances were held at the RMC on Saturday evenings once a month. Whilst on TEWTS (tactical exercises without troops) out in the countryside, directly we had studied the problem and worked out the answer, which usually took all of five minutes, Geoffrey Worsdell and I spent the rest of the time on the far more important problem of how to arrange for our chosen females to get to the next dance. As a JUO, his blue patrol epaulettes were now edged with silver braid, whilst mine were only red. However, Cadet Corporals as well as Sergeants had to take their turn as Orderly Sergeant, who wore a red sash whilst on duty. This added a splash of glamour, especially if you were Orderly Sergeant during the June Ball.

My father's pursuit of Gladys Parsons seemed to have languished, as had mine for her daughter Joyce. My partner for that June Ball was one Pat Gleed, whose brothers later became famous fighter pilots during the Battle of Britain in 1940. The Orderly Sergeant's duties lasted for a week, and one of them was to muster the lame, the halt and the dying for 'Sick Parade'. Every morning at 7 a.m. during my tour of duty, I would go round the Company, shouting 'fall in for Sick Parade', whereupon all those wishing to 'report sick' would fall in outside the Company, undergo the usual meticulous inspection and be marched briskly up the hill to the Sanatorium, about a mile away, for medical examination. Some would be admitted, others given M & D (medicine and duty) and be marched back.

192

During that last term, my desire to enter the Royal Tank Corps had become less and less. Much Regimental snobbery had rubbed off on us all during the past months, and I am ashamed to say that my feelings against it were mainly social. I did not wish to belong to a Corps which apparently everybody despised. Despite this, the two officer vacancies in it had been hotly contested. So when a friend came into my room and suggested that as there were two vacancies in the Highland Light Infantry, we take them up together, I agreed and went along to Pip Crouch to tell him of my decision, which obviously changed the entire course of my future life. He was furious. When I finally joined the HLI in October, I found my friend was not there. He had taken up my vacancy in the Tank Corps. I would undoubtedly been far happier in it than I ever was in the Highland Light Infantry.

A week before the end of that term, I awoke in the middle of the night with an agonising pain in my midriff, and was whisked off by ambulance to the Cambridge hospital in Aldershot where I was operated on as an emergency for appendicitis by that eminent surgeon, Mr Davis-Collier. I never discovered whether there was anything wrong with my appendix or whether the pain was caused by just something I had eaten. The appendix operation was a popular one among Army doctors, as an insurance against a sudden attack in some outlandish, remote and inaccessible part of the Empire. 'If in doubt, whip it out' was the medical catchword. I enjoyed my week in hospital, much enlivened by a beautiful nurse we all called Sunshine Susie. I had missed the passing out examinations and had to be averaged, which was lucky for I was placed 16th. I had certainly not done enough revision as I should have, to merit it. I was also a spectator at the Passing-Out Parade, watching my friends follow the Adjutant, Norman Gwatkin, on his horse, walk up the steps of the Old Building and into the hall, to the strains of 'Auld Lang Syne'. We had joined, a year and a half earlier, from different schools, with different ideas, hopes and ambitions, some 180 separate individuals. We emerged as a single product, the British Army subaltern officer, with all the defects of his many outstanding qualities. Even the A cadets had been assimilated.

16

My father groaned with dismay when the list of clothes and uniform arrived from the Highland Light Infantry. The various types of uniform seemed to be endless, from scarlet Mess kit to a hideous form of garment exclusive to the Regiment, known as 'marching pantaloons', a kind of baggy riding breeches made of the regimental Mackenzie tartan and worn with blue puttees. These were for 'battle order' and only worn by officers, ensuring they could be easily picked off first by the enemy. The ORs wore normal khaki. The regimental tailors were Hawkes of 1 Savile Row. In addition to uniform, many 'regimental pattern' suits and a blue blazer, were also required. A War Office grant would cover about half the items. We went up to London, where a host of little men in waistcoats with tape measures around their necks fussed about taking measurements.

Clothes for young men in the 1930s were stereotyped: dark suit, bowler hat and umbrella for London; in the country, a tweed suit on Sundays with a quiet tweed jacket and grey flannel bags during the week. Corduroys were just coming in as were suede shoes, but were considered rather 'pansy', what would be called 'gay' today. Lillywhites, the sports shop off Piccadilly Circus, carried a line of holiday clothes which were considered slightly pansy, though well cut. Most people wore a hat, often a trilby moulded into a kind of pork pie. The lower classes who went to football matches invariably wore a peaked cloth cap, which was utterly different in cut and shape from those worn by the gentry for shooting. I hated wearing a hat and avoided doing so whenever I could, causing much adverse comment. I was convinced, however, that the main cause of baldness, especially the ugliest type on the crown of the head, where everybody could see it except yourself, was caused by wearing a hat. I wished to keep my hair as long as possible.

It was now July and I had leave until early October, when I would join the 1st Battalion HLI at Dover. I asked my father if he would arrange for me to go to Germany and stay with a family. there to learn the language, of which I knew not a word. The previous year we had studied Germany to a considerable extent during our economics classes. The world depression had hit the Germans very hard. There were some seven million unemployed, much civil unrest and complete economic and industrial stagnation. The general opinion was that the country would at best become bankrupt, but more likely, turn Communist. However, in January 1933, a certain Adolf Hitler, leader of something called the Nazis, had been voted into power, and already, only seven months later, things seemed to be very much better. Through some educational agency my father discovered a family called von Dobeneck, who lived in the Wilhelmstrasse in Munich, who agreed to take me without a prior knowledge of German.

I had learnt from long experience that the only way to get my father to spend money was to persuade him that it was his own idea, was to be spent on something useful and of future value, such as learning German, or on something over which he had no control, such as all the gear for the HLI. Had I been going into an English regiment of course, or the Royal Tank Corps, much of what I had at the RMC could have been altered and used. Hence his groans at the tailors. Thus with some subtle and delicate prompting, he suddenly had this brilliant idea of putting the money to be used for the journey to Munich and back into buying a small car and motoring out.

So we hunted round for something suitable, which I would like and which would be reliable, and economical to run in the future. Our choice fell on an Austin Seven, perhaps the most famous of all cars. But this was no ordinary Austin Seven that we found gleaming in Jackson's Showroom in Guildford; it was a Brooklands model Austin Seven, of which only two had been made for the 1929 Motor Show at Earls Court. I longed to own it. In size it was not much bigger than a large bathtub, which it also rather resembled in shape. It had a long tapering tail, and red, cycle type front mudguards. The rest of the body was cream-coloured and the radiator carried a flying eagle mascot, which I was sure would appeal to the Germans, it being their national emblem. The upholstery was red leather, and I could see that my father also rather fancied himself at the wheel of this fetching little craft. It was the day of the hinged bonnet, which Mr Jackson opened with a flourish, revealing an engine the size of a largish mouse. The car had done about 20,000 miles, its number was UV 8054 and they wanted £50 for it. My father allowed me to use part of the money I had won for my scholarship to Sandhurst, to which he added the conjectured price of the Munich journey, and we bought it. Mr Jackson said 'it was very fast', and I was made to promise not to drive it at more than 50 mph. In practice, I found later that with a following wind and slightly downhill, one might get it up to 50. However it would trundle along all day very happily at 40, doing the same number of miles per gallon of petrol. The little car never let me down and I loved it dearly. Perhaps one's first car is always magical.

I cleaned it and its engine up to RMC standards. The engine had a number of brass pipes which could be polished with Brasso until they gleamed like gold. Even the tops of the sparking plugs were polished. Every grease nipple around the chassis was attacked daily in an almost religious fervour with a grease gun, and as carefully wiped clean. It amused me to pull into a garage for petrol, ask the attendant to check the oil and apologise for 'having rather a dirty engine'. Never was a car so cherished as UV 8054, only one of two such ever made. If I was to drive it to Munich, luggage was going to be a problem. With the hood folded down and the side screens in the boot, there was the minimum of room. I would have to carry my suitcase beside me in the passenger seat.

I drove it down to Pagham Beach near Bognor Regis, where my grandmother had bought a small four-bedroomed wooden bungalow among the pebbles, called Blue Peter. From here, every Sunday morning she would resolutely march us to the parish church of St Thomas à Becket, where the Saint had actually been vicar, before moving on to higher things, such as becoming Archbishop of Canterbury. She lived with her Pekingese Chang, whose eyes, if you pulled his forehead back, would almost pop out

196

of his head like marbles. My visit was not altogether unconnected with two rather attractive girls who came down at weekends to another bungalow nearby. My Aunt Gertie and Uncle Jimmy, along with Awdry and Kendrick Hughes, who often came down at weekends, dismissed them as belonging to a family of London fishmongers, '*machli wallahs*', unworthy of attention. The thought of introducing a couple of fishmonger's daughters, or even one, into Blue Peter was too much for me altogether. The acquaintance languished. In fact, they were highly respectable fishmonger's daughters, having been to Roedean, their father being owner of a large chain of fish shops along the South Coast. My grandmother also had a paid companion who lived with her and was always addressed as 'Mrs Palin', with whom I got on very well despite a number of large warts on her nose. She was a good German speaker and did her best to teach me a few phrases which I could use on my journey through Germany. It was a very happy time. I was 19, had done well at Sandhurst, owned a little car and was off to unknown adventures in it. Moreover I was eagerly looking forward to joining my Regiment, the culmination as it were of all my education: of the miseries of Walton Lodge, the struggles at Haileybury and the happiness of Sandhurst.

I set off for Germany in my little car in mid-August. The boot behind was stuffed with luggage, but the main bulk of it was in a suitcase beside me on the passenger seat. My father had seen a large signed photograph of Adolf Hitler in the *Sketch* or the *Tatler*, and suggested I frame it and put it on the top of my suitcase to impress the natives into believing that I was a young protégé of the Fuhrer. The effect was always dynamic. Whoever looked into my suitcase, slammed down the lid very quickly, clicked his heels, raised his arm and shouted 'Heil Hitler'. I duly replied in kind, but had a rather special salute with hand partially closed and two fingers outstretched ... On one occasion I was stopped on the road by a couple of rather unpleasant-looking young storm troopers, who officiously wished to search my luggage, but became all frightened smiles directly they saw old Adolf leering at them from the top of my suitcase. When I got to Munich, I told the von Dobenecks about the incident and they said I was very fortunate not to have been robbed, my car

197

stolen and myself left by the side of the road, all in one piece if I was lucky.

My immediate impression of Germany was how, after my journey through France, like England it was. Why, even my room in the little hotel at Freudenstadt in the Black Forest contained a chamber pot under the bed as in all English hotels, and unheard of in France, where a long drain down the corridor was provided instead, with a plank with a hole in it above, on which you perched in the morning. I had crossed the Rhine at Kehl, and driven up the winding road into the Black Forest. Freudenstadt was a riot of swastika flags draped from every window and flying on strings across every street. Columns of unwilling-looking small boys in Nazi uniforms were being marched along the roads by officious uniformed leaders. I was reminded of a village or town fête in England, with Boy Scouts instead of the Hitler Jugend. They slouched along with the same resentful, bored expression, but these seemed to possess a seriousness unknown in England.

Next day I continued through Ulm to Augsburg. All along the way, every hamlet, every village, every town, every city, was festooned with Nazi flags and bunting. The entire country seemed to be *en fête*, but in fact I discovered that flags everywhere was the normal condition. I stopped for another night at a village hotel, where sleep was made impossible by German regiments marching through all night on their way to summer manoeuvres, their bands blaring. In this it was totally unlike England, where in case they disturbed the inhabitants, the Army would either have to wrap their boots in flannel and creep round the edge, or not be allowed to march at all. However, during breakfast, which was served outside on a kind of patio, I kept bounding up to people, who by their dress and manner seemed to be English, only to be met with a smile and a shake of the head. One had a new Leica 35mm camera outfit using cine film, never used before in a still camera. The Leica was the latest photographic concept, able to use a number of easily changed lenses of different focal lengths and other gadgets, all easily portable in a fitted case. The Leica raised amateur photography to a new level, and was later to revolutionise the professional market as well.

If I had imagined that life with the von Dobenecks would be

198

similar to that at La Matholière, I was sadly mistaken. As for learning German, that was another mistake, for nobody seemed to speak it at all, but only English. All the other guests were Americans, including to my astonishment, Roger Black, the Rhodes scholar with whom I had been skiing the previous winter. Freiherr von Dobeneck had been an officer in the Bavarian Lehr Regiment, and was killed on the Somme in 1916. The Regiment later was expanded and became the famous Panzer Lehr Division in the next war. His widow. the Freifrau, now eked out a fairly prosperous living taking foreign guests who ostensibly wished to be taught German, but were not too put out if everyone spoke English. There were any amount of things to do in Munich at the time, besides having to bother with the language. The Freiherr had left three sons, Joachim, Klaus and Henning, all in their early twenties and over six feet in height. The title approximates to ours of Baron, the difference being that every male issue inherits it. Thus Germany was awash with Freiherrs and Herr Barons, and maybe still is for all I know.

Joachim was the eldest, and he and Henning, the youngest, had joined the SS. Klaus would have nothing to do with the Nazis, whom he loathed and despised at all times. He emigrated to the USA during the mid-1930s and came back to Germany with the American Army as an interpreter. Joachim was killed in a Waffen SS Division early during Hitler's invasion of Russia. Henning was taken prisoner at Stalingrad and not heard of for ten years. His wife, presuming him dead, had married again, causing all kinds of complications when he returned without warning. In 1956, whilst serving with the Argylls in Berlin, I went down to Munich to meet her and the Freifrau, now old and very frail. They told me that his return had not been a happy one as he never got over his ten years captivity in Russia and had once more disappeared. His son, however, was a charming boy of about 14, who clicked his heels and bowed on meeting me, in the best Freiherr tradition. As for Henning I never heard of him again, the millstone of having been in the SS would forever hang around his neck. Klaus, the clever one, who had sensed the direction of the wind and gone over to the other side, continued to flourish.

However, in 1933 the SS had not acquired the evil reputation it was later to achieve. It was 'the thing' to belong to, rather as our own Brigade of Guards, and was full of young German aristocrats, such as the von Dobenecks, von Lessings, von Dinclages and others that I met. Nor were they in any way anti-Jewish, though looking back, I doubt a Jew would have been very welcome, not for being a Jew, but a strange individual who would not fit in. During the two months I was in Munich, I scarcely heard Jews mentioned. Through the head of his Security branch, Heinrich Himmler, the Fuhrer had organised the SS, a body of men, spread throughout Germany, upon whose loyalty and devotion, sworn on oath, he could utterly depend, no matter the circumstances. The Germans are great oath-takers and usually abide by what they have sworn. To us, swearing such oaths would be so dramatic as to be a bit of a giggle. Furthermore, no-one could possibly doubt our loyalty under any and every circumstance, or ask us to carry out some act which was illegal, as the SS were later required to do. Thus many of the atrocities ascribed to them were carried out under orders, against which every instinct revolted. In those days too, the Germans took enormous pride in 'obeying orders', whatever their own opinion or inclination in the matter. Simply to obey to the letter, the orders of a superior was a virtue in itself, however stupid, brutal or unreasonable. 'Theirs not to reason why' in fact. In 1933, perhaps the most insufferable, conceited creature in all Europe was any small German boy who had been patted on the head by a German policeman.

Himmler had taken the Order of the Jesuits as a model on which to base the SS, and its organisation was largely on similar lines. The SS, an abbreviation of *Schutz Staffel*, means 'Protection Squadron', and into squadrons it was originally formed. These during the war, were expanded to become Waffen SS Divisions of some 17,000 men each, which fought alongside the rest of the German Army in the normal way, but also remained highly political, and always contained the most fanatical Nazis. Their commander was one Sepp Dietrich, an ignorant butcher. The general conduct of the Waffen SS, with some deplorable exceptions, should not be confused with the deeds of the Gestapo, the special SS Extermination Squads, or SS Concentration Camp Guards, all part of the SS and under Himmler's control. However, the whole organisation wore the death's-head badge of the Order, the same black Dress uniform, and the overall name of SS. In 1933, physical requirements for entry were very high. Candidates had to be under 25, of pure German Aryan stock for at least two generations on either side, and be of a general physical fitness of a high order. For instance, the SS Leib Standarte, Hitler's personal bodyguard, would not accept a man who had even as much as a single tooth filling. To me, Joachim and Henning were part of an elite, and I thoroughly approved of, even envied them. I knew all about being part of an elite. The whole of my education had impressed upon me that I was part of one, and it was my duty to live up to it, even to the privilege of being one of the first to die.

Besides the *Schutz Staffel*, who could be numbered in thousands, there was also the *Sturm Abteilung*, the SA, who numbered at least a million. The words mean 'Storm Division' and these are the men who will always be remembered as stormtroopers. They were recruited mainly from young men who would now be active as football hooligans, and it was two of these who had stopped me on the road to Munich. During the Nazis' rise to power, their chief enemy had been the Communists. In fact it was the fear of Communism and Bolshevik Russia that caused so many Germans, especially the upper and middle classes, to flock to the Nazi cause. Everywhere I went I heard, 'I am a Nazi because Hitler was the only one who could save us from the Communists.' To deal with the young Communists, who were especially numerous in all the large cities, it was essential to 'win the streets'. To do this, the SA was formed and had to fight cease-less running battles. I do not think the fear of Communism has ever been sufficiently emphasised in any account of Hitler's rise to power. The *Sturm Abteilung* were led by Ernst Roehm, a notorious, brutal, utterly ruthless, homosexual ex-Army officer who had been very highly decorated for bravery during the Great War. For the high moral tone the Nazis claimed to set, his blatant homosexuality was a continual source of embarrassment. Furthermore, commanding as he did, a force of over a million men throughout Germany, he was suspected of posing a threat to Hitler himself. Like Hitler, he sported a 'front line' tooth-brush moustache, denoting he had had to shave off the previous luxuriant growth beloved of so many pre-War Germans, in order to fit into a gas mask. To have such a moustache meant you had been a front-line soldier. Half the men in Germany seemed to wear them, whether to copy the Fuhrer or claim to have been front-line soldiers I never discovered, for it was a difficult question to ask.

Roehm wished to incorporate the SA with the Army, which under the Versailles Treaty could only be 100,000 strong, a move which caused consternation among the Generals. The Army was a highly trained, dedicated and carefully selected organisation of professionals; a training cadre which could be expanded tenfold almost overnight, by drafting in recruits. When Hitler became democratically elected Chancellor of Germany on 30 January 1933, one of the undertakings he gave President Hindenburg, who loathed him and described him as 'that Bohemian corporal', was that the Army would never be put under the control of the SA. Such an undertaking came easily to Hitler, and suited his methods entirely. By keeping almost every department of State continuously at each other's throats, it made his task of controlling them all that much the easier. To ensure the loyalty of the Army, every man and officer in it was made to swear an oath of allegiance personally to Adolf Hitler.

Whether Roehm intended to use the SA in a bid for power or not is hard to say, but certainly throughout 1933 and 1934, despite his outward show of almost abject loyalty at the Nuremburg rallies, Hitler suspected that he did. On 30 June, a year after I was in Germany, the Fuhrer decided to act. In May he had given the SA a month's leave. Roehm and a number of high-ranking friends had taken a villa on the Starnberger See, a large lake near Munich. That fatal night in June, 'the night of the long knives', the Munich SS, under secret orders, surrounded the villa, arrested Roehm on charges of 'sodomy and threatening to overturn the State'. He, together with all his companions, was taken out and shot, many protesting to the end that if Hitler knew, it could never happen, many shouting 'Heil Hitler' as they died, thinking they were being killed in an anti-Hitler SS coup. At the same time as eliminating Roehm, Hitler could not resist the temptation of disposing of anyone and everyone who could possibly be suspected of any kind of political opposition. Many died, including the completely innocent General Schleicher, who was shot down in front of his wife. Nobody escaped. The operation was too swift and too secret. Furthermore it served as a salutary lesson to discourage plots against the Fuhrer for some years to come. The Nazi-controlled Press made much of 'cleaning up Roehm's homosexual sink of iniquity', and that all the SA commanders on the Starnberger See had been found naked in bed with young men. Another prominent Nazi, Gregor Strasser, who had been Hitler's companion during his rise to power, and at one time an actual contender for the leadership of the Party, was also liquidated. His brother Otto was abroad and immediately fled to Czecho-Slovakia, from where he set up an anti-Nazi broadcasting station.

However for me in Munich, all that was in the future. At the time in Germany, all was bustle and promise. I felt they were building a new heaven and a new earth, compared to which everything in England appeared stale and apathetic. That the Germans were officious there is no doubt, always reporting on each other, or telling them what to do. So much was '*verboten*'. It was '*verboten*' to walk on the grass in the Munich Park, the 'Englischer Garten'. If you walked on the grass, at least a hundred Germans would tell you not to. I thought of a similar notice in France, which would ensure that everyone would walk on it, or in England where nobody would, but if they did, no-one would take any notice, pretending they had not seen. Although learning little or no German from the family, I had great fun gently teasing the Freifrau. She had an almost pathological grudge against the French and British, who had not only defeated the Germans, but had allowed, even encouraged, Communists to overrun Bavaria in the 1920s, from whom her friends in the various Freikorps, one of which developed into the Nazis, had delivered them.

Another perennial complaint was over the former German East African colonies, 'Vich you haf stolen from us.' Any least remark could be construed as a criticism of Germany, even something as innocent as wondering if it was going to rain that afternoon. '*Ach so!*' she would exclaim, 'You are feeble, you are effete, you do not like our Cherman vetter.' I liked her enormously, but could not help devising ways of bringing about paroxysms of indignation.

One such was the matter of the trams. For some reason the trams were an object of intense Munich civic pride. Apparently throughout the world there was no tram system to compare with it in speed, punctuality, price and general comfort. The Freifrau urged me to use this wonderful facility more often, to which I replied that I never used trams if I could possibly avoid it from fear of catching ringworm. This produced an outburst which kept her happy for days, until I managed to divert her back to '*Ach so,* you do not like our Cherman vetter.' However, I succeeded in setting her off again to fresh indignation by insinuating that the Changing of the Guard by the Lehr Regiment, in front of the Munich Town Hall, was dozy and idle. In fact it was first class, but I had no doubt that CSM Giddings would have bucked them up a bit.

There was always something to do in Munich. Most mornings I would go riding in the Englischer Garten. It was called that because it was supposed to resemble an English garden, but was in fact more like a large country house park. In the afternoons we would normally go swimming in one of the many outdoor bathing places. The period was the apogee of the '*Kraft durch Freude*' (strength through joy) movement, and thousands of young Germans could be found capering about, exercising themselves in the sunshine around the lakes and rivers where we swam. Nobody actually seemed to be enjoying themselves or would admit to it. All appeared to be in deadly earnest, preparing for the future glory of the Fatherland. Such sentiments in England would have been treated as an enormous joke.

In the evening we would either go dancing at the Regina Palast hotel, or to one of the many beer halls for which Munich is famous, the best known being the Hofbrau Haus. The city abounded in breweries, and I am afraid that I still consider the taste of German beer the best in the world, though drunk as it often now is in English pubs, it somehow tastes all wrong. The Hofbrau Haus was a huge long hall, holding perhaps over 500 drinkers. We sat on benches at long, scrubbed, wooden tables, linked arms and sang choruses to an oompah band in Bavarian costume, which played at one end. Soon a very strong head of steam would be raised by one and all. The beer was served in one litre (two pints approximately) stone 'steins' or tankards. Enormous Brunhildes of serving *Maedchen*, with legs and arms like hams, also in Bavarian dress, would dart from table to table, carrying six or seven such steins along each arm. We normally got through four or five steins of beer, and it was rare to be able to get back to one's bed in the Wilhelmstrasse without the world spinning around a little.

Getting slightly bored with the routine and wishing to see something more of Europe, I suggested to Roger Black that we take off in my little car, drive through Austria, visit Vienna, and then go on to have a look at Budapest. The Freifrau raised no objection, and even agreed we would not have to pay for our rooms and board whilst we were away. I had originally asked Joachim if he would come with me, but he said that no German could go abroad without paying a fine of 50,000 marks. This was done to save currency, but also produced a source of national revenue from those who had seen the writing on the wall and wished to flee the country. We crossed into the Austrian Tirol at Mittenwald. In 1933 people in the Tirol still drove on the left, whilst the remaining Austrian provinces used the right. It was rather as if Yorkshire had decided to drive on the opposite side of the road to the rest of England. The difference between Germany and Austria was striking. Everything seemed shabby and drab, the roads were ill-kept and full of potholes, whilst the inhabitants appeared to be without hope.

It was not until we reached St Polten, some 40 miles from Vienna, that we got on a road worthy of the name. We stayed in the city very cheaply at a small hotel. Everywhere in Vienna there were beggars. We went out one evening to the famous Grinzing, sitting at tables under the trees, drinking wine and listening to a band playing Strauss waltzes. Even here there were beggars, mostly young and attractive girls, going from table to table with outstretched palms and parrot cries of '*Nur essen, nur essen, nicht schlaffen*' (Only to eat, not to sleep). After the new heady prosperity and enthusiasm of Germany, it was very depressing. We moved on to Budapest.

If we thought the Austrian roads were bad and potholed, they were like billiard tables compared to those we found in Hungary. Furthermore they seemed strewn with nails and other pointed objects. We had two punctures within the first few miles, and no means of repairing the tyres. There was nothing for it but to put the vehicle in bottom gear, adjust the hand throttle on the steering wheel, and trundle along, walking beside it until we arrived after five miles, at a small town called Moson. Here an enormous crowd of children gathered around the car, never having seen anything like it, and the punctures were mended by the local blacksmith. On arrival at Budapest, we decided not to slum it as we had in Vienna, but to stay at the St Gelerts Hotel. This had a wonderful new out-door swimming pool which, every half hour or so, created artificial waves. We spent nearly all our time sitting around the pool, sipping beer and talking to a party of Mid-West Americans, who were 'doing Europe'. They had resolutely refused to reset their watches, and were as they boasted 'still on good old USA Mid-West time, and what was OK for Uncle Sam was good enough for them'. The rest of our time in Budapest we spent lying in the sun in the thermal baths on St Margaret's Island in the middle of the Danube. I even found time from these exertions to take a picture of the Hungarian Houses of Parliament.

Of our return journey to Munich I can recall nothing; except that there was such a headwind from the Austrian frontier that my poor little car was actually blown backwards. I spent a final week at the Wilhelmstrasse, making an arrangement with the von Dobenecks that, if in the remote possibility of England and Germany ever being at war again, and any of us made prisoner, we would contact each others' families. I had enjoyed my stay very much, and funnily enough had picked up more German on my way to Budapest and back than ever I had in Munich. I had heard or seen nothing of the evils even then being committed by the Nazi Party, and I left as an enthusiastic admirer of both it and its Fuhrer, Adolf Hitler. There was no part of my background, upbringing or education which might dispose me to dislike dictators. In one form or other I had been moulded by them all my life, telling me what to do, say, wear or even think. Nor was I alone in such sentiments about Germany. I never met anyone in England who had been there at the time who had not returned with similar opinions.

I still had a week or so before I had to report to the HLI. My father came with me to London, where we went to Hawkes for a final fitting and to pick up all my kit and uniform. He told me that he would make me the same allowance of £100 a year which his father had made him in 1900. On my pointing out that due to inflation it was worth about a third of what it was then, he was singularly unimpressed. Furthermore he was making clucking matrimonial sounds of which I was unaware, the object of his attention sadly not being the delightful Gladys Parsons, but an altogether different kettle of fish. She was Esther Logan, the divorced wife of Uncle Jimmy's brother Alfred, a Harley Street consultant for whom she had originally worked as a nurse. Whether my father considered this a form of life insurance or not, someone medically trained for his old age, I never found out. As for Esther, immediately after their first meeting, she told my grandmother, 'I'm going to get him!' From the day he married her, she began to poison his mind, drip by drip, against me. Never again was there our former friendly and easy companionship. If I were asked to pick a cricket team of horrendous women to play for England against the Rest of the World, then Twig's mother, Marjorie Corner, and Esther Logan, my father's new wife, would undoubtedly have opened our innings. Nor was Esther by any means either a raw hand when it came to bowling a googly.

17

Two dogs were copulating on the barrack square, surrounded by a crowd of Jocks yelling encouragment, that mid-October afternoon in 1933 as Dick Kindersley and I drove through the grim portals of Shaft Barracks in Dover. Apart from this, the place appeared completely deserted and without life. Looking back, it seems to have been a fitting introduction to the British Army of the day. I had met Dick as we both got off the train at Dover station and we shared a taxi up to the barracks. He had been to Wellington College and then to Trinity Cambridge, getting his Commission from there with 18 months seniority. He told me he lived on the Isle of Wight and had not wanted to join the HLI at all, but had tried for the 60th Rifles, where there were no vacancies. Furthermore it would seem that his main reason for wishing to join the 60th was because dogs were allowed in the Mess, but as I never saw him with a dog all the time I knew him, there must have been another motive. Dick was one of the most outstanding officers I ever met. He was also very handsome, irresistible to women whom he also found irresistible in large numbers, loved by the Jocks whom he never punished and to whom he was known as 'Cushy Dick', calm and utterly unflappable no matter the circumstances and with a great sense of humour. He commanded the 2nd Battalion during the war in the Western Desert and won the MC and a DSO. He also knew his job, which he may have learned whilst in the OTC at Cambridge, because I don't know where else he could have learnt it.

Shaft Barracks had been built during the Napoleonic Wars as a fort to protect Dover from invasion. It lay on the heights above the west side of the town, and was constructed almost completely underground, with hidden gun emplacements pointing out to sea all round its fortifications, their crews' quarters beside the guns. Two of these old quarters were now used as the officer's Mess. We wandered around for a time, even yelled encouragement to the dogs, until we met an officer wearing a sword, or rather a Scottish claymore, followed by an NCO with a red sash, the Orderly Officer and his Sergeant on their rounds. We introduced ourselves and were taken off to the Mess for tea. The room was crowded with officers in plain clothes. Nobody except the Orderly Officer wore uniform after lunch. Everbody stood up to greet us and we were treated as honoured guests. Tea was an elaborate affair, with wafer-thin cucumber and other sandwiches, scones and fruit cake. The tea was poured from silver pots, as was the milk. Every now and then Mess waiters in white jackets and tartan trews would replenish what we had eaten. The Mess had hired a civilian caterer called Mr Giffard, who was always around in tails and white tie, seeing that things were as they should be. He got paid £100 a year, the free run of his teeth and gullet, he drank but little, and the use of a small room where he slept with the cheeses under his bed. During the year I was in Dover, we could not have been better or more sumptuously fed had we been living at Claridges or the Savoy. How he managed to produce such meals on the four shillings a day subscription we each paid is beyond comprehension. How could anyone produce breakfast, lunch, tea and dinner, the last invariably of five courses, at a shilling (5p) each? He left us when we moved to Fort George near Inverness in November 1934, claiming that it was too far north and he hated Eskimos. I never found out what happened to him, but I hope he became a butler in some grand house, where he could continue to keep the Stilton under his bed, convinced that it not only made him sleep better but matured faster.

Of the many officers who greeted us that afternoon, I can only remember two. One was Tobias Matthews. If I had to describe a typical British officer of his day then Tobias would be the proto-type, all of whom possessed unknown, surprising and unguessable interests. Outwardly a Philistine of the Philistines, he secretly loved ballet and went to see it whenever he could. Aged about 34, he had joined the Regiment in 1918, just too late for the war, and after 14 years as a Subaltern had been promoted Captain. He had recently been posted back from the 2nd Bn in India where he had spent ten years, and as he boasted, had not managed to learn a word of the language, other than to be able to order his horse, a whisky and his bath. Small and compact, he had the little tooth-brush moustache sported by so many British officers, his face rather prematurely veined and somewhat purplish from heavy drinking, especially in India, where it was considered the only antidote for malaria and other unpleasant diseases. His fingers were stained by the innumerable Turkish cigarettes he smoked, the only ones allowed in the Mess, and always carried in a silver cigarette case, never a packet. Virginian cigarettes such as Players or Gold Flake were strictly taboo, and not considered the sort of thing smoked by gentlemen. He asked if we hunted, shot or fished. I diffidently said I had been out with the Chiddingfold, which he described as a 'birdcage of barbed wire', as also was the local Hunt. He regaled us with tales of pig-sticking in Cawnpore and seemed convinced that there 'was nothing an old dog fox liked more than being hunted', especially, I imagined, if it was going to be torn to pieces at the end of it.

In fact I gathered that Tobias Matthews was really only happy when he was chasing, shooting or catching some unfortunate animal, bird or fish and killing it, or another just like it, if possible every day. Off duty he was always as immaculately turned out as on parade, with tweed suit or check hacking jacket and grey flannel trousers, Highland Brigade or Regimental tie, and black highly polished Highland brogue shoes. His conversation was entirely confined to the slaughter of animals, horse-racing or London gossip. Of his secret yearning for the ballet we knew nothing. As with so many in the Army like him, his outward attitude had probably begun as an ingratiating pose, become a habit and then a way of life. A confirmed bachelor, he took no interest in women whatsoever other than insisting that 'a dose of clap was no worse than a bad cold'. He eventually retired to the south of Scotland, where he spent his remaining years otter-hunting. Of his profession he had been profoundly and deliberately ignorant throughout his career, insisting that 'the hunting field gave such an eye for country that it was all the training anybody ever needed'. He had finished the war commanding a battalion.

The other person I remember meeting that afternoon was a tall gangling Subaltern with a large bushy moustache and a mass of unruly dark hair, called Geordie Barclay-Lloyd, scion of an old Scottish family. He had a brother in a Guards regiment who disappeared under mysterious circumstances in Germany, and another who became a Minister. Geordie had adopted the pose of being a kind of military Oscar Wilde. 'Next time, dear boy,' he whispered as we were introduced, 'you simply must come and have tea with me in my room, but,' he went on, 'don't be surprised if you find me in bed with an elderly Gurkha corporal.' He undulated away, giggling. Some years previously, Geordie had been posted to the 2nd Battalion in India, where as he said, 'things became absolutely too much for me altogether, what with the heat, the flies and the natives'. He either actually went mad or feigned madness, for he was brought home by troopship in a padded cell. On landing he had rejoined the 1st Bn in Dover. Normally he would have been taken to the Army loony bin at Netley, but for 'the sake of the Regiment', the necessary strings had been pulled. For a time he had a civilian keeper who looked after him and kept him out of mischief when not on parade. His brother officers in the Regiment hid him from the sight of visiting generals or other awkward inspecting officers. By the time I joined he had recovered a fair level of sanity and the keeper had left.

Personally I always considered Geordie Barclay-Lloyd was much saner than he made out, nor by any means were his preferences solely those of Oscar Wilde. Geordie's were mainly part of a deliberate pose. He had a Schnautzer dog, and you would often see him and the dog sitting around the better Dover hotels waiting until some unaccompanied female came in who took his fancy. Directly she went to the women's loo, he would put the dog in after her as if it were a ferret after a rabbit, then hang about outside until she came out. 'Oh how awful,' he would say, 'my bad dog followed you in, and I daren't go in to let him out, do you think you could do it for me?' Nothing in Britain, of course, is a better ice breaker than a common interest over a dog. The rest was up to Geordie, and he said the system never failed.

These were then but two of the 35 or so 'brother officers' of the 1st Bn The Highland Light Infantry with whom I was going to share the next 30-odd years of my life. So absolutely divorced from reality did they seem, or the situation from anything I had ever experienced before, that I really wondered if I had arrived in a madhouse, or had stepped, like Alice, through a looking glass. Furthermore there were still some very peculiar characters waiting for me to meet.

Fully to understand the intricacies of life in the Army in the 1930s, it is necessary to explain how it was organised and armed at the time. If the thought of this brings irrepressible tedium, it might be advisable to skip the next few pages. In 1871, Cardwell, the Minister for War, had introduced the 'two battalion system' to police and guard the rapidly expanding British Empire, especially India, over which Queen Victoria had recently been made Empress. At that date, the British Regular Army had consisted of some 100 Infantry Regiments of the Line, each a battalion strong, of some 800 men, and each bearing a number which carried centuries of fighting tradition on its colours, most loathing and despising every other Regiment but their own, which was invariably 'the best in the Army'. For instance the 50th were known as 'the Diehards', because their Colonel, mortally wounded at Salamanca, had shouted to his men as he expired, 'Die hard Fiftieth!' Most had their own recruitment area in the UK, but few were named as such, merely known by their number, though some like the 71st were also called the Highland Light Infantry. They had also lost the kilt when made into Light Infantry. To become a Light Infantry regiment was a great honour in 1802, equivalent to that of Commando today. Quite why the kilt should have been considered an unsuitable garment for such duties is one of those perennial military mysteries so beloved of the British Army. The Highlanders had been galloping around the Scottish mountains in it for generations, making themselves a general nuisance to one and all. The loss of the kilt caused misery and heartache to the HLI for a hundred years to come. It was returned to them in 1947, only to be snatched away again ten years later, when they were amalgamated with the Royal Scots Fusiliers.

212

In addition to the Infantry of the Line, there were three Guards regiments, Grenadier, Coldstream and Scots, the two former having four battalions each, and the Scots, two. In addition there was the 60th Rifles of two battalions and the Rifle Brigade of four. There were also about 21 Cavalry regiments of 800 men each and numerous regiments of Royal Artillery and Royal Engineers, for all of whom the word 'regiment' was the equivalent tactical unit of an infantry battalion. To the uninitiated, it was, and still remains, very confusing.

The Cardwell reforms really only concerned the Infantry of the Line. All regiments with numbers below 26 now had two battalions, the rest were amalgamated with each other by twos, becoming the 1st or 2nd battalion, given a county or some other name and a training depot in the principal city of that county. Thus were born such famous fighting names as the Devons, the Gloucesters, the Middlesex and so on. In Scotland, six Highland Regiments were so formed, one of which was the Highland Light Infantry out of the 71st HLI and the 74th Highlanders, who became the 1st and 2nd Bns respectively, with their depot at Maryhill Barracks in Glasgow. The two former Regiments cordially loathed one another, and even in my early days officers were resigning their Commissions rather than be posted to the other, or paying volunteers large sums of money to take their posting instead. For me there was no comparison between the two, the 74th was always the better and I even have my pacemaker set at the magical number of 74. In addition to the six Highland regiments, there were five Lowland and some six Irish, all of the now stipulated two battalions.

No Guards battalions served further afield than Egypt, except to take part in various local or colonial wars such as the Sudan or South Africa. Nearly all the rest of the Army had one battalion in India, and the other at home which supplied fresh drafts of men to the foreign one as required. Both officers and men rotated between home and abroad. Cavalry regiments were posted back and forth as a whole. Keeping horses in the heat of India was considered bad for them. Furthermore, Regiments such as the Queens Bays or Royal Scots Greys had horses of a particular uniform colour. Nor could men be expected to be deprived of the animals they knew, cared for and loved, which would occur were they to take over the former unit's horses on arrival at the new station.

Terms of service for men were seven years with the colours and five in reserve, liable for immediate call-up if required. However, at the end of seven years many could, and did, sign up for 21 years' service. Officers served for their working life and their Regiment was their parent unit, whatever staff or other appointment they happened to hold. Thus the first question asked of any officer, often even before his name, was, 'What is his Regiment?' the social position of which would be immediately recognised but never spoken, and of which I gave a description in an earlier chapter. An officer could leave the Army whenever he wished, merely by writing a letter to his Commanding Officer resigning his Commission. In fact he was often required to do so rather than 'disgrace the Regiment', by facing court martial, passing a dud cheque, falsifying his orderly officer's report or sleeping with a brother officer's wife, which was highly frowned upon and likely to lead to Regimental discord. I found out in India, however, that there were degrees to which this last was acceptable, provided people set about it in the right way.

Thus with fewer men than contained in all their Legions at the height of the Roman Empire, the British Army, conquered, held, policed and defended a third of the population of the world. It was a remarkable feat, but certainly could never have been done without the acceptance of the peoples we governed, who also proudly raised forces of their own, such as the magnificent Indian Army, led by British officers who had all gone through the identical public school system. Some of them, especially such as those in the Gurkhas and the Corps of Guides, serving together, British officer and Indian soldier, father and son, for generations.

At the end of the Great War in November 1918, the British Army had consisted of some five million men, the greatest number in all its history, before or since. It had also lost nearly a million dead. During that war, the expansion had all been done on the Cardwell regimental system, each regiment simply raising and training many more battalions. For instance, the HLI raised 26 battalions, or some 21,000 men during the conflict. If you add the dead and wounded, the total is probably nearer 30,000. By the mid-1920s the Army had shrunk to its former pre-war size. By then the War Office had even begun tinkering with the Cavalry. Amidst a riot of apoplectic indignation, two regiments had been mechanised and become Armoured Car Regiments. The rest retained their horses but a number were amalgamated with each other, such as the 13/18th Hussars or 17/21st Lancers. Many such amalgamations did not run at all smoothly, officers being allowed to wear their old uniforms, and sitting glaring at each other on either side of the Mess table, or forming little regimental groups in the ante-room. In the late 1930s all the Cavalry lost their horses, were given tanks instead and became regiments of the Royal Armoured Corps, of which I would have been part had I joined the RTC from Sandhurst. I remember an early war cartoon in 1939 of an officer and a girl contemplating their broken-down car, and the girl is saying, 'Call yourself a cavalry officer and you can't even get it to go!'

Dick Kindersley and I were told to report to C Company at nine o'clock the next morning. In the Company HQ office we found 'Sixty' Smith, the Company Sergeant Major, along with CSM Giddings at Sandhurst the second of my two most vivid and unforgettable Army characters. Giddings did everything by the book, Sixty did nothing by it. He was unique in his methods, and the best CSM I ever knew, running not only the Company, but manipulating the Company Commander and the officers in exactly the way he wanted. He was ably assisted in this by Company Quartermaster Sergeant, CQMS 'Dusty' Miller. All named Miller in the Army were known as 'Dusty'. Sixty got his name from the last two digits of his number, to distinguish him from other Smiths on roll call, for instance 'Smith 21, Smith 43, Smith 60' and so on. Sixty was a small, stocky, immensely strong man of about forty, with an infectious chuckle. He had joined the 2nd HLI or 74th in 1912, and had gone to France in 1914, where he had survived all the main Great War battles with it, the retreat from Mons, the Somme, Paschendaele, without a scratch and a reputation for bravery and a charmed life. He had won the DCM and MM, both with bars, meaning he had earned them twice over. He rarely raised his voice, and always seemed to treat life as a huge joke. As far as discipline was concerned, he rarely if ever put a Jock on a charge, preferring to take him behind the barrack block and give him a good walloping with his pace stick. One of the better features of the HLI at Dover was the absence of bullshit.

Everyone from the CO downwards knew him as 'Sixty', but it was not for newly joined 2nd Lieuts to call him that. You had to gain his respect and friendship first. If the discipline, drill, and general running of the Company were in the hands of the CSM, its pay, clothing, and food were in those of the CQMS Dusty Miller, a rotund, red-faced, cheerful little man, who had also fought with the HLI from 1916 onwards. He and Sixty were part of the band of 'old sweats', magnificent NCOs who had served with either battalion in and out of the tropics, knew their job inside out, and who really ran the 71st. Sixty told me I had been given No 9 Platoon, but save for the Platoon Sergeant, Pollendine, another old sweat, and Private Dillaway, who became my batman, all the men were on the draft for India, leaving in the next few days. No 9 Platoon had been the future film star David Niven's whilst he was in the HLI, and Dillaway his batman. Niven had just fled to the USA after an acerbic altercation with a local General, and describes his life in the 71st wonderfully in his book, '*The Moon's a Balloon*'. Jim Dillaway remained my batman until I left for India in 1936, and rejoined me in 1940 in the 5th HLI. He stayed with me until 1944. During all this time he never stopped regaling me with stories of his beloved 'Mr Niven'. The Company Commander, Major Henry 'Bullet-proof' Hawkins MC, was also on the draft, a large athletic man who came in later, saw us with Sixty and said, 'Oh good, I'm glad you are getting to know each other.' He introduced me to our new Company Commander, Captain 'Fuzzy' Robertson.

Like Tobias Matthews, Fuzzy had just missed the war, joining in 1919. But he had been to Murmansk or somewhere, and had qualified for two war medals. A splendid photographer and better than a dab hand when it came to waving a Leica, as a military commander he was a positive disaster. He had only been given C Company because he was the next senior in line. Whenever there was a big parade, for he was incapable of giving a correct command, or important manoeuvres where Generals might be around, he was taken away and put in charge of some apparently

216

essential but innocuous job where he could do but little harm. His 2ic, Titus Oatts then took over the Company. The German War Academy classified the best kind of officer as 'being able and idle', the worst as 'stupid and industrious'. Titus earned full marks on both counts for the former category. Arriving for duty at 9 a.m., he was usually away home to his wife by 11.30 for his mid-morning gin. In fact 'doing an Oatts' became a Regimental synonym for sloping off early. We became great friends. To me he will always remain the very embodiment of Chaucer's 'veree gentil parfait knighte'. As for Fuzzy, he was of course a great Regimental asset, being more than somewhat wealthy, and having many friends and relations in high places who could pull all kinds of strings on our behalf.

The Battalion was in fact run by the Commanding Officer, who held the appointment for three years, and his Staff officers, the Adjutant, usually a Captain or Major, and the Quartermaster, Captain (QM) Innes. The QM was invariably promoted from the ranks with a Quartermaster's Commission. All the subordinate tasks were done by the Old Sweats, through the RSM, Regimental Sergeant Major McGarva, who gave orders to the CSMs. Under the QM there was also an RQMS (Regimental Quartermaster Sgt Major), who worked with the CQM Sergeants in the companies. In theory the battalion should have been 800 strong, but due to the defence cuts, the continual drafts to India, where the 74th had to be kept at full strength, it rarely exceeded 500 men. All British Infantry Battalions were then organised on 'the fours principle'. We 'formed fours' and marched in columns of four. There were four sections to a platoon (Pl), four platoons to a company (Coy), four Coys to a battalion (Bn), four Bns to a brigade (Bde) and four Bdes to a division (Div). Beyond that one got into the realms of outer space. This organisation was exactly that of the British Army of 1914. Some concession had been made to modern war, however, and one of the Coys was now a Medium Machine Gun Coy, comprising 16 of the Vickers water-cooled machine guns firing from a tripod, which had caused such deadly havoc in Flanders. These were now towed by Cardon Lloyd caterpillar tractor vehicles, which invariably broke down. In addition to the three Rifle and MG Coys, there was also an HQ Coy, comprising

217

Bn HQ with its attendant clerks, and other hangers on, such as the Signals and the Transport Platoons.

Other than the Cardon Lloyds, the whole of the transport was still horse-drawn. There were 'chargers' for the CO, Adjt and Signals officer, as well as one for each of the Coy commanders. Each week we had a route march of some 14 miles, and Fuzzy Robertson usually rode his horse most of the way. As commander of the leading Pl, no 9, marching right behind it, I got the full benefit of the animal's extremely smelly and noisy farts. I used to put tunes to them, and I reckoned 'it could fart all the Psalms, the best part of Brahms and the whole of the Moonlight Sonata'. It could also without the slightest provocation, produce enough urine to 'win the Swiss endurance piss'.

Besides Fuzzy's charger, there was another horse which pulled the Company reserve ammunition cart. Each man carried 100 rounds on him, and there were a further 50 in reserve on the cart. It was divided into two parts: one carried the ammunition, the rations and the rum ration in a large stone jar. Rum could only be issued under very exceptional circumstances, conditions of weather or stress. It was amazing how frequently these occurred. The second part of the cart consisted of a Soyer stove. Soyer was head Chef at the Savoy Hotel during the Crimean War in 1854, and had invented the stove for use by the British Army. It was a wonderful invention and continued in use until 1938. It consisted of a charcoal or coke slow-burning stove with a long chimney. A large pan of stew and another of tea were always ready for the men whenever required. It had performed the most wonderful service during the Great War.

Each of the Rifle sections of the Pl consisted of a Cpl or Lance Cpl, and seven men armed with the .303 calibre SMLE rifle which had been standard since the Boer War. In addition each section had a Lewis light machine gun (LMG), which was fed from a revolving drum holding 47 rounds of the same ammunition. Unlike the Vickers MG, it was air-cooled, and jammed constantly. It could be dismantled into its many component parts, and reassembled with no other tool than the nose of a round of its own ammunition. It had been our main infantry weapon from about 1915 onwards. Apart therefore from minor modifications, the

218

Infantry Bn was organised and armed exactly as it had been in 1918. Tactical thought too had never really left the trenches, where senior officers had learnt their skills or otherwise. The general belief was, as already stated, that there would never be another war, but if there was, it would again be the old familiar safe and happy stalemate in France, for those directing it. Our Commanding Officer was Lt Colonel Alec Telfer-Smollett, DSO, MC, who afterwards became a General. He lived in a huge house called Cameron, with a large estate along Loch Lomondside, which is now a luxury hotel. He would usually come in two or three times a week of a morning to see how things were coming along. He was a man of enormous charm and great influence. On hunting mornings he would come in to take Bn Orders dressed for the Meet, replacing his pink coat with his uniform jacket when men on various charges were brought before him for judgement. His Adjutant, Captain Roy 'walad' Urquhart – 'walad' means a boy in Arabic, from when he had first joined in Cairo – was a different cup of tea altogether. A deadly serious, highly professional soldier, working all hours of the day and night, he really ran the Bn through the Old Sweat NCOs. The Walad finally achieved fame in 1944 as commander of First Airborne Division at Arnhem.

Soon after our arrival he summonsed Dick and me to his office, and told us that 'we were the best Regiment in the Army, and how lucky we were to be in it'. When I rather naively asked him what we were best at, he flew into a rage and threw us out of the door. I admit that it was a difficult question to answer, for in the recent Brigade competitions for drill, shooting, marching or any other military activity you may care to name, we had been consistently last. At a tug of war contest the officer acting as anchor had slipped and fallen over, whereupon one of the Jocks had startled the bystanders by shouting, 'Pack it in boys, fookin' officer's doon.' As for being 'lucky to be in it', like David Niven, Dick Kindersley, many others to whom I had spoken, told me they had tried for other regiments, but had found themselves in the HLI, I began to wonder if I was the only one who had actually put himself down for it?

If tactical thought and armament were still that of 1918, socially

219

Alec Telfer-Smollett wished to get us back to before the Boer War, or as soon after as possible, anyway the early 1900s. The then CO had gone home on leave from Malta, where the HLI had been stationed, on three months leave. The only instruction that he had left, 'was to be always ready to entertain Royalty at short notice'. Like Muslims, who believe that the Messiah can only be born of a man, and where in many parts of the world the men wear baggy trousers with a large pocket between the legs in case he tumbles out unexpectedly, the orderly officer had to spend every afternoon in the Mess ante-room, lest Royalty called. It had happened only a few years previously, when the Prince of Wales, on attachment to the Guards, had suddenly appeared. So we were one up on the Muslims, who to the best of my knowledge have yet to produce anyone of significance in this way. Dick and I also had to make calls ourselves, leaving two cards with our name printed on them in copperplate at each of the other units of the Brigade, and one with the wives of our own 15 or so married officers. We would go round, praying that they might be out so that we could drop our cards and run, otherwise we would have to stay for tea, sticky cakes and polite conversation.

Officially an officer could not be married before he was 30. Even then he would have to seek his CO's approval, which if the girl was considered unsuitable, would not always be given, when he could either refrain, resign his Commission, or seek transfer to some more lenient Corps, such as the RASC or the Ordnance. No marriage allowance was paid to an officer under 30, but with sufficient private means and above all his Colonel's permission, he could marry. This was known as 'living in Army sin'. Without such means it would be quite impossible to pay his Mess subscriptions, maintain a wife and live the kind of social existence expected of him. With Other Ranks (ORs), only the senior sergeants upwards were married. It was quite impossible for the others on what they got paid. In the Highland Light Infantry, it was also virtually impossible for a junior officer to exist on his pay. Most had private means of at least £250 a year, some with much more. On the £100 my father gave me, I found things very difficult and was constantly in debt, but somehow managed and was never bailed out. In fact if it had not been for the kindness of my bankers,

Messrs Glyn Mills in Whitehall, I don't know what I would have done. They seemed to be financing half the Subalterns in the British Army. I had never earned any money in my whole life, regarded the Army as a continuation of my schooling, and my pay as pocket money. The HLI was considered 'rather a rich regiment', and we lived in a certain style with high Mess subscriptions. In the Tank Corps, few had private means and I would have been considered fortunate, rather than a poor relation.

The pay of a 2nd Lt was nine shillings and eight pence a day, or £14.50p a month. After three years he became a Lieutenant and received twelve and six a day. The increase does not seem much, but combined with a small private income it made all the difference. A Captain earned about £38 a month, and a Major some £63. Thus with my father's allowance, I had a monthly total of £22 10s (£22.50p) to live on. Quarters were free, but out of this sum I had to pay my Mess bill, which with various subscriptions and other things never came to less than £11, even if I drank nothing but the obligatory Highland toast on Pipe nights every week. I also had to pay my batman thirty bob (£1.50p) a month, and provide him with civilian clothes. There was in fact nothing left from my pay, and with the £8 allowance I had the upkeep of my uniform, plain clothes, entertainment, and try to keep up with my contemporaries. It was hard going. Fortunately we were paid in advance, so I found myself with a £14 'cushion' on arrival. Even so, without Glyn Mills I would have been scuppered.

Chances of promotion in the Army of the period were as dismal as the pay. Everything was in a state of stagnation. Advancement to Captain and Major was automatic, provided you kept your nose clean and passed the necessary tactical examinations, which were scarcely beyond the scope of an intelligent Lance-Corporal or a school OTC. Beyond Major, promotion was by selection, whether you had been to the Staff College at Camberley, and whom you knew who could pull a string or two, here and there, but especially in the War Office. COs of Battalions were usually chosen by a Committee of former senior officers of the Regiment, including its Colonel, usually a former General, and often included the Royal Colonel in Chief. Promotion however to Captain or Major, although automatic, depended entirely on whether there was a vacancy in the Regiment or not, and varied from regiment to regiment. The average was between 14 and 16 years, with perhaps another wait of eight years to Major. As only Captains and above could get Staff appointments, other than ADC which was a plum job for a Subaltern, the general lot of a junior officer was not a happy one: facing years and years of mind-numbing drudgery and boredom at regimental duty. Many went 'bushwhacking', as service with Colonial forces was called, in Nigeria, East Africa, Somaliland or the Sudan. It meant instant promotion, much better pay and a life of great interest. But it was not permanent, and an officer would 'drop out of regimental sight', coming back as a relative stranger, 'a bit of a funny, who enjoyed serving with natives and that sort of thing'. Most thought it better to stay with the mainstream, however sluggish it might be. That is whether after 14 years of regimental duty, they thought at all. I remember discussing it with 'Martha' Reeves, who appeared to be suffering from senile dementia and was still a Subaltern after 15 years. 'It's not too bad,' he said, 'for after twelve years they let me off doing orderly officer, so now I am able to do Captain of the Week instead.'

Despite all its drawbacks, the system obviously worked. Many officers studied hard, regarding their profession as a vocation. Nobody could accuse them of being in it for the money. Unfortunately, such people were often regarded rather as 'swots' had been at Haileybury. Only a few years later, however, after a few early hiccoughs, it produced the finest set of Commanders during 1939 to 1945, that this country has ever known, especially Monty, without whom El Alamein could never have been won, and the Allied landings in Normandy in 1944 as great a shambles as the earlier raid on Dieppe.

18

In November we moved to Connaught Barracks, perched on the cliffs above the Castle, on the other side of Dover, where it collected every icy north-eastern blast of wind straight from Siberia. Dick and I were put on a junior NCO's cadre course to learn the rudiments of the .303 rifle and the Lewis light machine gun. It was everything that I had loathed about the OTC at Haileybury, slow, pointless and impractical, in that we never actually fired either weapon, and what we learnt could have been as equally well done in a couple of mornings, instead of a fort-night. It could also as easily have been carried out in a barrack room, instead of outside in the freezing wind. I felt too that we had been put on it simply from want of any idea of what we might be given to do. The utter mind-numbing futility of my existence slowly began to sink in; for there was literally nothing for us to do. The Battalion ran itself. Officers were in fact given half the day's pay of a normal civilian as a retainer to set, should the unfortunate need arise, a good example to the men in battle by getting them-selves killed first. Our hours of work were not strenuous. At 9 a.m. Dick and I would be in the Coy office, ready to greet Fuzzy when he came in half an hour later. 'Go out and see what the men are doing,' he would order. Nearly all the men would be occupied on fatigues of one kind or another, but some would be drilling or training under their NCOs. At Sandhurst I had thought that this would be our future job as young officers. I also at first marched smartly about, with my silver-topped regimental 'swagger cane' under my arm, and stamped my feet as I had been taught at the RMC. I was told it was 'unofficerlike to be smart on parade', and soon became as languid and limp as the rest, adopting the right kind of 71st HLI slouch, tapping my cane against my leg as I watched, with utter and barely concealed boredom, the Jocks being put through their paces. But it did make me wonder how the men could be expected to be smart if their officers 'were dozy and idle', as CSM Giddings would have put it.

At 12.30 we knocked off for the day and went to the Mess for lunch. Work was over. Every other week, Dick or I would be detailed to pay out the Company on Friday afternoon. This was a most elaborate procedure. One would sit at an Army trestle table covered with a grey issue blanket, with CQMS Dusty Miller beside. The men would line up, and two would be chosen at random as witnesses to stand behind us. As each name was called out in alphabetical order, the Jock stepped smartly forward and stood in front of the table. Dusty called out the amount due, the officer paid the man from a pile of notes and coins on the table. Dusty then entered the amount called on the Acquittance Roll. The Jock would salute and say, 'Pay correct Sirr.' It was the duty of the witnesses to see that Dusty marked the Acquittance Roll with the amount called. At the end, each witness got paid himself and signed the Roll to certify all was correct.

The pay of a Private soldier was about 2/3d (12p) a day, but there were usually various stoppages for uniform upkeep and barrack damages, reducing it somewhat. The normal weekly sum I paid out was about 14s (70p), after which those with a 'plain clothes pass', and others in their 'walking out dress' of trews, spats, khaki jacket and Glengarry bonnet, were 'away doon the toon looking for their wee hoor'. A 'wee hoor' was quite a friendly term and could apply to a current girlfriend or someone they met in a pub. A prostitute was just a 'hoor', with no 'wee' before it. Dover being a port, the place abounded in whores, with sailors and the soldiers of the garrison, Seaforths, Royal Scots, the Buffs and HLI as clients. Cases of VD were numerous. Provided a man went to the Early Treatment room run by the MO in each Battalion, for prophylactic treatment on his return to barracks, venereal disease did not count as a Self-Inflicted Wound (SIW), and a soldier would not lose his proficiency pay for his skill at shooting. Treatment for VD, especially gonorrhoea or 'the clap', was made as painful and ignominious as possible, *'pour encourager les autres'*.

It was not difficult to pick up the Jocks' vocabulary, which mainly consisted of two words. Anything good was 'wee', especially as in 'my wee hoor'. Anything and everything else began with the word 'fookin'. But it was the subtle way that this word was pronounced which gave it an almost limitless meaning to the cognoscenti. I am told that Chinese is much the same: a single word has many meanings, depending on the emphasis given to its pronunciation. I first discovered the subtle use of the F word by the Jocks whilst out on a route march. We had been given permission during a ten-minute 'fall out' to drink from our water bottles, normally forbidden. Suddenly one of my platoon cried out, 'Wha's the fooker 'as got me fookin' fooker?' Without a moment's hesitation another Jock threw him back his corked water bottle, with the words, 'Heer's yer fookin' fooker, yer fooker.' It was impressive stuff, for pronounced even slightly differently the words would have had an entirely different meaning. Thus chimpanzees and the higher apes communicate with each other by astute difference of cry or grunt. Though not for a moment am I suggesting that chimps use the F word.

Once a fortnight or so, we would have to do Orderly Officer. 'Extra Orderly Officers' were also awarded as a punishment. There was in addition, a Captain of the Week, allotted to a senior officer, who did separate duties, usually in a most lackadaisical fashion, twice a week. The Orderly Officer was not permitted to leave barracks, other than on Fridays, when with an escort, he would go to the bank and draw the Battalion's pay in canvas bags, and distribute it to the Coys. He began the day accompanied by the Orderly Sgt, inspecting the Jocks' breakfast, then the issue of the day's rations to the Sgt Cook, the original old sweat of old sweats, almost rotund, called Sgt Winter. After this came inspections of lunch and supper. The food was much the same as we had at Haileybury, meat and two vegetables, with custard on all the puddings. It looked quite disgusting to me, but was certainly plentiful and the Jocks seemed to like it. As we approached each table, the Orderly Sgt would bang on it with his stick, saying, 'Any complaints'. Whereupon the man at the head of each would leap to his feet, stand to attention and say 'no complaints Sirr.' If there was something to complain of, it had better be good, or whoever made it would be charged with 'making a frivolous complaint'. For most, the food was far better than anything they would have found at home in those days of unemployment and depression. The next task was at about 5 p.m., to mount the Quarter Guard outside the Guardroom at the main gate, the final duty being to turn out the Guard at sometime after 11 p.m. What with one thing and another the Orderly Officer was pretty well occupied all day.

Apart from the three hours, reputed as work, we did on weekdays, Saturday morning would be taken up by that amazing Army function known as 'Interior Economy', barrack room inspection and generally cleaning the place up. Few senior officers would be involved unless the CO was inspecting the Coy lines. Every Sunday there was a church parade under the Captain of the Week, when everyone below him in rank had to attend. Once a month or so, the CO would hold a church parade, when everybody had to attend, and our three bands, bugle, pipe and military, would take turns in marching us to the Presbyterian service in the garrison church, bugles blaring, bagpipes skirling and drums thudding. There were also a number of Roman Catholics in the Battalion, and these had to be marched every Sunday to their church in the town, usually by the next for duty Orderly Officer, but a task often awarded to others as punishment for a minor misdemeanour.

However, the part of regimental life that I found most boring, useless and frustrating was the five hours or so, often much more, which we spent every weekday over dinner. We had to be in the ante-room at 7.30 p.m., dressed in our Mess kit of very tight trews, boiled shirt and stand-up collar, black tie and scarlet bum-freezer jacket, ready to greet the CO or Senior dining member. On Mondays there was Band night, when the Military band would play to us, and Thursdays were Pipe night, at first an especial bugbear. I knew nothing about bagpipes and cared less. In fact to me they always sounded the same, similar I imagined, to Chinese boys being buggered, which I was stupid enough to remark, thinking it witty. In a very touchy Highland Regiment, this was much the same as joining the Vatican staff and letting it be known you weren't too impressed by the Holy Virgin.

On Pipe nights, at the end of the meal there would be a

tremendous squealing outside, and suddenly five or six pipers would come marching in and go round and round the long polished table, gleaming with all the regimental silver. So deafening was the noise that I have often seen English guests almost fall off their chairs in astonishment. Each piper carried a Company Commander's coat of arms as a banner on his drones, and the Pipe Major carried the Regimental banner. After the Marches, the pipers stood behind the CO and played a series of Strathspeys and Reels, after which came the Pibroch or lament played by a lone piper. This was an agonisingly slow, drawn-out event, and if you were unlucky you might get 'the desperate battle of the birds', when the dawn would come up and the wretched creatures would still be hard at it. The Pibroch finally over, the Pipe Major would drink a large neat whisky from a quaich, handed him by the CO, and then give the Highland toast '*Slainte na Gael*'. We never drank a Royal toast in the HLI. As the first Clan Regiment to be formed after the 1745 Jacobite uprising, it was felt such toasts might be pushing loyalty too far. Nor did we get up when the National Anthem was played. Apparently George III dined with us on board a ship, and the ceiling was so low that nobody could get up. The tradition lingered. After the Pibroch, the pipers would play another set of Marches, Strathspeys and Reels. Then came the tricky bit. The CO would ask some unfortunate Subaltern for a choice of pipe tune. I used to write down a selection in pencil on my boiled shirt cuff and look at it surreptitiously. The bagpipes are an acquired taste and sound. At first it is impossible to distinguish one note from another, but suddenly they make sense. In a very short time I was, and always shall remain, a rabid devotee of their wild music, which I find the most moving, stirring and savage in the world. I also feel a sense of sorrow and sadness for those who cannot understand or appreciate it. As battle music goes, I have only to hear a March such as the 'Black Bear', to wish to run around and stick a bayonet into someone as soon as possible.

Once a month there would be a Regimental Guest Night, at which some influential officer such as a General or Brigadier, would be invited, whose entertainment we would all find on our Mess bills under 'Mess Guests'. There was even a little doggerel about it.

Have another glass of port, Brigadier.
I really feel you ought, Brigadier.
My Subalterns will pay,
They get ten bob a day.
So have another glass of port, Brigadier.

As well as the monthly Guest Nights, there were special Scottish occasions such as St Andrews Day, Burns Night and Hogmanay or New Year's Eve, at which all hell was let loose after the pipers had played. There was much drink taken, Reels danced and general horseplay, much of it, I realised later, highly homosexual, at which tight trews were split and scarlet jackets torn. Dick and I knew nothing of Scottish Reels, and were put under instruction by the Pipe Major. At first my attitude to this was fiercely hostile. I felt I had not joined the Army in order to learn to dance, but in the end I became, as with the pipe music, a fanatical dancer of every kind of Scottish country dance, and despised those who did not know all the steps, just as my brother officers must have despised my own early and clumsy efforts. At weekends, a buffet supper would be served for which we would have to wear dinner jackets. One evening, wishing to go to the cinema, some of us persuaded Mr Giffard to serve us supper in the library. When it was discovered we had actually eaten without a dinner jacket, there was a terrible rumpus. We were marched in front of the Adjutant by the Senior Subaltern, given extra Orderly Officers, and confined to barracks until we had mowed the Mess lawn with nail scissors.

If Sandhurst had been all substance and no froth, the Highland Light Infantry seemed to me to be all froth and no substance. Its entire emphasis appeared to be on the wrong things. For its officers, it was nothing short of a glorified Government-subsidised country club. Apart from those officers actually concerned with running the Battalion, such as the CO and Adjutant, there appeared to be no interest in the Jocks whatsoever, either with their welfare or their training. I discovered too, that at least a third of my brother officers were homosexual, '*waermer bruedern*', or 'warm brothers', as the Swiss would say. I found this almost overt homosexuality hard to stomach, especially after hearing two old Majors arguing as to whose tent should be next to Dick

Kindersley's on the autumn manoeuvres. In those days, homosexual acts between men were a criminal offence, and an officer had recently been forced to resign his Commission for being found in bed with his batman, which was considered highly detrimental to good order and military discipline. Such close fraternisation with the men was frowned upon. Officers so inclined either kept it among themselves or took it up to London. A very senior Major, 'Rector' Mathel, was a Mess joke for his importuning of young officers, whilst another, whom David Niven describes so well in his book as the 'Weasel', kept pornographic photographs of small naked black boys in the drawer of his desk in the Company office. Homosexual acts have never really been high on my priority of occupations. In fact I have always found it impossible to understand how people can choose to make use of the body's main sewer as their playground. Whatever the case may have been with other public schools, the opinion at Haileybury against it, when I was there, was very strong. Although such acts between men were criminal, women were not included. Apparently when the Parliamentary Act was placed before Queen Victoria for signature, it did include women, but she refused to sign, saying 'Such things are impossible'. So the lucky old lesbians had been able to carry on regardless.

I have always thought that the HLI suffered from a kind of 'Highland Complex', of which I soon found myself part. Although accepted, albeit rather grudgingly, by the five other Highland regiments as a member of the Highland Brigade, this was not the case with the rest of the Army, which considered that Highland regiments wore the kilt and had their depots in the Highlands. The HLI wore trousers and had its depot in Glasgow. Ergo, it was a Lowland regiment. I must confess, so little did I know about it when I joined, that I thought this myself, and was unconvinced when I was told that it was not the kilt which denoted a Highland regiment, but the white spats worn with our trews. As both my grandfather and father had been in a most distinguished Lowland regiment, the Royal Scots Fusiliers, whilst another, the Royal Scots, was the oldest regiment in the world, I could not understand what they held against them. Thus the HLI were more Highland than the Highlands. Most of the officers fell into two categories.

They were either so Highland that they slept wrapped in Mackenzie tartan plaids, or so 'horsy' that they used saddles instead of pillows. I also found to my amazement that the most vociferous Highland ones had rarely come from north of Watford, and the horsy ones were scarcely ever seen near a horse. There was however a tightly knit, undoubtedly homosexual, horse clique, which dominated Regimental politics for the next two generations. The impression that all this conveyed was one of deliberate and intense amateurism, that they were all 'just putting in a few years in the Army, whilst awaiting to inherit vast estates and grouse moors in Perthshire or other fashionable parts of Scotland'.

The Army training year began in January with teaching the men in the Platoons their individual weapon skills. This progressed through the year to Company and Battalion field exercises. In July and August the men shot for their proficiency pay as a supplement to the basic rate. The standards to be aimed at were, Marksman, first, second and third class shots. None was very high, and I was astonished at the lack of interest in what seemed the essential skill for a soldier. I became a Marksman with little difficulty. When I arrived I half expected the Battalion shooting team to compete at Bisley and be treated rather as bloods had been at school. In fact such a team did not even exist. Most weeks, every Wednesday, there would be a route march of 15 or 16 miles. The entire Battalion would be involved, and we would move in columns of four by Companies behind the three bands. The Bugle band was headed by Bugle Major Bendy, a huge and magnificent creature who held the Army heavyweight boxing title, was also Army shot put champion, and holder of the 100 yards freestyle swimming record. The bands took it in turn to play us along, but when they were silent, the Jocks would sing in a quavering repetitive monotone,

'Whiter than the whitewash on the wall.
Oh whiter than the whitewash on the wall,
wash me in the water you washed your dirty daughter,
and I'll be whiter than the whitewash on the wall,
with my big kidney wiper,
and half a yard of foreskin hanging down to the ground.'

230

In September Brigade manoeuvres were held, and we moved into a large tented camp near Ham Street in Kent. As we were marching out to it, up the hill outside Dover, who should come riding up but none other than the Brigadier, Sir Hereward the Wake. He was a direct descendant of the Hereward who had fought so gallantly against William the Conqueror during 1067, in the fens around Ely. 'What are the pipes playing?' he asked Sixty, who was marching beside me. 'Glendaruel Highlanders Sirr!' Sixty said, without a moment's hesitation. 'Are they really playing that?', I asked afterwards. 'I haven't the faintest idea,' Sixty replied, 'but then neither has he, and Generals like quick answers, it saves them having to think.' My chief recollection of those manoeuvres was the endless marching. Sixty said it was worse than the retreat from Mons, and the waving of red flags to denote anti-tank guns, of which the Army had none. We saw no tanks either, so I wondered why they kept waving the flags. On one occasion the Battalion was acting as enemy to the whole Brigade on an exercise which was not scheduled to start until after midnight. For this the entire Mess was transported to a windy hilltop. The Brigadier was guest of honour and Mr Giffard presided in white tie and tails. We had a five-course dinner, the pipes played, the Highland toast was drunk, the port was passed round, and then we all got up and went off to do battle until dawn. Not that there was much battle at that, for either the Brigade got lost in the dark, or we did.

Leave for officers in the Army in those far-off distant days was generous. Everyone was entitled to two months a year, either consecutively or in bits. To go on leave you had to get your Company Commander's approval and enter your name in the leave book in the Adjutant's office. He and the CO would have to sign it before you could go. There had to be a reason for your leave, and some were so cast-iron as to be impossible to refuse. Top of these naturally were hunting, shooting and fishing. Polo was also a good gambit, as were golf and skiing or a cricket tour. Perhaps best of all was to attend the round of Highland Balls held in Scotland during September. At Christmas that year I managed to wangle three weeks to go and ski at Chateau d'Oex again, where I spent my twentieth birthday and the New Year. I knew

231

most of the British colony living there and spent much of my time skiing with 'Wiggs' Beauchamp, sister of Barbara, Roger Black's girlfriend, who was now in the grip of a ferociously jealous lesbian called Joan. Wiggs, too, was reputedly engaged to some boring Assam tea planter by the name of Plunket. Not that it seemed to worry her too much, and she used to wear my Glengarry instead of a ski hat. Wiggs died the following April from septicaemia, which began as a simple little spot on her cheek. Nowadays, penicillin would have cured it in a few hours. Barbara always claimed that she died from all the various cocktails, Sidecars and White Ladies, we had drunk every evening at Petay's Cafe in Chateau d'Oex.

As we had done no weapon training at Sandhurst, all newly joined officers had to do a six weeks Young Officers' course at the Small Arms School in Hythe. My time there did much to restore my faith in the British Army, which was fast beginning to wane. In a way it was rather like being back at Sandhurst, because all those one knew were also on the course, now as 2/Lts. The discipline was much more relaxed, but there was the same exhilarating feeling 'that nothing but the best was good enough'. There were also the same type of absolutely first-class NCO instructors. We were divided into squads of about ten. I was delighted to find Geoffrey Worsdell was in our squad, along with Skip Taylor of the Royal Sussex, and Percy Seymour of the Wiltshires, afterwards Duke of Somerset. Our squad instructor was CSM Instructor 'Hoppy' Hopkinson. The whole course comprised some 60 young officers, and most of us were billeted in digs around Hythe.

We learnt all about the SMLE rifle, and the Lewis gun, threw live grenades out of trenches, were subjected to poison gases with our masks on in special gas chambers, and stuck our bayonets into innumerable straw dummies, with blood-curdling yells. It was everything I had always hated at OTC and in the HLI, yet because Hoppy taught it so superbly, it became intensely interesting and I loved every minute of it. At 11 a.m. every morning we had a 15-minute break, when the Naafi brought us hot sausage rolls, and ever since, whenever I have eaten a sausage roll, I have been reminded of those happy weeks at Hythe. At the end of our course, six of the instructors put on a display of rapid fire rifle shooting that can never have been surpassed. Each one fired 50 rounds in a minute at targets 300 yards away, and every round was either a bull or in the inner ring. To obtain such speed and accuracy takes years of practice and dedication, the bolt action on the rifle being manipulated entirely by the thumb. It must also be remembered that the magazine had to be refilled every ten shots. Fifteen rounds a minute was considered highly proficient for a good shot, and was the standard rate of fire of the BEF which devastated the German infantry in 1914.

When I got back to Dover I was agog to pass on all I had learnt at Hythe. No-one was even interested. I had done my YO course and that was that. I discovered throughout my career in the Army that what was taught on courses, even the Staff College, had little to do with reality. What was learnt on a course was what could be achieved under ideal circumstances, with no conflicting interests, where every unit was fully up to strength, men were not away on fatigues or unavailable for other reasons, and all the necessary equipment was there in working order. Reality was that such a combination could never happen. It left me wondering why one had been sent on the course in the first place, other than the realising how interesting and absorbing any instruction can be made if properly taught, by officers and NCOs who really know their job and love what they know. Every course I ever went on was of this standard, and the ignorance I always found on returning to normal duty, the greater shock.

Whilst at Dover I experienced a phenomenon for which I can offer no reasonable explanation. Our rooms were sparsely furnished and for thirty bob (£1.50p) I had bought a very old arm-chair at a secondhand furniture store in Dover. A few days after its arrival, the Senior Subaltern 'Chunk' Colvin, who had the room below, accused me of 'moving furniture around all night', and ordered me to march the Roman Catholics to church in town the next Sunday as a punishment. I denied all knowledge of moving furniture, but noticed that every morning the chair was in front of the window as if someone were in it looking out. One night, from my bed in the little room next door, I thought I actually heard it move, and jumped out of bed to rush into my sitting room. There it was as usual, turned around towards the window, instead of facing into the room. A few nights later, I got John Milman and Dick Kindersley to mark rings around the chair legs with chalk. We went out and came back after midnight. There, sure enough, it had moved to the window. This was obviously a case for the Padre. The next day we called him in and left him alone with it.

I don't know what he said or did, but he was a staunch Irish Protestant and maybe threatened it with having to march the Roman Catholics to church, three Sundays hand running, for it certainly never moved again. When the Battalion was posted to Fort George the following year, I left the chair behind for the benefit of the new occupant. I met him many years later, long after I had forgotten all about it. 'That was a funny old armchair you left in your room at Dover,' he told me, 'very comfortable, but it used to move around the room on its own all night. Made such a rumpus that in the end I had to get rid of it. We put it on the bonfire and as it went up in flames, do you know, it looked for all the world as if there was an old man sitting in it.'

The main social events of that summer of 1934 were the annual Regimental Dinner, held at a well-known London military club, and the Caledonian Ball at Grosvenor House in Park Lane. This was opened by a set Eightsome Reel from the six Highland Regiments, all in their pre-1914 full Dress uniform, plaids, dirks and everything else. There was not too much of this old finery about, but many of the older officers had worn it before the war as their normal parade uniform, and all chipped in with what they had got. We were the only ones in trews, but with the long Mackenzie plaids over one shoulder, frankly I thought we looked the most distinguished of the lot. My Scottish dancing had progressed so much that I was one of the four to be chosen 'to dance for the regiment'. Now there's a distinction for you! Our names had been published in *The Times*, as well as those of our partners, four of the Season's Scottish Debs, the names picked probably out of a hat, but who were all considered better than raw hands when it came to dancing reels, or should I say raw feet.

A few days before the Ball I had injured my ankle playing rugger for the Dover Garrison against Betteshanger Colliery, and was limping about in considerable pain. It was too late to

234

withdraw from the Ball, so I gritted my teeth and carried on. In fact, what with the occasion and an odd glass of whisky or champagne, I scarcely felt it, but when we returned to Dover at dawn, I could scarcely walk. The next day I was carted off to the Military hospital in Shornecliffe, where I shared a room with a most amusing officer from the East Surreys, Peter Wreford-Brown, who had just got himself engaged to some famous woman golf champion. Personally I could not understand what he saw in her, for to me she looked perfectly square and kind of hammered down. Not that I mentioned this to him. My right fibula was found to be broken and I spent a fortnight in hospital, being discharged in plaster for a further three weeks sick leave. I spent the time at my grandmother's little house on Pagham Beach. When I got back, to my surprise, the Adjutant was furious. Instead of praising me for my fortitude in dancing for the Regiment against all odds, he stormed, 'It seems you can dance all night without any bother, and then expect to be off duty for over a month. The time will count against your leave, and you will do extra Orderly Officer for the days you missed.' I really felt I was home again, as the incredible futility of it all came flooding back.

The Regimental Dinner, later in the year, only confirmed my belief that I was, like Alice, living in Wonderland. The guest of honour was the Colonel in Chief of the Regiment, the Duke of Connaught, Queen Victoria's youngest son, now in his eighties and slightly bewildered. To greet him was the Colonel of the Regiment, Major General Balfour and our own CO, Lt Col Alec Telfer-Smollett. The room was full of past and present officers of the Regiment, some going back to the Zulu Wars of 1879, to me at the time, further away than the Stone Age. The Duke had served for a time in the 60th Rifles, and was also their Colonel in Chief. He seemed confused at times to know whether he was with the 60th or dining with the Highland Light Infantry. We were soon to know. At the end of the meal, he made a long rambling speech, about how delighted he was to be back among his old friends in the 60th and how there was no regiment in the British Army to compare with it. We gazed dumbfounded at each other across the table.

General Balfour got up to reply. He must have thrown his

original notes to the wind, for not by a single word did he imply that the Duke had made a mistake. Furthermore I hope the old boy never found out, for he was a kindly old man at that, and it would have distressed him greatly. The Royal family are Colonels in Chief of so many regiments that it must often be confusing to know which one they are with. Shortly after our dinner, the Prince of Wales came down to Dover to inspect one of his regiments, the Seaforth Highlanders, impeccably turned out in their uniform, except that he was wearing a Royal Scots Fusilier Glengarry. And this was even before he had met Mrs Simpson.

19

Newly joined officers were not allowed to have cars until they had been with the Battalion for over six months. The object of this was to ensure that we kept to the Mess for as long as possible. For me it meant the expense of having to keep my car in a garage somewhere. Others such as 'Cocky' Charteris, a dark, curly-haired little man related to the wine industry, simply kept their cars secretly in lock-ups in Dover, and used them from there. Something, stupidly, I had never thought of doing. Cocky had the most beautiful light blue four-seater open MG Magnette, which induced even greater paroxysms of indignation among the senior officers than my own poor little vehicle. From the uproar it caused the moment I appeared in it, sometime in April 1934, one might have been forgiven for thinking a major calamity had befallen us all. Admittedly, instead of being the regulation black, it was, of all horrors, 'a coloured car', with a cream body, a tapering tail, and bright red cycle-type mudguards. It also looked to some extent like a perambulating bathtub. Rector Mathel, rather drunk in the Mess one evening, was very rude to me about it, urging my brother subalterns 'to paint it all over with pink spots'. Funnily enough, my brother subalterns did not object to it at all. When Cocky Charteris duly appeared, with further uproar over his light blue MG, and Dick Kindersley's white Wolseley Hornet saloon, the tumult subsided. Personally I could not see what was so wrong with my little car. My father, that stuffiest and most conventional of old gentlemen, had helped me choose it. My uncle Jimmy, ex-cavalry officer and pillar of the Cavalry Club, who had been born middle-aged, liked it. None of my cousin Awdry and Kendrick Hughes' Guardee friends were rude about it either.

The objection to 'a coloured car' was that it 'drew attention', and the 71st HLI had an absolute horror of anything which did so. This attitude even extended to its own existence. That summer, the Dover Brigade held its annual King's Birthday Parade in June along the seafront. The other three Battalions marched through the town with bands playing and colours flying. Not so the HLI. To avoid drawing attention, we crept down through the back alleys and returned the same way, hoping nobody would notice us. I was commanding the Colour Party, and bitterly resented only being allowed to uncase the Colours when we arrived at the parade ground, and then having to encase them again before marching back to barracks. If ever there was a day for foot-stamping and general panache, then surely this was it? As for my car, I swapped it some time that summer for a dark green, six cylinder open Wolseley Hornet, through envy of Cocky and Dick's far more powerful machines, the better to be able to entice girls from the dances at the Leas Cliff Hall into it. My little bathtub had cut no ice at all, only giggles.

There was a dance every Saturday evening at the Leas Cliff Hall in Folkestone. As well as the dancing, there were mass singalongs when old songs such as 'Roaming in the gloaming', and 'A bicycle made for two' were sung. Most of the girls went to it to be 'picked up' in the parlance of the time, which would also include them under the generic and somewhat derisive term, as 'shop girls'. Cocky even met one called Doris, for whom he resigned his Commission and married. Everyone thought he was barmy, and the marriage was a disaster. Such a thing, however, was the exception, Girls at that time were divided into two categories: those 'who did it' and those 'who didn't'. It was very difficult for a girl who got a reputation for being one 'who did it' to get married. However, the girls we picked up at the Leas Cliff Hall were 'shop girls', of a lower social background from ourselves, and even should we, like Cocky, become entangled and wish to marry one, the CO would never even contemplate permitting it. The main problems therefore, were avoiding getting one of them pregnant or contracting a dose of clap. Perhaps the oddest feature of all this was that the girls themselves played by the rules. They may have been happy 'doing it' with young officers, but would never have

238

dreamt of doing so with their own social equals. Besides the girls, however, there were others. On some evenings one would see the Weasel on the prowl for suitable young men, despite his preference, judging by the postcards in his office drawer, for little black boys.

Refreshingly straight amongst all the homosexuals was a senior Captain called 'Seedy Sam' MacWhirter a small rather wizened man who wore gold-rimmed spectacles and boasted an almost insatiable sexual appetite. Most weekends would see him up in London, patronising the better class of whore, who charged in guineas rather than pounds for her services. However, he was not averse from time to time to sampling the odd enthusiastic amateurs from the Leas Cliff Hall. With what he called 'The Sam MacWhirter Patent Anti-Clap Machine', a device which he had invented and constructed himself, he felt safe from any form of VD. Tobias Matthews may have described a dose of clap as 'nothing worse than a bad cold', but for an officer, any cure had to be undertaken secretly and was also very expensive. A certain giveaway sign of someone undergoing treatment, was when he knocked off alcohol. Certain civilian doctors specialised in VD, whilst others carried out secret abortions, the going rate for which was £50. An officer consulting a military doctor with VD, mainly clap or syphilis, risked being court-martialled for making himself unfit for duty, a SIW. The disease would also have to be entered on his record of service as 'likely to effect his future efficiency as an officer', reducing his promotion chances considerably.

Such civilian practitioners were known as pox doctors, highly regarded and in considerable demand, especially by Guards and Cavalry officers, who would allude to them as 'prick-farriers', and could afford their exorbitant fees. For the doctors it became a nice little earner on the side and was, moreover, perfectly legal. Seedy Sam relied entirely on his Clap Machine to save him from infection. He scorned French letters, the word condom was unknown, describing them 'as eating a toffee with the paper still on'. He took the machine with him, packed in his suitcase wherever he went. It was a most extraordinary contraption of glass retorts and rubber tubes on a small metal stand. On returning to his room after a night of indulgence, whatever the hour, Sam would hook himself up to his machine, which with gurgles and hiccoughs flooded the appropriate parts of him with a strong solution of pot permanganate crystals, or Condy's fluid, turning everything a lurid purple in the process. Seedy Sam told me that on one occasion in London the colour had not faded from the previous weekend, and catching sight of this terrible bright purple monster leering at her, the poor girl had fled shrieking from the room.

In these days when everybody seems to jump into bed with everyone else at the drop of a hat and maybe sooner, and where there is no further need for pox doctors as it is all on the NHS, such things may sound bizarre. Despite it all, the professional sex industry is stronger than ever. In the days I describe, there was little else but the professional sex industry, supplemented here and there by the enthusiastic amateurs. Girls were regarded more as objects than people. There were the ones you bedded and the ones you married, and you hoped neither the twain would meet. If they 'did it' you didn't marry them, and if they 'didn't' you might, provided you were over 30 and the CO approved of her. It all really began at Sandhurst, where as I wrote in an earlier chapter, cadets would go to London and return, boasting that they had 'had a woman', as if it were a piece of steak for lunch. It was an attitude very Edwardian, almost Victorian in its concept, which is hardly surprising as most of the senior officers had joined in Edwardian times. Furthermore military thought processes, such as they exist, are always some 30 years behind the rest of the population.

Officers of the more expensive regiments, especially the Guards and the Household Cavalry, mostly stationed in London, would have coteries – the Cavalry naturally called them 'stables' – of girls more or less exclusive to them, who would be passed from one to another by recommendation, and agree to go to the Regimental pox doctor for regular check-ups. Many of these girls were highly sought after and carried considerable social cachet. For instance, a Sandhurst cadet who could induce a well-known whore to attend the June Ball as his partner, would earn much rakish kudos, as readers of David Niven's book will recall. Some at the June Ball were even the object of raffles. None minded being called a whore and would usually allude to themselves as

240

such. The word 'prostitute', an Americanism, was just creeping in, and applied only to the lower class of person on a five-bob rate, instead of guineas, seen hanging around street corners in Piccadilly. Your Cavalry Club girl would be highly indignant at being described as one.

In November 1934, the Battalion moved up to Fort George near Inverness. The posting was hailed with delight by the older officers as giving untold opportunity for the really serious business of life, such as shooting and fishing, and groans of dismay from us younger ones, torn from the fleshpots of Dover and London. Fort George was miles from anywhere. It was built in the second half of the 18th century, to hold down the Eastern Highlands after the Jacobite rising of 1745. Situated at the extreme end of a small promotory sticking out into the Moray Firth, about 12 miles from Inverness, opposite Fortrose on the Black Isle, it was one of the many fortresses built around Europe at the time on the design of the French military engineer, Vauban. They were always constructed as low as possible, with thick turf banks before the walls for concealment and as a cushion for cannon balls. Behind the outer line of fortifications was a deep moat protecting the inner keep. Batteries of artillery were in strong emplacements at every corner, so that any attack could be swept by cannon and musket fire from a flank. A Vauban fort was the last word in 18th-century military engineering skill. I was interested to see that the German defence system in the Channel Islands, nearly 200 years later, was based on the same principles. Fort George, like Connaught Barracks in Dover, collected every icy blast from Siberia, but being nearly 700 miles further north, was even colder. We shared the barracks with the Seaforth Highlanders, whose Regimental Training Depot it was.

The first thing we had to do on arrival was to get ourselves a civilian kilt, so that we could attend, properly dressed, the various balls, dances and routs to which we would be invited by the local gentry. A representative from Willy Anderson, the military and civilian tailors, came up from Edinburgh to measure us for kilt and doublet, plus hose, sporran and all the other Highland accoutrements dreamt up in Victorian times, having as little to do with Highland custom as had the elaborately designed clan (sic) tartans. The original Highlander was little more than an unwashed savage who wore a kind of blanket wrapped around his middle with the end draped over his shoulder. The women who wove the blankets varied the pattern from clan to clan, ensuring instant recognition in battle. Bonnie Prince Charlie, when first dressed up as a Highland Chieftain for propaganda purposes, is reported as saying, 'Now all I have to do is to begin scratching!' All this was developed by Victorian romanticism and commercial interests, into the many and various 'tartans' known today. Many of us had no right to wear a tartan whatsoever, but it was amazing how, as in my case, they managed to dig up the odd grandmother with Scottish connections. To wear one's grandmother's tartan was entirely permissible. My father's mother could wear the Robertson tartan, and my father even managed to produce a civilian kilt he had worn as a young man. Willy Anderson's rep fastened on it with a whoop of delight; 'Such beautiful vegetable dyes,' he said, 'nothing like that about these days.' It needed very little alteration to fit me, and now, over a hundred years after it was made, is still going strong. At that time, the kilt was only worn as civilian dress by the gentry, and never south of the Highland Line, which began at Stirling.

We had taken over our barracks from the Kings Own Scottish Borderers, the KOSB, and had also inherited their Beagle pack. 'Swaggers' Swettenham, a subaltern of some eight years service, became Master, with Dick Kindersley, Cocky Charteris and Mark Hollis as whippers-in. This entailed further outlay with Willy Anderson, in the shape of bottle green coat, white breeches, special running shoes and other paraphernalia. Personally I wished no part of the Beagles whatsoever, as I have always considered it about the most boring form of exercise it is possible to take. Furthermore I always felt so sorry for the poor hare, which had never done any harm to anybody, and after the hounds had finished with it, could not even be eaten. Not only that, but a hare seems to have no sense whatever, running round in a complete circle, with the hunt in full cry after it, back to the very place it started. Why bother to chase it at all, when by staying where you were, you could catch it when it returned? The gentry from miles around, flocked to the drinks party we gave in the Mess before the

Opening Meet, their daughters in force, to give the marriageable form a once over. They were the most forbidding collection of females that I had ever seen. Most were almost square in shape, their shiny brick faces devoid of any suspicion of paint, powder or make-up, and legs like those usually seen holding up the more solid kind of dining room table. Apart from their heavy brogue shoes, they were entirely clad from head to foot in thick hairy tweed. Even their stockings were made of tweed, and one could hazard a guess, probably their underclothes as well. One with bright red hair was so absolutely hideous as immediately to earn the soubriquet of 'Monkey's hole'. After six months at Fort George we became quite used to them, and in a further six months began to find them, even Monkey's hole, positively alluring.

That winter I went skiing with Skip Taylor of the Royal Sussex Regiment, whom I had met on the Small Arms course at Hythe. Apart from Dick, whose taste for expensive winter sports hotels I could not afford, nobody in the HLI was interested in skiing. We had to go before Christmas, as I was due for a PT course in Aldershot at the beginning of January. We had chosen Kitzbuehel in Austria, then scarcely known. It had no ski lifts, but nor had any other resort, as such things had not even been invented, but it did have a cable car up to the Hahenkamm. When we arrived there was no snow. It was very early in the season, and a disadvantage of Kitbuehel is its relatively low altitude. We took the train to Garmisch-Partenkirchen in Germany, and then the mountain railway to the hotel on the Zugspitze at over 8000 feet, where there was plenty on the Schneeferner glacier.

Germany at this time was incredibly cheap for tourists, as the Nazi government was trying to obtain foreign currency, especially pounds and dollars. The exchange rate given was 25 marks to the pound. Our stay in the rather luxurious hotel on the Zugspitze glacier was about ten shillings (50p) a day. The skiing was very limited, the normal run being to the Knorrhuette, a couple of thousand feet down the glacier, with a long trudge up again on sealskins. There was a long run which required a guide over the edge of the glacier and down to Ehrwald in Austria. This meant taking the cable car back to the Austrian side of the Zugspitze and a semi-crawl through a long tunnel back into Germany. There was a Customs Post at each end, with much stamping of passports and 'Heil Hitlers'. Among the guests at our hotel was an attractive American woman of about 35, who took a great shine to Skip Taylor. He was singularly unresponsive, considering her middle-aged. Not so three Frenchmen, who almost swooned whenever she went past, whispering to each other with despairing sighs, '*Ah, la belle vagine Americaine!*'

We spent a week on the Zugspitze and then went back to Austria, where there was still no snow except at over 6000 feet. We took a bus from Innsbruck into the Sellrain valley, and from Gries had to walk, pulling skis and suitcases on sleighs, for three hours in the moonlight up a barely distinguishable snowy track, up to the Jagdschloss at Kuehtai. There was nobody about. We were alone in a desolate wilderness, and thought we could hear wolves howling in the mountains around us. We resolved to sell our lives dearly and devised an anti-wolf drill. On the command 'Wolves action!' we would stand back to back with our sledges before us, holding our ski sticks like bayonets in the 'On guard' position. After a few rehearsals, we got so good at it that we rather hoped the wolves would attack, to see what would happen. Kuehtai is now a first class ski resort, high enough always to have good snow. Then there was nothing but the Jagdschloss, a hunting lodge which had belonged to the Emperor Franz Joseph. Today it is a luxury hotel owned by his grandson, the Graf Stolberg-Stolberg. There was also, lower down, a climbers' refuge called the Dortmunder Huette. The skiing is wonderful over the whole area, and I spent my twenty-first birthday there.

At the end of 1934, over three years still remained before the Anschluss, when Austria became part of Nazi Germany. The Nazi underground movement there was very strong, especially in the Tirol, and almost every Austrian I spoke to was an ardent supporter of Hitler – after all, he was an Austrian! Compared to Germany, nothing in Austria seemed to function properly. In some manner, the Jagdschloss was involved in some form of clandestine activity, and there was much coming and going between it and Gries, where the buses from Innsbruck stopped. I discovered later that Gries was actually the secret headquarters of the Tirol Nazi Party, which was very highly organised. One evening when we

244

were in the bar at the Jagdschloss, they call it the *Stube*, a posse of Austrian police suddenly arrived, arrested everybody in sight and took them off to the gaol in Innsbruck. It was only with difficulty and by waving our passports that we did not share the same fate.

At the end of my leave I only spent long enough at Fort George to collect my things, before heading south again for my course at the Army Physical Training School at Aldershot. The Commandant was a most splendidly bibulous old Lieutenant Colonel from one of the Highland Regiments, with bushy moustache and a relaxed attitude to physical fitness. It did much to alleviate the bright-eyed and bushy-tailed enthusiasm of the rest of his Staff. After a hard morning in the gym, seeing him warming his bottom at lunchtime by the fire in the Mess ante-room, as he knocked off the pink gin, helped to restore one to reality. The course lasted six weeks and consisted of some 50 young officers. Like the one we had done at Hythe, it was meant to supplement our time at Sandhurst, so all one's old friends were on it. We did free-standing exercises, as well as those on the horse, parallel bars and other pieces of gym equipment. Again, the emphasis of Army PT was explained to us as being 'the harmonious development of the body to meet all physical demands upon it, of balance, strength, agility and endurance'. Muscular development for its own sake was actively discouraged as merely having to carry around unnecessary muscle. The course also infected me with an enthusiasm for physical fitness that has lasted through life.

Throughout my career in the Army I enjoyed going on courses. They always showed how things could be, not as they normally were. I especially enjoyed my PT course and was very sorry when it finished. Directly the day was over, we worked during the afternoon at games, athletics and classroom studies, we were free until parade the next morning at 08.30. I lived in the Mess of the 79th Cameron Highlanders, and found their attitude to life as different from the HLI as being on another planet. Away from all regimental restraint, students were into their cars and off up to the London night spots, just as soon as they could change into white tie and tails, or maybe sooner if they kept them up there. They would stagger back in the small hours – nobody in those days worried about 'drink and drive' – to snatch a couple of hours' sleep before work the next day.

None of us was over 22 and at that age it is amazing what the system will stand. This going up to London was not something I often indulged in, because I simply could not afford to do it. One of us, 'Oscar' Holderness, was usually in London night after night. There was an exercise in the gym which he could never do. This was to haul himself up onto a shelf and then lower himself neatly down again. One day there was no Oscar on parade. Halfway through the morning came the shelf-climbing exercise, and there to our amazement lay none other than Oscar, dressed in boiled shirt, white tie and tails, fast asleep, his opera hat over his eyes. The Staff Sgt instructor who demonstrated every exercise before we did it, was up first and seemed not to notice and, none of us said a word. Oscar was merely reported as being absent from duty. He managed to square it somehow with the Commandant, probably over a pink gin or two, for he continued the course as if nothing had happened. He had, however, no further difficulty with the dreaded shelf, leaping on and off it with the best of us.

In addition to all the physical work we did, we were also shown how to take classes ourselves, how to judge boxing bouts, how to improve our athletic performance, how to swim and dive in the garrison pool, and how to judge diving competitions. It was the first time in my life that anyone had ever taught me a physical skill. At my various schools and Sandhurst, I had played rugby, football, tennis, cricket and hockey, without ever being told how to do it or to improve my game. At the PT School we were shown not only how to improve our own performance, but how to coach others. The previous year I had won the 100 yards, 220 yards races and the long jump on our regimental sports day. By learning how to improve my start, we dug little holes in the ground with trowels – there were no starting blocks – I knocked over a second off my time for the 100 yards. We were also taught bayonet fencing. This was done with a large wooden weapon shaped like a rifle, and approximately the same weight and size. At one end was a spring-loaded 'bayonet', with a large knob on the end of it to prevent injury. We were heavily protected by padded clothing, thick gloves, and a heavy helmet with bars across the face. The

246

general effect was very much that of a moon astronaut. The rules, feints and thrusts were much the same as épée fencing, the whole body being the target. Bayonet fencing became my great enthusiasm.

When I got back to Fort George, I was as keen to put all I had learnt into practice as I had been after my course at Hythe, to be met with the same apathy and total lack of all interest. However, I did manage to raise and train a bayonet fencing team which I took down to Edinburgh, where we won the Scottish Command championship. One of the worst features of the tedium of regimental duty was the seeming endlessness of it. Day after day went by in stupefying boredom, during which one felt nothing had been achieved whatever; other than perhaps being social and making the right Highland noises. Rector Mathel had left the Mess and lived in a small house at Ardersier, the nearby village. He used to take Dick sailing on the Findhorn and give small dinner parties. Stories began to circulate of young subalterns having to use their sporrans to rap his knuckles as he tried to creep them under their kilt. For some reason, no homosexual has ever made a pass at me. Perhaps they found what they saw distasteful, or judged from my attitude that such advances would not be popular. Many years later I met an old friend who had known the 2nd Bn in Peshawar, and she told me, 'Do you know, out of the whole HLI we reckoned you were the only one who was not queer.' My own view is that homosexuals do not suit military life, there are too many opportunities at hand. It gives rise to cattiness, gross favouritism and tightly knit unpleasant cliques.

How much homosexuality there was among the officers of the 74th in India is hard to say, for it was never spoken of other than in jest. There is no doubt however that a good number of them were that way inclined, highly convenient in a country where girls were scarce and fiercely competed for. That I was the only one with a girlfriend meant nothing. Dislike of women, either feigned or actual, was actively encouraged in the Army. Women enticed young officers away from Mess life and those really important aspects of military training, hunting, shooting, polo or pig-sticking, luring them instead into various forms of poodle-faking at the Club, such as tennis, lying around the pool or dancing and other effeminate pastimes. That an officer disliked women by no means meant he was homosexual, but merely fashionable. After all, Field Marshal Haig, former Commander of the BEF in the Great War, though happily married, made no secret of the fact that he loathed and despised women at all times.

As May came round, it was time for the Caledonian Ball in London again. My name was sent forward to dance in the set Eightsome reel to open the Ball, and my partner was Daphne Hancock, one of that Season's Debutantes, whom I knew well. This year however, another treat was in store for us. All we young oficers were to be presented to King George Vth at a special Levee on 31 May, the day after the Ball. For the Levee we had to wear pre-1914 full Dress uniform, but that was no problem, for it was the same as that we had worn for the dance: tight trews, scarlet doublet, and plaid fixed with a huge silver brooch. For the Levee there was, however, one addition, the Tschako, or helmet that the HLI wore instead of the feather bonnet of other Highland Regiments. Members of the Post Office at the time also wore a Tschako as their official headgear, so with our trews and plaids, we looked like a collection of Highland postmen. All this gear was lent us by officers who had served prior to 1914. Someone produced a Tschako for me. I never noticed that it had gold braid around its top, which fitted, so I put it aside without a thought, to wear for the great occasion. The next morning some six of us, after being carefully dressed by an army of helpers, set off from Grosvenor House, across the Park for St James Palace, where the Levee was to be held. Here we were met by General Balfour, Colonel of the Regiment, who was to present us to the King. Many officers from other regiments were also being presented, and we formed up in a long line in an anteroom according to our regimental numbers. As the HLI was formerly the 71st, we were some way back.

The procedure was august and intimidating. There on a dais, on a small throne, which seemed too tight for him, sat the King-Emperor, by the Grace of God George V, in the uniform of a Field Marshal. Behind him stood his four sons, the Prince of Wales, future King Edward VIII, in the uniform of the Welsh Guards, beside him was the Duke of York, afterwards King George VI,

248

dressed as an Admiral of the Fleet, then came the Duke of Gloucester in Hussar uniform, and next to him, the Duke of Kent, dressed as an RAF Air Marshal. The King looked sick and ill. He had only a few more months to live. It was his last Levee, and the last ever to be held. The long line of officers, bareheaded with their helmets under their arms, shuffled past the group on the dais. As each officer reached the throne, he turned towards the King and his name was called out, he bowed and was rewarded by a perfunctory nod. The Prince of Wales looked bored out of his wits, and one of the first things he did on his accession was to put an end to all such presentations. As for me, I left the throne room with a feeling of exhaltation and pride, shared by all those who had the privilege to be there on that awesome occasion.

My exhaltation was not for long. On our way across the Park a photographer had taken our group, and the picture appeared the next day in several newspapers. My Tschako with the gold braid round the top stood out clearly from the others. When I got back to Fort George, all hell broke loose. Marched by the Adjutant in front of the CO, I was told that 'I had insulted the King by appearing before him improperly dressed.' It was a real HLI row, where something trivial and of no importance whatsoever was blown up out of all proportion, whilst something of real significance was scarcely noticed. This attitude was very prevalent in the British Army at the time. I was to meet it again in 1942 at the training centre of the Glider Pilot Regiment, when good men were returned to their unit (RTU), a disgrace, for having 'idle bootlaces'. When I protested, I was told, 'if you let men get away with twisted bootlaces, where will it all end?'

My 'crime' and insult to His Majesty was that my Tschako had gold braid around the top of it, something only to be worn by Majors and above. In vain I pointed out that I had received the helmet in good faith and could hardly have been expected to tear the gold braid off someone else's hat; that General Balfour had seen me in it and had said nothing. Furthermore it had been tucked so firmly beneath my plaid that it was scarcely likely that the King could have even seen it. I was told he had an eagle eye which nothing escaped and was conversant with every minute detail of uniform of every regiment in the Army. I made matters far worse, and thought the Adjutant would have a fit, by pointing out that in this case His Majesty was unlike the rest of his family; for the Duke of Connaught had not known whether he was dining with us or with the 60th Rifles at the last Regimental dinner, whilst the Prince of Wales had gone to inspect the Seaforth Highlanders wearing bits of Scots Fusilier uniform, such as their Glengarry and badge, as his headgear. It was no use. I was confined to barracks and given fourteen extra days as Orderly Officer. I now realise that my superiors were simply obeying the old Army principle of covering their backs. Perhaps someone at the Palace had noticed, and might take official action or complaint. It scarcely bore thinking about, and was the equivalent of 'losing one's name to the King'. In such an event they could say, 'The officer in question has been severely disciplined', quite irrespective of justice or justification.

1935 passed quietly on. We did platoon and company training, qualified the Jocks for their shooting on the ranges, marched the 60-odd miles to Tain for the Battalion camp, did one exercise, stayed three weeks eating raspberries and cream, and marched home. I competed in the Inverness Highland Games and won both sprint events and a satisfactory sum of money. This I found rather embarrassing but used it to buy a silver Dunhill cigarette lighter and had the date and the events engraved upon it. That way it seemed I had won a prize and not money. We Highlanders danced ourselves silly at the Northern Meeting in September.

One morning at lunchtime, Walad Urquhart came into the Mess anteroom and said to me, 'You're for the Shiny – for India, along with Mark Hollis, Charles Wilson and Major Stewart.' Peckham Stewart was a portly man with a round red face and the standard 'officer pattern' toothbrush moustache. He was to command our draft of 200 Jocks being sent out as replacements for time expired men of the 2nd Bn, or 74th Highlanders as it preferred to be called. The Walad went on to tell us that we had a month's embarkation leave each, and to arrange the dates among ourselves when we took it. I left mine as late as possible, so that I could go skiing. We were to sail on the maiden voyage of a brand new troopship called the *Dilwara*, from Southampton. I organised a large party of both sexes, and as Germany was so cheap, we went to Garmisch-

Partenkirchen, where there was a big cable car, serving all the Olympic runs, for Garmisch was to be the site for the Winter Games at the end of January 1936.

When we arrived there just after Christmas there was no snow, so it was back up to the Schneefernerhaus hotel on the Zugspitze glacier. When the snow came, it never stopped for days. After it cleared, three Germans, despite warnings, left to ski down to the Knorrhuette and got caught in an avalanche. Two died, but the third managed to struggle to the hut and sound the alarm. I went out with the rescue party to try and dig out those still buried, hoping they might be alive. The rescuers worked in a line, each two feet apart holding a long iron rod with which they prodded the snow to discover anyone below. We found the men, but both were dead. Somebody stuck a safety pin through one man's tongue and pulled it out to prevent it being swallowed, before starting artificial respiration. The man was beyond help. His tongue froze with the pin sticking up, rather grotesquely, into the air. I thought how sore he would have felt if he had been brought round.

Among those from the HLI in our party was a certain John Royle, one of the wild young men of the 1930s who were to do so well in the coming war. Later during the spring of 1936, he, Rhoddy Rose, also of the 71st, and Sheemie Lovat of the Scots Guards, were to set Cairo alight with their escapades. John would often get extremely drunk at dances and other functions, then find some quiet corner where he could sleep it off. Unfortunately if woken, he was inclined to hit the first thing he saw, and as he was a large and very solid man, the result was likely to be disastrous for anyone who woke him. Sometime in 1937, he joined us in India, and during a dance at the Club in Rawal Pindi, he was sleeping inoffensively in a corner, when a Major in the Indian Army woke him up and told him to go home. John's reply was to flatten him. At the subsequent court martial Royle was dismissed the Service. I next met him in the train going up to Aberdeen to enlist in the Gordons as a Jock in September 1939. I was on my way to Fort George. From the Gordons, John went to the 5th Bn Scots Guards, a hotch-potch unit, waiting to go to Finland to fight the Russians in December 1939. He became a Regimental Sgt Major in the Scots Guards, a feat probably more difficult and praiseworthy than becoming a Field

251

Marshal. He regained his Commission and became a Major, serving with me in the Glider Pilot Regiment. He died with great gallantry, leading a patrol at Arnhem in September 1944.

We boarded HMT *Dilwara* at Southampton Docks early on Tuesday, 28 January 1936, a day and date which will ever remain in my memory. She was a large white ship of some 20,000 tons. We sailed early that afternoon. As the gap widened between the ship and the quai, I suddenly realised that I was as far away from my life in England as if I were already in India. The ship was spacious and comfortable, the food wonderful. We junior officers were three to a cabin, living in comparative luxury. The Jocks and others slept in hammocks and lived between decks except for boat drills, when they emerged blinking like moles. Every third night we did Orderly Officer, and went round the HLI deck to see that all was well. It is said that a slave ship could be smelt from afar and was the worst smell that could ever be experienced. I wonder, however, if whoever wrote or said that, had ever sampled that of a hundred pairs of Jocks' sweaty feet after a long day in rubber plimsolls, lying in their hammocks on a hot and steamy night, on passage down the Red Sea and into the Indian Ocean? My money would be on the Jocks every time. Besides our draft there was a large RAF contingent aboard, bound for Basra on the Shatt el Arab in Iraq. With the detour we would have to make for that, our voyage to India would take a month.

Our first stop was at Port Said after a week of sailing. The weather had been atrocious and the *Dilwara* showed evident proof of her inadequacies by rolling, pitching and corkscrewing to every wave. Most people were sick and the stench was appalling. She was a pig of a ship in rough weather. Directly we docked, a number of us went ashore. The minute we stepped on land we were beset by a crowd of yelling, jostling, shrieking men in turbans or fezes, and long nightgowns: 'Just look Mister, feelthy picture you no find better', or offers, 'You want jigajig my sister all same inside like Queenie Victoria'. Others were offering their small brothers, 'All same inside like King Georgie'. We resisted such blandishments and visited Simon Arzt. On our return to the ship we found it swarming with fortune tellers and *gulli-gulli* men producing chicks from under fezes. I was instantly transported

252

back to my childhood, when as a little boy of eight on the *Scindia*, we had stopped at Port Said on the way back from India. Now I was returning there.

Terror of the sun's dreaded Actinic ray directly we got East of Suez still dominated medical thought. As soon as we entered the Red Sea, every man had to wear a pith helmet, a solar topi, if they were on deck during the day. The next stop was Aden, which the pipe tune 'The Barren Rocks' describes most perfectly. A mass of small shops run by Indians, all along the harbour front, sold goods even more cheaply than at Simon Arzt. We kicked ourselves for having bought there. Aden was a desperate Outpost of Empire at which to be stationed, hot, fly-ridden and with nothing to do. Even bathing was dangerous and had to be done behind a shark net. We heard that only a week before we arrived, a shark had broken through the net and had had the effrontery to eat a Group Captain's wife. The ship ploughed on up the Persian Gulf, which was cold, wet and stormy, to deliver the RAF replacements at Basra. Then on to India, where we berthed at Karachi exactly a month after leaving England. Nowadays the journey is hardly an overnight flight. In the 1930s, even P&O liners took a fortnight. Personally, as a form of travel I would always prefer the sea voyage, even on the *Dilwara*.

20

We entrained in the Frontier Mail, one of the most famous trains in India, at Karachi. The journey took two days, and all the old sights, sounds and smells I had known as a boy came flooding back. Unfortunately I had forgotten every word of Urdu. I hoped that it, too, would return in due course. The Indian railways were exactly as I remembered them. We four officers of the draft shared a large half carriage with the usual pull-down bunks and a compartment for the tin bathtub and the lavatory. The train was met at Peshawar by an officer in Mackenzie tartan shorts, cut so amply wide that they resembled a kilt as closely as possible, tartan hose with green flashes, a thick grey flannel shirt with open collar and rolled-up sleeves. On his head was the inevitable pith solar topi, embellished by the red-and-white Regimental hackle on one side. With the pipe band skirling at our head, we were marched to Roberts Barracks, the men dispersed to their quarters, whilst Charles Wilson and I were allocated a quarter in a bungalow, No 68 at the extreme end of the Mall. Mark Hollis was housed in another. We shared it with two others, Jerry Beale, who was attached to us for a year before going into the Indian Army, and Dick when he arrived on the following troopship a month later.

Next day, we three junior officers were marched in front of the Adjutant, Captain Fortescue-Green, who lectured us on how we were to behave whilst in India. He said that he gathered that some of the Jocks had been seen 'leaning out of the carriage windows during our journey up without wearing their solar topis. Did we not realise how dangerous this was? It would have been our fault if one of them had died of sunstroke.' He went on to explain that if it did not actually kill, 'the actinic ray could turn people as black as a native and maybe blacker, why,' he added, 'only last month an officer in Lahore had walked across to the Mess from his bungalow just a hundred yards away, without his topi, and by the time he got there he had turned blacker than a yard up a chimney.' As to making friends, he told us, we were to make friends within the regiment. If we wished to make friends outside it, then the officers of the 13/18th Hussars at Risalpur near Nowshera were perfectly acceptable. Under no circumstances could we be friends with those from the Indian Army, the Royal Tank Corps or the RAF. If we did so, he hinted, we would be letting the Regiment down. In fact nothing in India had changed since my father's day. The social hierarchy was identical. All the old prejudices and snobbery, even their acceptance as normal, remained the same. The only difference I could see, due possibly to inflation, was no more dog boys.

To me, Peshawar was like coming home. From my earliest years I had been told tales of the North-West Frontier. My grand-mother had been married in Peshawar Cathedral, my cousin Twig Birch was now in my grandfather's old No 3 Mountain Artillery Bty, in Kohat, just up the road. I had probably been conceived, early in 1913, as tribesmen's bullets thudded against the iron-shut-tered windows of the fort at Shabkadar. The North-West Frontier of India was to the British much the same as Hadrian's Wall had been to the Roman Empire. It was the boundary line over which the barbarians could not be permitted to cross. In our case, these were the wild Pathan tribes of magnificent warriors, who lived in the desolate mountains between British India and Afghanistan, the Mahsuds, Wazirs, Afridis and Mohmands. Peshawar was the main garrison for the northern end of this defence line.

There were two completely distinct parts of Peshawar, the city and the cantonments, about two miles apart. The City was entirely native and consisted of some 300,000 inhabitants. No Europeans lived there and only visited it as sightseers or tourists to buy goods from the various bazaars and street sellers. Each trade or industry had its own street, such as the 'street of the brassworkers' or of goldsmiths, tinmakers and so on. Young tribesmen, feeling awkward and naked without a rifle slung across their back, would swagger through the throng of people, or sit smoking 'hookahs' or water pipes and sipping mint tea at the cafes. With these the brothels did a brisk trade, especially the boy brothels. Those seeking such pleasures would carry a single rose across their mouth or behind one ear as an indication to the innumerable swarming pimps. The language of the North-West Frontier is Pushtu, and when learning it later, an Afridi whom I paid for conversation, told me 'that the day the British left India, there wouldn't be a virgin remaining between the Khyber and Lahore. Not that we Pathans reckon much to virgins anyway, preferring boys and goats.' When asked why, he said, 'Have you ever seen our women?' 'This might explain the boys, but not the goats,' I continued. His answer was, 'Boys are scarce, goats plentiful, and you really should see our women!' Many of the Afridis are blue-eyed and fair-skinned, direct descendants of Alexander the Great's soldiers who came through the Khyber around 325 BC. This would explain not only their homosexuality, for which the Greeks were notorious, but also their predilection for goats from the mythical satyr, a creature half-human, half-goat.

Just outside the city lies the fort, built of baked mud bricks, looking as imposing as any medieval castle. In its dungeons lay the entire reserve stores of small arms and artillery ammunition for the whole of northern India. There was a permanent guard on it of a platoon from the British Regiment stationed in the cantonment. One's turn for this tour of duty came round about once a year. It was usually a subaltern's first independent command and was highly popular. Still, as a legacy from the Great Indian Mutiny of 1857, no Indian Army unit was ever given the opportunity to seize the fort and its contents.

The cantonments were situated on the Kajuri Plain, which stretched some 30 miles to the mouth of the Khyber Pass, where lay Jamrud fort, shaped like a crouching lion, at its entrance. The fort was permanently garrisoned by a company of infantry from one of the Indian Bns in Peshawar, commanded by a single British officer who could say, 'Carry on Subadar Sahib,' jump in his car and away to the Peshawar Club for *tiffin*, whenever he felt like it Jamrud was considered too desolate a place for British troops. Apart from such small outside detachments, the entire garrison was stationed within the cantonments, and surrounded by a thick belt of barbed wire. In 1931 the Afridis had swept down from the Khyber right up to the wire, slaughtering everything in their way, and had with difficulty been driven back. Lately they had shown their contempt for our military vigilance by lifting two camels across the wire one night, leaving them tethered inside to be found in the morning, the camels having been stolen from within it two nights previously.

The barbed wire encompassed a huge area, as beautifully laid out and tended as only the British can do it, as far as possible a replica of England but giving due heed to local conditions. During the cold weather when all the Memsahibs were there, it was a mass of roses and other flowers, tended by a horde of *malis* or gardeners under control of the PWD, the Public Works Dept, whose officers were even further down the social ladder than those managing something called 'grass farms'. Within this area lay the whole Peshawar garrison, as well as an RAF airfield, the cricket ground of Test Match proportions, a cathedral, the entire civilian apparatus which controlled the North-West Frontier Province (NWFP), including Government House and the Governor, Sir John Cunningham, the Peshawar Club with its famous horse-shoe bar, the Peshawar Vale Hunt and its kennels, two military hospitals, British and Indian, a native bazaar, innumerable bungalows and officers' Messes, servants' quarters, a large hotel for Europeans, Grindlays Bank and a shopping centre. Probably some 15,000 people lived within the cantonment wire.

The military garrison consisted of HQ the Peshawar District and Mountain Division, commanded by a Major General. The Division contained three Bdes, the Peshawar Brigade commanded by Brigadier Dick O'Connor, who in 1940 won such a wonderful victory over the Italians in Libya, A Brigade at Nowshera, commanded by Brigadier H.R.G. Alexander, who afterwards became Monty's boss at El Alamein and then Lord Alexander of Tunis, and a Bde at Landi Kotal at the head of the Khyber Pass on the frontier with Afghanistan, commanded by Brigadier Molesworth. If you had asked me then which of the three really knew his job, I would have picked Brig Molesworth every time, but he retired as a Brigadier. There was a cavalry Bde at Risalpur, the name means 'cavalry town', of one British and three Indian cavalry regiments, the British being the 13/18th Hussars, among whom Fortescue-Green had told us we could find friends. As well as the Peshawar Bde in the cantonments, there were a number of Divisional units, the 16th Cavalry, the Peshawar District Royal Indian Signals Regiment, a field regt Royal Engineers, a squadron of the Royal Tank Corps with light tanks, and No 20 Army Co-operation Sqn of the RAF, equipped with Hawker Hart Variant aircraft. The Mountain Regt RA also had its HQ with Peshawar Div plus one Bty, the other three being out with Bdes. There were, in addition, Coys of the Royal Indian Army Service Corps, RIASC, known as the Rice Corps, who dealt with all matters of supply and transport, and the Royal Indian Army Ordnance Corps, RIAOC, who took care of rifles, machine guns and artillery. Not to be left out was a large Army vetinerary establishment to look after the many horses and mules, civil and military, and in addition, the foxhounds of the Peshawar Vale Hunt, the famous PVH.

The 16th Cavalry were in the process of being 'Indianised', and the only two British officers remaining were the CO and the 2ic. Indianisation had been going on for some years, with the object of a phased and orderly handover of power, both political and military, to India. As British officials and officers retired, they were replaced by Indians who had been educated and trained in Britain, the military officers at Sandhurst, Woolwich and RAF Cranwell. They were awarded the King's Commission and ranked in every way as equals of their British counterparts. The idea was that in 10 to 15 years, India would attain self-government with Dominion status, similar to that of Canada and Australia. How much better would this have been than the cowardly skedaddle by our Labour Government in 1947, when over a million died in internecine strife during the partition of India and Pakistan.

The whole NWFP area was on a semi-war footing and all units were fully up to strength, each Battalion containing some 800 men. The Army was still organised on the 'fours' system as explained in a previous chapter. Thus each Bde had four Bns, one British and three Indian. The Peshawar Bde consisted of Bde HQ and:

2nd Bn The Highland Light Infantry (74th Highlanders)
4th Bn 15th Punjab Regt.
1st Bn Bombay Grenadiers (known as Bombay Grinders)
1st Bn 19th Hyderabad Regt (known as the Hydraboodles)
Peshawar Mtn Bty Royal Artillery of eight 3.7 inch 'Screwguns'
Bde Signal Section, Royal Indian Signals.

Ancillary troops were added from divisional resources as and when required. The transport was entirely by mules or horses. The artillery pieces of the Royal Artillery are of special interest. They were quick-firing guns, which could be unscrewed, taken to pieces and reassembled in a very short time, so that they could be carried on mules. The officers were all British, but the men Indians, usually Sikhs. The field pieces had to be screwguns with a high trajectory for use in the mountains. The other two Bdes of the Peshawar Division were organised on exactly similar lines. The British Bn at Nowshera was from the Duke of Wellington's Regt, and that at Landi Kotal from the Cameronians.

The infantry battalions in India were all armed and equipped in the same way, on the 'fours principle'. Each consisted of a HQ Company, three Rifle Companies and one Machine Gun Company. There were four platoons to a company, each of four sections of eight men led by a corporal or lance corporal. In a British battalion there were some 35 King's Commissioned officers, Coys being commanded by a major or a captain with a subaltern officer in charge of every platoon. The CO was a Lt Colonel, with a captain or subaltern as his adjutant. The Quartermaster was invariably an ex-ranker, promoted from the supply side of the administration. There were only 12 King's Commissioned officers in an infantry battalion of the Indian Army, four of whom were generally away on leave or courses. Except for those regiments, such as the 16th Cavalry, undergoing Indianisation, all King's Commissioned officers were British and usually Sandhurst-trained. Each Coy would therefore be commanded by a British officer, as was the CO, Adjt and QM, in this case not an ex-ranker. All the other officers were Indian, holding a Viceroy's Commission. However long their service, some of over 20 years, festooned with decorations and medals, even the VC, they always remained junior to the most recently joined King's Commissioned 2/lt from Sandhurst. The Indian officers of any regiment were the most wonderful body of loyal, brave, disciplined, dignified and knowledgeable men it is possible to describe. At their head was the Subadar Major, the CO's right-hand man. With each Coy there was a duplicate company commander, a Subadar, with a Jemadar commanding every platoon. The Subadar bore two 'pips' or stars on his shoulders, the Jemadar one. They were invariably addressed by all ranks, even Field Marshals, as 'Subadar' or 'Jemadar Sahib'. The Indian officers really ran every battalion, just as the RSM and senior NCOs ran every British one. The officers were merely there as ornaments and to answer with their heads if anything went wrong. Young British officers on joining the Indian Army would be 'put back for instruction under a Subadar or Jemadar'. Woe betide him if he failed to heed what they said.

Although many Indian Army regiments went by grandiloquent titles, such as Bombay Grenadiers, Mahratta Light Infantry, Coke's Rifles, 9th Jats or 45th Rattray's Sikhs, the name was usually a hangover from a previous epoch. Tradition was as cherished as it was in British service. 'The Bombay Grinders' had as little to do with Bombay as they had with Bradford, probably less. Most battalions consisted of two Coys of Punjabi Mussulmans (Moslems) known as PMs, the bedrock of the Indian Army, a Coy of Sikhs, and possibly a Coy of the ethnic group from which they took their name. The Frontier Force Rifles recruited tribal Pathans, and the Rajputana Rifles, alias the 'Large Banana Trifles', recruited Rajputs. Due to their really outstanding thieving skills, the 40th Pathans were affectionately generally known as the 'Forty Thieves'.

All infantry units throughout India used the same ammunition for all their weapons except revolvers. This was the .303 inch, rimmed, mk 7, sharp-nosed, nickel-plated bullet fired from a brass cartridge. Every man had his own personal rifle with which he had fired his annual course to earn his proficiency pay. The rifle was the Short Magazine Lee Enfield (SMLE), which had been the standard weapon throughout the Great War. In 1936, the Lewis light machine gun (LMG) was being replaced by the Vickers

Berthier or VB, a Czech-designed magazine-loading weapon, better known throughout World War Two as the Bren. (A combination of Brno in Czecho-Slovakia and Enfield.) There was one VB to each rifle section. The Machine Gun Coy was equipped with 16 Vickers belt-fed medium machine guns (MMG), water-cooled and firing from a tripod, unchanged since the Great War. All officers carried as their personal weapon a .45 inch calibre Colt revolver, the size of a small howitzer. It fired a heavy lead bullet, which on exiting from a man's body would tear a hole in it the size of a large soup plate. Such was the kinetic energy contained in such a bullet that it would knock a man flying, even if it only hit him in the hand. A weapon such as this was the only thing that could stop a charging Pathan once he got to close quarters, attacking with the relentless fury of a wounded tiger.

And what of the enemy against whom this massive British force was organised to fight? The enemy was the Pathan tribes who lived in tribal territory, outside British jurisdiction, yet having to obey it under British political officers and advisers. They lived in the wild and desolate mountains on either side of the Khyber Pass. A lateral road skirted this area, and there were two roads through the Pass itself. The roads were in British India by treaty with the tribes, but to stray off them even for a few yards risked kidnap or murder. The Pathans lived in clans and septs, not unlike those of the 18th-century Scottish Highlanders. They were, also like those clansmen, probably the physically hardest people in the world, who could run up and down their mountains as fast as the herds of sheep and goats they loved so much, and maybe faster. These animals, and perennial lack of rain, had stripped the mountains of all vegetation, except in the 'nullahs', dry beds of mountain streams which flooded from time to time, in which scrub grew. What corn or vegetables grown were sown and tended by the women on terraced fields around the small villages made of sun-dried mud bricks, with a mosque in the centre. Pathans are devout Moslems. The women wore long black garments, which had to be hitched up as they bent down to work in the fields, disclosing bright red trousers below. The men would lounge in the shade of a wall to watch them, making sure they toiled and did not get up to any hanky-panky.

No man in tribal territory would move without his rifle, his cherished possession. The most eagerly sought-after type was the SMLE. Just off the road between Peshawar and Kohat, but in tribal territory, there was a rifle factory which made exact copies of the British model out of bits of wood and scrap metal. The barrel would be bored out with an ancient drill worked by a strung bow. Those who made such weapons were real craftsmen, working on the floor with a combination of hands, feet and toes. The rifles actually worked with fair accuracy, but wore out very quickly. However the greatest prize was to steal an Army rifle, and it was a disgrace for a unit 'to lose a rifle'. The tribesmen were such expert thieves that men had to sleep on their rifles, and even then they would get them out without disturbing the sleeper unless it was also chained to his body. Tribal territory was also the land of the blood feud, which continued between families for generations. A deliberate murder, or even an accident, in which a man or boy was killed, would start one off. Women naturally did not count, nor were ever murdered in revenge killings. The Pushtu word 'khuni' for a murderer was included with those 'denoting an honourable profession', which formed its plural by adding 'ian'.

We had been fighting Pathans ever since 1840, and a curious love-hate relationship had built up between us, based on mutual fighting qualities. Around Peshawar, these small wars would begin by the Afridis or Mohmands raiding into British India in search of loot, or there would be strife among themselves threatening the stability of the whole region, which could not be permitted. Some of these were accepted as part of everyday life and, provided they did not get out of hand, were tolerated. For instance, two septs of the Afridis living on either side of the roads going through the Khyber to Landi Kotal, loathed and detested each other. There were continual blood feuds and sniping between the two. Each village had an ancient muzzle-loading cannon, but only one cannonball between them, which they took it in turns to fire, obligingly stopping to allow Brig Molesworth to drive through on Thursday and Saturday mornings on his way to hunt with the PVH. This was all regarded as whimsical good fun, and nothing much done about it. The Indian Government kept an elaborate establishment of spies among the tribes, who were well known to one and all. Often a tribal headman would complain bitterly to the Political Officer that their own particular batch of the ones engaged to spy on them was not being paid as much as those of the neighbouring tribe.

Every now and again, however, some Fakir or 'Holy Man', would appear and proclaim 'a holy war or Jihad' against the 'British Infidel'. Such had happened in 1935, just before I arrived in India, when both the Peshawar and Lahore Divisions had been used to suppress the Mohmands, a medal being issued for the campaign. In 1937 the Fakir of Ipi did the same on a much larger scale in Waziristan, calling out the whole of the Wazirs and Mahsuds. The campaign against them dragged on for nearly two years. Hostilities usually began in the same way by the Pathans ambushing a British column as it passed through some narrow valley. In Waziristan it began by the ambush of a number of tanks as they negotiated a narrow pass, the Shah Tangye, by blocking the road before and behind prior to attacking. As well as the tanks, there were a number of three-ton trucks carrying infantry. We took heavy casualties, and someone who was there told me later that the Pathans had been shooting at them from behind boulders and other cover all day from about 30 yards, yet such was their skill as guerrilla fighters that he never laid eyes on a single one.

The NWFP was a wonderful training ground for the British and Indian Armies. Enough people got killed and wounded to keep everybody on their toes. There was always the chance of winning a decoration and the certainty of a campaign medal. Many a military reputation had been built on a Frontier war. Even VCs could be won, but invariably posthumously, in which I have always considered there is but little percentage. Whenever trouble flared up with the tribes, the first into action were the RAF who were sent to bomb the villages involved. This was an elaborate procedure, the tribal elders being summoned by the British Political Officer to a '*jirga*' or conference, and warned that if their young men did not behave themselves, action would have to be taken. If this warning was ignored, certain villages would be picked for bombing and leaflets dropped on them, giving the date and time of the action, so that all the people and livestock could be moved to safety before it began. Such action was more of a nuisance value than anything else, because the mud brick houses could easily be rebuilt.

Most at risk were the pilots and observers of the aircraft involved, for in the event of engine failure there was nowhere to make a forced landing amid the bleak and jagged hills, full of wild, hostile and fanatical tribesmen, who would hand them over to the women for torture. Some of the women were experts, able slowly to flay a man alive and conscious for at least 48 hours. Cutting off the eyelids, smearing the face with honey and tying a man over an ants' nest was another favourite pastime. Every air crew on operations carried a letter offering a large reward for his safe return to the nearest cantonment or British unit. Red-headed airmen on the other hand were considered very lucky and often put out to stud. Muslims who have been on pilgrimage or Hadj to Mecca are permitted to dye their beards red, and it is a holy colour. The same kind of torture and mutilation was meeted out to any British or Indian soldier captured during ground operations. The greatest disgrace any unit could have befall it, equal to 'losing its Colours', was to leave a man wounded or lying dead on the hill – a disgrace that would resound from the top of the Khyber to the southernmost tip of Ceylon and which would linger for decades wherever soldiers met.

If bombing from the air failed to produce results other than enraging the inhabitants of the villages who had had their houses destroyed, then a Brigade Column was sent out to continue the war. It always met with stout resistance, and from many an early ambush, at which the Pathans excelled, along with other military disasters, great and small, we had worked out and perfected a most excellent and nearly foolproof system of mountain warfare. Yet when the ill-fated British force was sent to fight the Germans in Norway in April 1940, not a single mountain warfare expert went with it. Not that it is likely that it would have made any difference had advisers been sent, for the troops were completely untrained in the difficult art of mountain warfare, and were up against the crack German Mountain Division, who really knew their onions.

The main body of the column had to operate in a long thin line along rough tracks only fit for horses, mules or men, at the bottom of the valley. On each side were steep, shale and boulder-strewn hills on which little or no vegetation grew. In summer shade temperatures reached 120° Fahrenheit and up to 100° in winter, with freezing cold at night. There was little or no water available, though the villages, perched on terraced fields on the mountain sides, had wells. From the high ground on each side, the tribesmen would snipe and harrass the Column below. The answer lay in the short sentence, 'piquet the heights'. This meant that all ground from which the Column could be attacked must be occupied by our own troops before the Column could move forward. Imagine a long woollen tube being endlessly turned inside out upon itself. There would be a small advance guard moving along the valley floor, followed by the piqueting battalion. Each Coy in turn would be used, and each piquet consisted of a full platoon. The officer would be shown the exact location of the piquet by means of a 'pointer stick', which separated into two exactly parallel halves, each with sights on it like a rifle. The Coy Commander would sight the exact position for the piquet, and the officer who was to go there saw precisely the same place on his half of the pointer stick. There could be no mistakes or excuses that it had not been properly explained. Then, up would race the platoon. In the mean-time, the ground they were to climb over was covered by the machine guns of the Bn and the screwguns of the mountain Bty RA. Any hostile action would bring down a curtain of fire in front of the advancing troops.

As the piquet would have to remain in place until the whole Column had passed below, the first thing the platoon had to do after posting sentries, was to build a '*sangar*', a breastwork of a stone wall, built in a circle, which would give cover if attacked. The hills overlooking these valleys were dotted with such *sangars*, remains of former piquets, and if you were lucky you might find the remains of one still standing after 50 years. When the leading battalion had sent up all its rifle platoons, the next took over the task of piqueting, and so on, each one taking its turn. At the rear of the Column flew a large red flag. Directly you saw that past your piquet, you came running with your men, absolutely flat out, down the hill, for the enemy would be on the *sangar* you had just left, from the other side, just as soon as you could say 'Jack Robinson' and maybe sooner. Thus as the last piquets were coming down at the rear, the first piquets would be going up at the front of the Column in a continuous procedure. It was amazing the speed at which the soldiers could tear up and down a mountain. Best at it were undoubtedly the Gurkhas, who were born and bred to it, but I was astonished how well our Jocks adapted, and we could certainly hold our own with anybody. The whole process was a well thought-out, rehearsed and perfected drill, in which everybody knew their part. It was practised over and over again during peacetime manoeuvres around Peshawar, and our skill at it was a matter of pride to everybody.

The system, however secure, had one great drawback. It was very slow, and rarely averaged more than ten miles a day. Attempts to speed things up nearly always ended in disaster. Night camps therefore had to be constructed, with strongly held piquets on the heights all round. Everyone set to, building a stone wall for protection of the camp. Based on the ancient Roman model, every unit and every HQ was always in the same place, and could be contacted almost blindfold from prior knowledge without having to ask. For this method of mountain warfare to function properly, however, there had to be well-nigh perfect intercommunication. Each unit was responsible for providing this within itself, with the Royal Corps of Signals providing it above battalion level. Wireless was not used except from Bde HQ to the Air and to Divisional HQ. In any case, in the deep valleys, wireless would have been well-nigh useless. When not on the move, all HQ, even down to Coys, were connected by field telephones with rather primitive handsets, activated by rotating a handle at the side. These telephones were always coloured a rather bilious green. Every battalion had its own Signals Platoon, carrying all its equipment on mule back. Two signallers would be allocated to each piquet. All signalling was done by using the Morse code, and signallers became so expert that I have even seen one reading a newspaper as he received and tapped out messages with his other hand. On the Frontier, there were three methods of using the Morse code, by heliograph, flag and Aldis lamp. Far the most widely used was the heliograph. With almost every day of cloudless sunshine, this was the obvious method. By a cunning combination of sights and mirrors, signals could be received and sent from any direction. The recollection of the heliograph winking from the piquets all round, will be for me, an ever-abiding memory of the Frontier. At night the heliograph would be replaced by the Aldis lamp. Flags were reserved for the rare days without sun, but the Morse code was used with them and not semaphore.

Night was the time for the *sangar* to be attacked, not so much to overrun it, that would be costly and difficult, but in the hope that a relief force would be sent out from below, which could be ambushed, with stragglers cut off, their rifles and ammunition stolen and men captured for the sport of the women. Thus if attacked, a *sangar* would have to fight it out on its own, its fire-power infinitely greater than anything that could be brought against it. On occasion, sporadic fighting would continue all night, the *sangar* garrison relatively safe behind their stone wall. To the Pathans, it was more or less all part of a game. Quite often the leader of the attackers would come in the next day under a flag of truce to see the Brigadier, and ask him to congratulate the young officer who had carried out so doughty a defence of his piquet the previous night. He would like to invite him to a *pilau tiffin* or lunch in his village when hostilities ceased.

Now, I was considering quite seriously transferring to the Indian Political Service, where eating *pilau tiffins* was all part of the day's work, until I attended one of these lunches myself in a Pathan village. Time means nothing in India, and it was interminable. Cooking did not even start until the last guest had arrived. As nobody knew how many or who had been invited, this took considerable time. All the while, the unfortunate fat-tailed sheep which was to provide the meal was tethered outside, bleating its head off, for every guest to admire as he came through the door. If you asked a Pathan why their sheep had fat tails, he would tell you that as they always grazed facing uphill because of the heat, the fat melted and ran down into their tails, forming like a camel's hump, a wonderful reserve of food in time of famine. A sign that at least something was happening for the lunch was when the unfortunate creature was ritually slaughtered and taken away to be skinned and cut up into small squares, which would be boiled and served with pilau rice. When it eventually arrived, the food was quite eatable, but its taste was irretrievably spoilt by the memory of the pathetic and piteous sounds of the bleating of its main ingredient. The Pathans were convinced that the British lived on nothing but hard-boiled eggs, so whilst waiting for the other guests to arrive, we were offered, and from politeness had to eat, an endless succession of hard-boiled eggs, which left one constipated for weeks. I often wondered if this was the Pathan idea of a splendid joke.

21

The 74th was a very good battalion. This was thanks largely to its new CO, Lt Col Berney-Ficklin, known affectionately as 'Berney' or old Huntin', Shootin' and Ficklin'. He had been brought in from the Norfolks on accelerated promotion, taking over from the most charming former Olympic fencer Guy Greville, who closely resembled the film star Aubrey Smith playing the part of many a bluff old British Colonel in various Hollywood productions, such as *Bengal Lancer* and *The Four Feathers*. Guy had come to us from an Irish Regiment. He had to give up command after a bad riding accident whilst out hunting with the PVH, his horse rolling on him in the way that horses love to do in such cases, and had to be invalided out of the Army. The arrival of yet another 'foreigner', in the form of Berney, was too much for many of the officers to accept. In revenge, one of the senior Majors, called Macartney-Filgate, promptly ran off with the poor man's wife. By the time I arrived in Peshawar, he had found another – he was not the sort of man to let grass grow under his feet – a beautiful if excitable Russian, named Ileana. She had a stage Russian accent, and the mercurial temperament of an operatic diva. She slept in a huge bed, with peach-coloured silk sheets and pillow cases, with Berney next to her on a narrow camp cot, with his saddle as a pillow.

I got on very well with her until the unfortunate episode of the tennis tournament. For some reason I had been appointed tennis secretary at the Club, and one of my duties was to arrange and run the annual tennis tournament. This was a rather grand affair, for which there were entries from all over the NWFP and beyond, even as far as Lahore. One of its strict rules was that any competitor arriving more than 20 minutes late for their match was automatically scratched. Ileana was playing in a mixed doubles. Her opponents had arrived, as well as her partner. We waited the statutory 20 minutes, plus an extra 10, after which I awarded the match to her opponents. When she eventually turned up, saying she had mistaken the time, I broke the news to her as gently as I could, but realised she was not best pleased and was working up a fair head of steam. However, rules are rules, and how could I make exceptions, especially as she was my CO's wife? It would look like blatant favouritism. Actually I did not think much about it. As the Colonel's wife she must see my point of view. Unfortunately, for some reason I was actually staying with them in their bungalow at the time. When I turned up that evening to change for dinner, I was met at the door by an almost demented female, wild of eye and frothing at the mouth. 'Out!' she shrieked, 'Out! Out! Out!' prodding me with a scarlet tipped, bony forefinger, 'You are nozing but a snipe guttaire. Out! Out!' I fled to look for another roof under which to lay my head that night. Peshawar rocked with the news. I had become quite a celebrity, possible future subject of a Bateman cartoon, 'the subaltern who scratched his CO's wife from a tennis tournament'. The general opinion was that it was the right, if somewhat foolish, thing to have done. As for Ileana, she never forgave me, and my future off-duty relations with Berney always felt awkward

The 2nd HLI had been in Peshawar for a couple of years before I arrived, and was a hardened Frontier battalion. It had marched there from Razmak, some 220 miles, where it had spent a year on perpetual semi-active service duties amid the bleak Waziristan mountains, policing the unruly Mahsud tribes. Just prior to my arrival it had taken part in a small war against the Mohmands, for which a campaign medal had been granted. All the men were experienced professional soldiers of at least three to seven years service, the NCOs, especially the more senior ones, were rock-like, steady 'old sweats', who knew what to do in any situation without having some ignorant officer to tell them. It had a magnificent Regimental Sgt Major in RSM McIver, the CO's right-hand man. He and the Adjutant, Fortescue-Green, ran the unit, through the CSMs with a few kind words from time to time to the Coy commanders to make them think they were doing it. This left the officers almost unlimited time for mayhem and intrigue. At least a third were homosexual, including a very 'horsy' and unpleasantly snobbish clique which controlled social events and promotion in the Regiment for many years to come. The remainder appeared to spend much of their time bed-hopping with each others' wives. In fact, it seemed to me at least a month before I saw any of them use a door. They were too busy leaping in and out of windows.

A couple of months after we arrived the hot weather began. All the Mem- and Miss-Sahibs departed for Kashmir or other hill stations, the heat being considered too much for their delicate constitutions. Furthermore it was well known that it turned their skin as yellow as old parchment or maybe a banana, and who wants that? There were only two seasons in the NWFP, hot weather and cold weather where, unlike other parts of India, there was no monsoon, and it hardly ever rained. The hot weather began towards the end of April and finished in mid-October, when the cold weather began. It would be hard to find a greater contrast, the hot weather being uniformly horrible, and the cold uniformly delightful. During the hot weather, the day temperature in the shade rarely fell below 112° F (45° C), and 80° F (27° C) at night, whilst the cold weather had glorious crisp sunny days like a fine English summer, with frosts at night. The hot weather, too, was the time for mosquitoes, many of them malarial, and sandflies, whose bite often carried a very unpleasant flu-like disease called sandfly fever. Air-conditioning was of course unknown, but we did have ceiling fans which stirred the hot fetid air. Most officers had their beds moved out onto the lawn and slept under a mosquito net. What the Jocks did I am ashamed to say I have no idea, because nobody took the trouble to find out.

Parades were held at 5 a.m. and lasted until 9 a.m., to take advantage of what coolth there was. We then had breakfast, spent an hour or two in the Coy office, and work was over for the day. Officers and Jocks fired their annual course with rifle and light machine gun to earn their proficiency pay. I remember writing home to say that if I could travel as fast as a rifle bullet, I could be back in England in under four hours, instead of the three weeks it took then. Yet within my own lifetime, travelling by Concorde, it has been possible to do it even faster. Days of work and leave were the same as they had been in my father's time. Thursday was a holiday as well as Saturday and Sunday. Ten days leave was always available and did not count against one's entitlement, but it had to be for some proper purpose, such as a polo tournament, pig-sticking, shooting and so on, and not for anything frivolous such as poodle-faking. Leave entitlement for an officer was two months every year, and eight months 'home leave' every third year.

There was no leave for us newly arriveds that first year, but I did manage to escape the heat for ten days in Kashmir with Jerry Beale. We hired a broken-down old car and drove to Srinagar, where we took a houseboat on Nagim Bagh, the nearest place to paradise I have ever encountered. We spent the time swimming in the warm waters of the lake among the water lilies, basking in the sun of a climate that must be the most perfect in the world, amid scenery that would make the Alps of Switzerland or Austria look like a slum. Furthermore a Kashmiri houseboat was entirely unlike any other similar accommodation to be found anywhere. For sheer luxury and comfort it could not be surpassed, being made of sweet-smelling wood, with beautifully carved and polished ceilings to all the rooms. These consisted of a large, well-furnished sitting room with big, opening doors looking out onto the lake, a dining room, two or three bedrooms, a bathroom and loo. The roof was flat, covered with an awning and provided with comfortable wicker chairs. Electricity was supplied from a connection on the mooring. There was no running water, but there was the usual *bhisti* to provide this and heat the bath water, as well as the low-caste 'untouchable' *mehta* or sweeper, for other unmentionable duties. The owner of the boat was called a *manji*, who acted as bearer to look after one's clothes, ran the other servants, cook, *khidmatgar* or waiter, arranged all *bandabusts* and acted as a general factotum. The cost of hire varied between four to six rupees a day per head (30 to 50p), depending on the luxury provided. The price included all meals plus a large and satisfying tea in the afternoon.

The houseboat I always hired was called the *Triumph*, which had three bedrooms and cost us each about 40p per day. Our *manji* was one Amadoo Wagnoo, a young man who tended to our every comfort as well as providing superb food. Other amazing qualities of these *manjis*, and of Indian servants in general, was the impossibility of surprising them. You could arrive an hour or two late for a meal, with 15 unexpected guests, and in no time at all the most delicious food would appear as if by magic. The same applied to other arrangements or '*bandabusts*'. You could call Amadoo and say, 'Day after tomorrow we go trekking in the mountains to such and such a place, please make a *bandabust*.' You would set off around 10 a.m., to find on arrival tents up, tea with scones, butter, jam and cake ready, all your kit and sleeping bag laid out, hot water for a wash, and comfortable canvas chairs to sit on around a camp table. Dinner would usually consist of four courses, cooked over a log fire in a stone hearth, and the price still only about a rupee a head over what you paid on the houseboat.

Srinagar lies at an altitude of some 6000 feet, with a climate that is unimagineably perfect, hot, cloudless sunny days, enough rain to keep everything green, cool nights, snow and frost in winter with excellent skiing up to 13,000 feet at Gulmarg nearby. Lying on a flat plain amid a maze of lakes and canals, Srinagar was the leave centre for officers of all the cantonments of northern India from Lahore upwards. It is a kind of mountain Venice, and the main way to get about was by gondola. These were called *shikaras*, and would carry four passengers. They were paddled by three men, sitting at the back using large, heart-shaped paddles. They were called by exotic names, culled from the Persian classics, written on a board nailed to the canopy, such as 'Eating the meat of the pheasant makes the teeth golden' – gold teeth apparently being highly prized by the Mughals. They all advertised 'fully sprung seats', and the canopy had drawable curtains all round, giving complete privacy. Many a young girl, fresh from England, lost her virginity on these all-sprung seats, to some sex-starved subaltern, even captain, up on leave from the dusty plains, on a warm June night on her way back from a dance at the Club. In fact, as Kipling might have put it in his song about the Old Moulmein Pagoda, 'you could hear the hymens snapping from Rangoon to Mandalay' – well, as far as the Srinagar Club on

273

the Bund, anyway! The fact that there were three Kashmiris paddling behind the curtains made no difference, for servants somehow, did not exist. These *shikaras* were very cheap to hire. For a rupee a day (about 8p), you could have one plus crew attached permanently to the houseboat, ready and cheerfully willing to row you wherever you wished to go at any hour of the day or night. How these men could live on such a sum and support a family is beyond comprehension. Whilst working with a house-boat, they would live in the servants' boat, moored nearby, where all the cooking was done. I always became very friendly with these men, who reminded me of the *jomponnies* in Naini Tal when I was a child, and would often sit with them in the back and row the *shikara*. In return they would present me with little bags of walnuts from their village, and wonder why the Sahib would wish to paddle. He was clearly and undoubtedly insane.

As for the soldiers, there was nowhere for them to go at all, nor could they have afforded it if there had been. Although it did not worry me at the time, in fact I accepted it as the normal state of how things were, it does now greatly trouble my conscience. For the officers, there was everything, clubs, tennis courts, hunting, shooting, polo, dances, leave and cars. Above all for the unmarried ones were the girls, still known as the 'fishing fleet', who flocked out on the P&O liners at the start of the cold weather, to stay with parents, uncles, brothers or sisters. Even so, with about one girl to every panting, sex-hungry officer, it meant that any even remotely presentable female was snapped up as quickly as a chameleon snaps up a fly, and maybe quicker. This gave rise to the somewhat curious cult of sour grapes among those men who missed out, pretending to loathe and despise women and poodle-faking at all times.

However, there were no girls from home for the soldiers. None of those who came out to stay with their officer relations would have dreamt of going out with one. It would have been quite unthinkable. Even if they had done so, there was nowhere to go. ORs could not be members of any club, and the hotel in Peshawar was far beyond their pockets. There were no leave centres, no home leave every third year, for them. They did their stint of four or five years and went home with the draft. Some stayed on and became 'old sweats' of NCOs, hard-bitten and pickled in the ways of the Service. There were a few girls to be had, often very beautiful Eurasians, children of those who ran the Indian railways. They went to Sergeants' dances, their faces covered with so much powder to make themselves look white that they appeared to have fallen into a flour bin on the way. Many of these girls married NCOs, who after leaving the Army often remained in India, getting a job on the railways.

On reflection, perhaps the fact which amazes me most is that there did not appear to be any resentment among the Jocks for the difference between their lives and ours. Or if there was, they did not show it. In fact the more exotic, wild and eccentric the officer, the more his doings were talked of, the faster his car, the swifter his polo ponies and hunters, the more popular with the men he seemed to be. Although he was never in India, a classic example of this was the regard the Jocks had in the 71st for David Niven in Malta and Dover. During the cold weather we organised games such as rugby and hockey for the men. There was also a very good Regimental football team, it being their national game. The 74th, in addition, had an outstanding swimming team, of which I was captain, and we won every swimming cup in northern India.

For women, the men mostly had to rely on the raddled bazaar whores at four annas a time (2p). Whilst on duty at Peshawar fort, I discovered that the Jocks were hauling girls from the nearby city up and down the walls in wicker baskets. I suppose I should have interfered, but as they posed no security risk, did not do so. Funnily enough, nor was there any VD as a result. The pimps who arranged such matters made sure the girls were not infected, for the benefit of their own future sales.

For six weeks every hot weather, each company moved up into the hills to Cherat, not far away. At about 4000 feet, it gave the men some relief from the stifling heat of Peshawar. I had been posted to A Coy, along with Dick Kindersley and Jerry Beale. We were commanded by the Weasel, and our CSM was Neilson. We three junior officers shared a bungalow, perched on the very ridge of a mountain, looking over the arid plain thousands of feet below. There were no mosquitoes or sandflies, and at night a cool breeze blew through the windows. After Peshawar at the height of the hot weather, Heaven was a dry skin!.

One of the first things I had done on arriving in Peshawar was to start learning Urdu again. I told my bearer, Mohammed Said Khan to find me a '*munshi*', a teacher. A few days later an extraordinary apparition appeared at my door, dressed in the baggy white trousers with shirt worn outside which was normal Peshawari dress, but wearing a solar topi and carrying a large umbrella. There are some who will claim that this should be called a 'sola topi', from the pith it was made of, but solar or sola, 'a hat by any other name will shade its wearer just as well'. 'Sir,' he said, 'may the light always shine upon your darkness, may you have many fine sons. I am Munshi Sahib, come to teach you Urdu. I am pukka European fellow, wearing topi wristwatch, loving Jesus veree much.' I discovered afterwards that he was a devout Muslim, and his act was all part of a show put on for the Sahibs, who loved it. I paid him 15 rupees a month (£1.15) and we did an hour's tuition five days a week, plus a good deal of homework, over which he was very strict. Urdu is not a difficult language save for the rather complicated Arabic script, and childhood memories of it must have been retained in my subconscious, for in three months I took and passed the Lower Standard Urdu exam, obligatory for all prospective Indian Army officers during their year's service as Unattached List Indian Army (ULIA), with a British Regiment. I was the only one in the 74th who bothered to learn even a few words of the language.

The Lower Standard was almost entirely military, with enough Urdu to allow an officer to command his men, tell his *syce* the way to the polo ground or a Meet of the PVH. I imposed a system of fines on my bearer. Each time I had to speak to him in English, I would pay him four annas, and each time he addressed me in it, he would be fined one anna. I cannot recall him ever speaking English to me again. Childhood prejudices from my parents were still very strong, and I hated Indians speaking to me in their slightly comic sing-song English, which was an insult to me and seemed to rob them of all dignity. Within six months I was completely fluent again, and was even accused by a shopkeeper in the bazaar of being a '*dacey admi*', a local. Perhaps the final accolade was when, with evident distaste, Fortescue-Green one day said, 'Willoughby, you sound just like a bloody native.' I then turned my attention to learing Pushtu, the language of Peshawar and the Pathan tribes, whose greeting is 'May you ever be rich', to be answered by 'May you ever be fat', and whose farewell is 'May good be upon your face'. I told my *munshi*, alas I forget his name, that my grandfather Birch had been a proficient Pushtu speaker in the 1890s, and that my mother had spoken it and Urdu from birth. He returned next day, very excited: 'Was your grandfather not Major Birch Sahib of the mountain artillery? He is still remembered as that *Shaitan* Birch, that Satan Birch, who could dress and speak like an Afridi, spying on us and all we did.' I told him that my grandfather was indeed as described, and my stock rose a hundred points.

I was just as strapped for cash in India as I had been in Britain. To make matters worse, at home we had been paid in advance, and in India we were paid in arrears, in case I imagine that we died of one of the many available diseases and the Indian Government found itself out of pocket. Thus the first thing I had to do was to ask the manager of Grindlays Bank for an overdraft, and it was his kindness and forbearance which financed me throughout my time in Peshawar. In the end, it was only by selling my horse, my car and practically everything else, that I was able to clear my debts before I left. In August 1936, after three years in the Army, I had been automatically promoted to Lieutenant, and my pay rose to 13 rupees a day (£1). It helped, but was not nearly enough, and even with my father's allowance I was always in debt, as were most of us, in accordance with the basic rule 'that outgoings always rise in excess of funds available'. Pay for the Indian Army was at least 50 per cent better than ours, and promotion much quicker, with double the pension at the end of it. But who wanted to be in the Indian Army? Military snobbery from Sandhurst days and my qualms about the Royal Tank Corps had bitten deep into me. When Fortescue-Green had told us we could not have friends in the Indian Army, I had agreed with him, though funnily enough those I did things with from Peshawar, such as go on leave or climb mountains, were ULIA.

To help us out with essential purchases the 74th had a

wonderful system called the Polo fund. Every officer paid a small subscription into it, whether he used it or not, and over the years a considerable sum had collected. Large amounts could be borrowed from it and paid back on one's Mess bill in small, interest-free instalments. There had, however, to be tangible proof that you had bought what you requested the loan for. You could not borrow, for instance, to go on leave in Kashmir. Its main purpose was to buy polo ponies or hunters, shot guns, polo sticks, saddles or other similar items considered essential to military proficiency, with the rather grudging admission of cars. I had to make up my mind whether I would hunt with the Peshawar Vale (PVH) or play polo. I could not afford to do both. I decided on hunting, as I only needed one horse for the two days a week it hunted. Accordingly, for 150 rupees (£11.50), borrowed from the Polo fund, I bought a large, fat horse, an Australian 'whaler', of over 16 hands, called by the appropriate name of General Goering. Also with 150 rupees, from the same source, I bought the most beautiful old 1929 model, open two-seater Lagonda, which ran for two years without a service or addition of oil, mainly because I was completely unaware that such things were necessary. It gave me no trouble, though in the end had a tendency to jump out of third gear. I eventually sold it for more than I had paid.

More as a joke than anything else, I wrote to the German Consul in Calcutta, requesting permission to continue calling my horse after the General. A couple of months later, I got a letter from him saying 'that General Goering has graciously consented that your horse continue to be named after him'. Next year the good General was promoted Reichsmarschall, and without any further prompting from me, there appeared one morning in the post a beautifully inscribed 'Commission' in lovely Gothic script, signed by no less a person than Goering himself, stating that, 'the horse General Goering has now been promoted Reichsmarschall'. Who says the Germans have no sense of humour? Unfortunately the certificate was lost during our move to Palestine in late 1938.

In mid-October, the cold weather began. Wives and girls had been returning in dribs and drabs from Kashmir and other places in the hills, whilst a fresh lot of girls arrived from home. The Mall lay as a kind of central axis through the cantonment, a long, wide road shaped like an Australian boomerang, with pavements on either side shaded by neem trees. At its apex lay the Peshawar Club, centre of all social life as 'the Club' was in any station, however small, where there were British throughout India. It is impossible to exaggerate the importance of these clubs upon our existence. A feature of membership of one, meant honorary membership of all clubs throughout the country. No Indians were allowed to be members – the thought of them dancing with white girls was wholly repugnant and too much for anyone to stomach. Furthermore 'they might even go swimming in the pool, and the colour of their skin come off in the water!' Such rules were beginning to pose a considerable problem for the Committee when refusing to allow King's Commissioned officers of the Indianised 16th Cavalry to become members. As one of them said to me, 'We are members of the Cavalry Club in London, yet here, dogs are welcome, but not us.' In protest their British CO and 2ic refused to join, and eked out a lonely existence in their bungalows. The decision not to allow them to join was supported by the vast majority of Club members. Considerable political pressure was put on the Committee to reverse it, but they were not to be persuaded. My own feelings at the time were part approval, part indignation at something which was so manifestly unfair. I certainly did not want attractive and rich young Indian officers from the 16th Cavalry 'messing around with our girls', especially Rosemary Collin, a beautiful redhead with green eyes I had met at the first dance of the season. I was having enough trouble fighting off hungry predators such as Dick Kindersley or Bobby Dalrymple as it was, without adding to the list.

Dances were held at the Club every Saturday night. For men white tie and tails were obligatory, as were long dresses for the women. Every one was given a card with a little pencil attached, on which you wrote the name of whoever you invited to dance, and she wrote your name on hers. The dances were foxtrots, waltzes and the occasional tango for the cads. The evening usually finished with a gallop. No one was a very good dancer, as it was considered rather bad form to be so, and likely to earn you a bad annual Confidential Report from your CO. A good dancer was an object of intense suspicion, as being some kind of a 'dago'. Thus the unfortunate females were generally pushed backwards around the floor with much pumping of the left arm, quite irrespective of time, rhythm, or type of dance. Around 2.30 a.m. everyone had breakfast of mulligatawny soup, followed by scrambled eggs and bacon. Then it was back to the bungalow to snatch a couple of hours sleep before changing into hunting clothes to go to the Meet of the PVH, which usually took place at 7 a.m. Scent died very quickly in the heat as the morning progressed.

I had been introduced to Rosemary by Henry 'Bulletproof' Hawkins, whom I had met shortly when I joined at Dover. He was now commanding D Coy of the 74th. She was just 19, and her father, Major Ted Collin, was 2ic of the Royal Signals regiment in Peshawar. He was a most amusing man with a keen sense of humour which he had passed on to his daughter, and a lover of Damon Runyon, whose books, '*Guys and Dolls*' and '*More than Somewhat*' were just appearing. Rosemary was undoubtedly the most attractive girl in the cantonment, and we clicked instantly, threw away our dance cards and danced the rest of the evening together. From then on we were inseparable until her father was posted in April 1938 to Shanghai. We went on leave together to Kashmir for two months, sharing a houseboat with a convenient American called Amanda Boyden as a chaperone in those days considered essential. Amanda came in very handy from time to time, reading Runyon to us in its native tongue. Later Rosemary's father and mother came up and stayed with us on the houseboat, and we climbed a number of mountains together. There was gossip about us and conjecture, but nobody seemed to mind, and her parents certainly did not wish to see her married to a penniless subaltern of 23 with a career to make. However we did get on wonderfully well, even though she used to complain from time to time that I was turning her into a squaw. On arrival in Shanghai, she quickly consoled herself with a young officer in the Seaforth Highlanders – why hang around when you are as attractive as she was? – whilst I wrote her pathetic letters from Palestine, bemoaning my loss and exaggerating the danger from the flying bullets of the Arab terrorists, or freedom fighters, depending from which side you look at it. She joined the WRNS at the start of the War and, being highly intelligent, waltzed through the ranks to become a 2nd Officer in Western Approaches at Liverpool, where I met her once more in 1942. She was then heavily involved with a one-legged Roman Catholic Lieut Commander in the Navy, whom I named the 'Papal Bull'. She eventually, I believe, married a Naval Officer called Bell, but whether he had two legs I do not know. I never heard of her again.

Besides the Club, the other centre of social activity was the Peshawar Vale Hunt, the PVH, famed throughout India. Instead of foxes we hunted jackals, many of which came down from the hills and would often give hounds a seven to ten mile point. I am told the country was not unlike that of the Meath in Ireland, huge double banks with an irrigation ditch running down the middle. You had to jump onto the bank, change legs to take the ditch and down the other side. We met very early on Thursday and Sunday mornings, and I do not think I missed a single Meet the two seasons we were in Peshawar. General, now Reichsmarschall, Goering was a wonderful horse and carried me everywhere quite faultlessly. Not so in the point to point, however, when I was right up in the lead, and might easily have won, he refused to jump a tiny little rill not 18 inches wide. There was nothing I could do to get him across, and I had the ignominy of seeing the whole field streaming past. He did exactly the same again at the same place the following year. Perhaps keenest to hounds was the Master's wife, who was heavily pregnant. Rumour had it that hounds were running a six mile point and she had no chance to dismount, but gave birth in the saddle, the child born hanging to the horse's mane for dear life, as hounds killed.

Early in 1938, Titus Oatts and I were sent down to Risalpur for a fortnight to act as umpires for the 13/18th Hussars in the Cavalry Brigade manoeuvres. These were probably the last large-scale horsed manoeuvres to take place in the British Army, for afterwards all the regiments were mechanised and became tanks or armoured cars. A notable feature of these manoeuvres was the Balaclava charge of the 16th Cavalry against dug-in and wired Vickers Machine guns of the Dorset Regiment, who were acting as enemy. Had it been for real, not a man or horse would have survived.

I thought the 13/18th Hussars the most charming and delightful people I had ever met in the Army, and got on with them like a house on fire. The difference between their attitude and the one I had become accustomed to in the HLI, where everyone went around looking for the nearest back to stick a knife into, was as if they came from another planet. As a British cavalry regiment, they were as near the top of the social pecking order as makes no difference, yet they were without any form of regimental snobbery at all. They provided us with splendid horses, and in no way looked down on us as 'infanteers', nor did they look down on the Indian Army or anybody else. Had I been able to, I would have gladly transferred to them on the spot, and both Titus and I were very sorry when the manoeuvres were over. They were even more fun than hunting, and after riding 40 to 60 miles every day for a fortnight, we were as fit as we had ever been in our lives. Naturally, even during manoeuvres Sunday and Thursday were still a holiday, and I managed to get away each time to hunt with the PVH. It was the only occasion in my life when I felt that being in the saddle was more natural than walking.

A memory of that time which will never fade was the sight of the Royal Horse Artillery going into action. Our own squadrons had kicked up a cloud of dust behind us as we advanced, and through this dust at full gallop, six horses to each limber, came the four guns of a section of the battery supporting us. Round in a half-circle at full tilt they went, bringing the guns up to face the enemy. They unlimbered and were in action within a couple of minutes, their proud boast, '*Ubique*! Everywhere the Cavalry goes, we can go.' It was pure theatre, and alas, even then, as out of date as the battle of Waterloo.

22

One morning in November 1937 I was summoned to the Orderly Room by Fortescue-Green. On the way I wondered what enormity I had committed to merit such an honour, and how many extra Orderly Officers I was going to be awarded? Perhaps I had been seen at Peshawar Races without a hat or chosen the wrong pipe tune at the last Mess pipe night. Band and pipe nights were the same as at home, and we still took five hours over dinner. To my surprise he greeted me with some warmth. 'Brigade want you,' he said, 'apparently Brigadier Molesworth told Dick O'Connor that you spoke Urdu and Pushtu, so they have asked for you as Brigade Intelligence Officer – BIO. Report to Peshawar Bde HQ in the morning, and good luck!' I had joined the gilded Staff, who wore blue armbands with BM (Brigade Major) or SC (Staff Captain) embroidered on them in red letters. Mine would have BIO on it. What bliss! It was a splendid job and would get me away from the soul-destroying drudgery of regimental duty. Above all, no more Orderly Officer!

I reported next morning at 9 a.m. to 'Tochi' Barker, the BM, Brig O'Connor's chief Staff Officer, who ran the operational side of the Bde. He was a big man in his early forties, with a round, moon-like face and a beaky nose, who came from the Gurkhas. Tochi had got his name from being at some time in the Tochi Scouts, an irregular unit of wild and cutthroat Pathans, who operated in the mountains looking for trouble. He was a fluent Pushtu speaker. The SC, Major Brian Godley, was also from the Indian Army, a slight, thin man who always seemed to have the troubles of the universe on his shoulders. He was responsible for all matters of supply, equipment and discipline.

283

'What are my duties Sir?' I asked Tochi when I arrived. 'You tell me,' he replied, 'you are supposed to be the Brigade Intelligence Officer.' I felt we had reached an impasse. In the end I became a kind of dogsbody, doing all the jobs nobody else wanted, and learnt a great deal by it. All I knew of Military Intelligence was that you had to know all about the enemy, in this case the Pathan clans who lived in tribal territory. The difficulty was that however much I learnt about them, nobody would pay the slightest attention to anything I had to say. If anyone wished to know what the Pathans were up to, they would go along and ask 'Pansy' Cox, who was head of the Political Agency which dealt exclusively with the tribes and how best to control them.

Pansy Cox was a very good tennis player, and when he wasn't playing tennis at the Club he was usually to be found eating hard-boiled eggs at some Pathan headman's *pilau tiffin*. In fact, I consider that Pansy must have eaten more hard boiled eggs than anyone else in the NWFP, unless it was the Governor, Sir George Cunningham, who had also been in the Indian Political Service, and was a well-known egg-eater. Furthermore, when he wasn't eating these eggs, Pansy was probably knocking back Californian Syrup of Figs to counteract their effect. Whenever the tribes gave signs of becoming unruly, he would call a '*jirgah*' or meeting of all the elders, to hear their complaints. These meetings usually took place in tribal territory so that the men could come armed with their rifles, without which they felt naked. The Political Officer would sit on a chair, probably under an umbrella, with the elders sitting on the ground in a half-circle before him. Most of the complaints were about the theft of goats or sheep by one village or another, or about murder, which could start a never-ending blood feud, unless an agreed indemnity or blood money was paid in settlement. Cox would have to pass a suitable judgement. By far the most common cause of complaint was the salary of the 'secret' spies, employed by the British to pass on information from the villages. 'Why were the spies in such and such a village paid more than in ours?'

My correct action should have been to have asked to go on an Intelligence course, held at intervals, somewhere in the sloth belt of southern India, but this was the last thing I wished to do. For a

284

start it meant missing six weeks of the hunting season with the PVH. This had by now, almost become an obsession, especially as John Royle, who was away on a machine gun course, had lent me his wonderful horse, Half Note, which at one time had won the Indian Grand National, as fierce a course as the one at Aintree. This saved the Reichsmarschall having to hunt two days a week. Then there was the question of abandoning Rosemary Collin to the wolves of Peshawar. I would spend my time missing her sadly and madly, torn by the pangs of jealousy as to what she was up to whilst I was away. Perhaps above all, my experience of Army courses, supremely conducted as they always were, had convinced me of their utter futility. Nothing one ever learnt or did seemed to have any bearing or relevance on what one found on return to real Army life. I had no doubt that an Intelligence course would be the same.

Experience had also taught me that when in doubt about anything in the British Army, 'look busy and indent for something'. My office was a large spacious room with a balcony, leading off from the BM's. I accordingly indented for 'Boards. Map. Cork. Rectangular 15ft × 10ft. Quantity. One.' This was duly fastened to the wall with much shouting of instructions and confusion, by a Havildar (Sgt) of the Bombay Sappers and Miners – plus eight of his men. To this I affixed a large-scale map covering the entire Peshawar Divisional operations area. I then went along to see Cox, whom I knew well, as I played tennis with him at the Club, and explained that I wanted to mark up all the Pathan tribes and septs, they are called *Khel*, the Pushtu for 'people'. Thus one sept called itself the *Adam Khel*, 'the Adam people' or 'Children of Adam', similar to the Mac of Scottish clans. '*Excreta tauri astutos frustrantur*' which can be roughly translated as 'Bullshit baffles brains' replied Pansy who, having been a Wykehamist, was proud of his Latin quips. However he let me have a goodly selection of his *khel*, and printing their names on little flags, I pinned them onto my board. The next step was to put in coloured pins to show the location of all our own troops in the area. By the time it was finished it looked a very fine and impressive display indeed. Now of course things are even more impressive in the Army if they are 'Secret'. Although there was nothing secret about my map, I indented for a roller cover for it, locked with a small padlock. It was now the 'Secret Operations Map', and visitors would be brought in by Tochi Barker, who naturally took the credit for the whole idea, to view it.

Whenever I could do so, I went skiing in the Pir Panjal mountains, an offshoot of the Himalayas, in Kashmir. Most of the skiing was done above Gulmarg, at Killanmarg, where the Ski Club of India had built a refuge at 10,000 feet. This was quite large and consisted of a living room and two dormitories with bunks. It could hold about a dozen, all told. Next to it was another hut comprising the servants' quarters, for it was unthinkable that Sahibs could ever have to fend for themselves. Thus the inevitable '*bandabust*' would have to be made, a letter written to Amadoo Wagnoo, my HB Triumph *manji* in Srinagar, telling him to have all prepared for so many Sahibs, Mem- or Miss-Sahibs, giving dates and times. We would be met at the bottom of the hill below Gulmarg by coolies to carry our skis and luggage, and begin the 6000-foot trudge through the Gulmarg pine forest up to the hut, which took some six or seven weary hours. On arrival there would be a smiling Amadoo and cook, a huge tea ready and the stove crackling. Bedding rolls would be whisked away from the coolies, beds made up on the bunks, toothbrush, paste and razor all laid out neatly in the *ghussal khana*, with piping hot water for baths. Above 10,000 feet, the Pir Panjal seem to be a mountain range without rocks or trees, just turf, a perfect base for ski-snow, which extended to the highest point, Apharwat at 13,500 feet. Here the air felt thin and we panted for breath. We usually went skiing at the end of March or early April so as not to interfere with hunting or the point to points. The skiing was superb, and only in the Lebanon have I found spring snow conditions to equal it. We would set off at 6 a.m. for the 3500-foot climb to Apharwat, the snow as hard as concrete under our feet from the night's frost. By the time we reached the top three hours later, it had begun to melt, and one skied down with perhaps a quarter to half an inch of soft snow on a hard base, the most blissful of all conditions. Naturally there were no ski lifts, nor would we have dreamt of carrying our own skis. We had the baggage coolies to do that, and it would have been unfair to have deprived them of the revenue. Besides his

Sahib's skis, each coolie carried a Dewar's whisky tin tray. After handing his skis over with a flourish and receiving his *bakhsheesh*, he would crouch on the tray and whizz off down the mountain, shouting with laughter, faster than any skier, and, if possible, enjoying it even more.

It took about 20 minutes to get back to the hut and a huge breakfast, after which pipes would be lit and we would sit in the sun to admire the magnificent view of the Himalayas across the valley. It was dominated by the towering mass of Nanga Parbat at nearly 27,000 feet, which seemed to go on for ever and reach into the sky. The Germans had been trying to climb it for some years, without success. One whole expedition had been wiped out by an avalanche. Later, if the snow was still firm enough, we would climb the 1000 feet or so to Lillywhite Shoulder, on which there were a couple of little birch trees, and do another run. By midday the strong sunshine had turned the snow into almost unskiable porridge. It is difficult in these days of overcrowded pistes, long lift queues, expense, ballyhoo and the commercialism of modern skiing, to describe what it was like to have an entire mountain to yourselves, and ski it under perfect conditions. A Mughal Emperor once said of the Shalimar gardens in Srinagar, 'If there is Paradise, then this is it, this is it, this is it...' It was the way I felt about the skiing at Killanmarg. Could anything spoil it? For every rose there is a thorn. On one occasion, skiing down alone from Lillywhite Shoulder, I suddenly came face to face with a large Himalayan black bear. It would be hard to say which of us was the more astonished, or who took flight the faster, the bear up the hill and myself down it. The entire incident was watched from those basking in the sun outside the hut, shouting encouragement to the bear.

The hut was a new one, situated on a small plateau at the edge of the tree line, before the slope plunged once again down to Gulmarg some 4000 feet below. In 1936, a huge powder snow avalanche had come roaring down from Apharwat, taken the roof off the hut, filling the interior, and instantly killing all those inside. Three Sahibs and their servants died. To get some idea of how instantly they were killed, one was found sitting at the table writing a letter, a second had a mug of cocoa still held to his lips, whilst the third was lying in his bunk reading a book. Frozen into these postures, it was hard for the rescue party to fit the bodies onto stretchers. However, willy-nilly, it had to be done, and down the hill they went, one still drinking cocoa, another writing his letter and the third with sightless eyes, holding up his book between stiff and frozen fingers. A little Indian doctor had come up with the rescue team from Srinagar, complete with a supply of medicinal brandy in case anybody needed reviving. Finding them all dead, he exclaimed, 'Pitee to waste it,' and drank the lot, to be carried down the hill on a stretcher along with the other corpses.

The position of the new hut was considered to be safe from future avalanches, but they are a risk that must always be accepted anywhere in the mountains. The one which had destroyed the former hut roared on over the plateau into the thick pine forest below, cutting a swathe through the trees and throwing them about as if they were matchsticks. We had to pick our way through a trail of devastation on the way up. The leader and organiser of our party was R.L. Holdsworth, who was in his early forties, lean as a greyhound, with a thin, craggy face and bushy eyebrows. He was a skier and mountaineer of some repute, who was headmaster of Ismailia College in Peshawar. He had been one of a party which had reached the summit of Kamet at nearly 27,000 feet, then the highest mountain to have been scaled. He had even smoked his pipe on the summit! An inveterate pipe smoker, his pipe never seemed to be out of his mouth, even when he was eating. He was one of the very few people who could climb uphill on his skis and smoke a pipe simultaneously. At a time when five out of six men smoked a pipe, this was a remarkable feat. The other members of our party were 'Kodak' Webb, photographic officer of 20 AC Sqn RAF, Paddy Boden from the Rifle Bde, Rosemary Collin – there was no way I was going to leave her behind to face the competition in Peshawar – Joan Richardson, the British Resident's daughter from Srinagar, and myself, plus of course an attendant coterie of servants to pander to our every whim.

When I got back to Peshawar, Tochi Barker called me into his office one morning and said, 'We want you to run a two-week Intelligence course for all the units in the Brigade.' Nor were two weeks excessively long. No work was done on Thursdays or at the weekend, or in the afternoon. This left eight mornings for the course. Now, knowing absolutely nothing about Military Intelligence myself, I was obviously the right person to pick for such an undertaking. The five years that I had spent in the British Army had taught me that its fundamental advantage was 'that there was always someone available to carry out an irksome duty you did not wish to perform yourself'. For some reason, Tochi had decided that the belt of barbed wire around the cantonment was the responsibility of the BIO. This meant a long and tedious bicycle ride of 20 miles in order to verify and report on its condition. Another chore awaiting me was the sorting and cataloguing of all our maps. Both these items would be given a high priority on my course.

The first essential was to get the Brigadier involved. I asked him to give the opening lecture, 'So that we would know exactly what was wanted.' As it was his own Bde HQ course, he could not very well refuse. Furthermore the course was now at 'Brigadier level', about as high as it could get. I could demand compliance for attendance and equipment from any and all of the Bde units, which would otherwise not have been possible. Furthermore I had a fair suspicion that little Brig O'Connor might know even less about the subject than I did. Sure enough, a few days later, I saw him in a huddle with Tochi and Brian Godley, discussing the matter. Tochi called me in later. 'The Brigadier,' he said, 'simply has not got the time to think up a lecture for your course, and has told me to prepare some notes on the subject for him. I am very busy at the moment, so you can do it for me.' I accordingly wrote out exactly what I was proposing to do and handed it in, so that Tochi could rewrite it in his own handwriting and pass it on to the Brigadier. My principal aim for the course was to get other people to do all the work whilst at the same time giving the impression that I had done it myself. The students consisted of three from each of the four infantry battalions of the Bde, plus some ancillary Arms such as Artillery and Signals. All would have to talk English, as few British soldiers had much knowledge of Urdu – members of Bn Intelligence sections of the Indian Army were mainly picked for their knowledge of English. So that was no problem. The HLI section was led by Cpl Dick Mathie, whom I immediately seized upon as course assistant. He was also part of my ever-victorious swimming team. He later obtained a Commission and finished up as a Colonel in Nigeria.

I got Pansy Cox to start each week with a lecture on the Pathan tribes in our area, their customs, life, philosophy, tactics and making or obtaining weapons. Tochi Barker gave a talk on how the Bde would operate against them. Officers from the Artillery and Signals added their views. Kodak Webb lectured us on aerial photography and 'photographic interpretation', where, by the cunning use of special glasses and two photographs of the same area taken from a slightly different viewpoint, a three-dimensional result instead of a flat image could be obtained. We did a lot of practical work on this. Other practical work was 'map coordination'. A horde of us descended on Tochi's office to rearrange and catalogue all our maps in their pigeon holes to correspond with numbers marked up on the 'Secret Operations Map' in my office. This dealt with one of my chores. There only remained the Cantonment barbed wire. I gave each Bn Int section a length of it to survey, sketch and report upon as homework, to bring in the next day. The result was a beautiful, detailed map and plan of the whole defensive wire around the garrison, much of it in a very dilapidated condition. Orders were sent out to those concerned to get it repaired.

My Intelligence course was voted a huge success, and everybody seemed to have enjoyed it. It could hardly have been otherwise. Even if it had been a disaster, too many senior officers had become involved in it to admit otherwise. Pansy Cox was so delighted that the military were at long last taking an interest in his beloved Pathans, that he invited Dick O'Connor and his Bde Staff to an especially long and tedious '*pilau tiffin*' with one of the local headmen, for which two unfortunate sheep were slaughtered, and whilst waiting for the meal to arrive, we had to eat so many hard-boiled eggs that we were all constipated for weeks afterwards.

Our generation was the last to serve that now much derided institution, the British Empire, for which so much guilt is felt. The previous generation, those born in the 1880s and 1890s had mostly perished in the carnage of the Great War. It was probably the finest generation that this country has ever produced, nor

290

could any other have stood the sacrifice it had to undergo without breaking. Perhaps its short life at the apogee of Empire had something to do with its spirit. During the late 1930s, as war with Germany in the near future became obvious to us, we too expected to face the same carnage and were perfectly willing to do so, in fact proud that we would. Moreover, the new war would be exactly like the last, trenches and costly assaults. As not a single one of the military manuals dealt with trench warfare, this was another splendid reason for not studying them. Of course no-one dared utter any such patriotic sentiments or they would have been considered very odd indeed, but we felt very privileged to uphold an organisation which ruled a quarter of the Earth's land surface, a third of its population, and whose Royal Navy undoubtedly ruled the oceans with the largest and most fearsome fleet. The British Empire brought peace, justice and prosperity throughout the length and breadth of its dominions, those three essentials for human happiness, that they had never known before or since. It was our generation that fought the 1939–45 war, but we never expected that within 20 years, all that we had striven to uphold 'would be one with Nineveh and Tyre'.

The British attitude towards those they governed altered subtly during the second half of the 19th century, reaching its zenith in the years just prior to 1914. Before the 1850s people had gone out, made their pile and come home as rich men, or died abroad of some noisome tropical pestilence. After the Indian Mutiny of 1857, we ruled for the benefit of those we had either conquered or acquired. This was especially the case in India, whose people flocked to serve us. No British civilian administrator or soldier was 'in it for the money' – they were too miserably paid for that, even proud they were so. Most officers had to have a private income merely to exist. The disadvantage of this was that they worked at their profession on their own terms, which were to lead the life of a country gentleman, the sons of whom they usually were, and indulge in the pursuits they had always known, of hunting, shooting and fishing. To this, in India, they added polo, pig-sticking and tiger or leopard shooting. The country was infested with these animals, with constant pleas from the villagers for some Sahib to come out and shoot them. In fact we regarded the Army as a kind of glorified Country Club. Few were interested in their profession, and those who were, were considered slightly peculiar, and to 'have been bitten by a mad soldier'. Furthermore they were 'keen', the worst epithet that could be levelled at anyone. The majority, gallant though they were, knew how to keep their men clean and tidy, their buttons and equipment polished, and the correct words of command for parades. Beyond that, the Art of War was a mystery they did not wish to explore. I was as ignorant as any, and in 1939 found myself having to teach minor tactics to officer cadets in Dunbar, probably knowing less of the subject than they did. I used to have to mug up each lecture before I gave it, and dreaded awkward questions. Such ignorance had been no real handicap against poorly armed Fuzzy Wuzzies, Zulus or Pathans, but against Germans it was a different kettle of fish altogether, and led to many disasters.

Whether by accident or design, successive British Governments had devised a system whereby those who upheld the Empire could not obtain too much status, power or wealth for themselves. Thus those in the Civil Service had enormous status and power over huge areas, but were poorly paid. The Army, too, had great status but was even worse paid. Its power was limited to itself and never exercised outside, unless requested by the civilian authority. Finally there were those who indulged in trade, the 'box-wallahs', whose status was low, their power very limited and their wealth great. In this manner, no section could attain all three, status, power and wealth. It was the system used by the Romans to ensure that 'little Caesars' could not set themselves up in remote parts of their Empire.

None of us gave any thought to this at the time. In fact we were proud of 'not being money grubbers' and, as we said, of 'having to pay to be here'. Furthermore we lived the kind of life that could only have been lived by normal civilians with 20 times our incomes. Everything was made easy for us. We had enormous status for our age, with innumerable Indian servants to perform, most cheaply, any and every irksome chore. After the Club, the centre of bachelor life in Peshawar was his bungalow, which was shared by four. Each quarter contained a large, high-ceilinged sitting room with a big roof fan at its centre, a bedroom, and a bathroom or *ghussal khana*. The quarters were fully furnished, with cloth '*durries*' (carpets) on the stone floors, plus a desk, a sofa and two large armchairs in the sitting room. The house and furniture were provided free. The bungalows were long and low with a deep verandah, designed to keep out the heat during the hot weather. It also got extremely cold in Peshawar in the winter, and each sitting room had a fireplace. Every building was surrounded by a large garden, called 'the compound', lovingly tended by the *mali*, who was on the shared payroll.

The servants lived in a separate building close by. One's bearer one paid oneself, the rest were paid by the Mess, and you found your share on your monthly Mess bill. Although we had electric light, there was no running water or flush loos. The *bhisti* heated and poured the water into our tin baths, *mehtas* or sweepers cleaned the loos as well as sweeping the floors. They were considered unclean by all other natives, but as people, I always found them quite charming. They were born to their work and could do no other, nor was there any escape from their fate. Such is the Indian caste system. There was also the *chowkidar*, or night watchman, always an old man, who slept on a *charpoy* on the verandah. There were also stables for hunters and polo ponies, each one having its own groom or *syce*. These were also paid individually by the Sahib concerned. Your bearer got about 22 rupees a month (£1.75), but was provided with his Mess livery by his master. The *syces* got about £1. Apart from the dog boys, and a slight increase for inflation, the system was identical to the one I had known as a child. But then I was on the same level as the servants, their children were my friends and companions. Now I was 'one of the Sahibs', a being apart. I was arrogant and unpleasant enough to accept the situation as my birthright.

In May, Ted Collin was posted to command the Royal Signals in Shanghai on promotion to Lt Colonel. He took Rosemary with him. For a time I was utterly desolate. We had been constantly together for almost two years. Then being without her became almost a relief. I could now concentrate on climbing mountains. The previous year I had managed to drag her up one or two 15,000-foot peaks in the Pir Panjal, but I could hardly claim that she had enjoyed it much, preferring the sloth and the swimming from the houseboat on Nagim Bagh. There were a number of unclimbed summits I wished to attain. The first of them was 17,600-foot Malika Parbat, at the head of the Kaghan valley. I persuaded two ULIA officers, John Lind and 'Frankie' Franks to join me. My fellow HLI officers were extraordinarily unenthusiastic. A short time previously, the German Nanga Parbat Expedition had passed through Peshawar on its way to that mountain, and I tried my best to get myself attached to it as liaison officer in charge of the porters; but to no avail. Malika Parbat, although 9000 feet lower, was the next best thing. Various attempts had been made to climb it without success. We were lucky, and found an easy way though a narrow crack in the rock leading up to a steep snow field, over which we cut steps. We left our camp at 5 a.m. and did not get back until 10 p.m., utterly exhausted. Out porters had come up from our camp to light us down with hurricane lanterns.

The most unforgettable moment on that trip, greater even than the excitement of reaching the summit at about 4 p.m. that afternoon, came the next morning as we sat outside our tent eating a huge and leisurely breakfast. About 600 yards below our camp was a large boulder, and beside it, their den must have been in its hollow, were a family of snow leopards, perhaps the rarest of all the big cats; a female with her three cubs gambolling together on the patches of old snow around the rock. Through field glasses we could watch their every move. After a while, the mother led them away into a belt of scree, and we saw them no more.

1938 was the year I should have taken my eight months leave in England, having completed my two years' stint abroad. I had given it up, mainly because I did not wish to leave Rosemary Collin, but also because I much preferred life in India to anything I could find at home. However, my two months Indian leave was unaffected, and this I spent in Kashmir, climbing mountains, notably Haramukh at 15,500 feet, above the Wular lake, a much climbed peak. In fact there was a book at the top kept in a biscuit tin, in which you signed your name. I shared the climb and our old houseboat, the *Triumph*, with my cousin Twig Birch, now in his grandfather's old battery, the 2nd Royal Kohat Mountain, RA. '*Ubique et quo fas et gloria ducunt*' and all that. We had become intensely interested in photography. Twig even managed to convert part of the houseboat into a darkroom to process his films and enlarge his negatives. We both used Contax 35mm cameras, then the latest thing, with easily changed lenses on a bayonet mount. They took standard cine film. The original camera had been invented by a certain E. Leitz in Germany, which later became the world-famous Leica.

My ambition was to climb a 21,000-foot mountain called Mechoi, on the outskirts of the Zoji La Pass. In fact we could use the *dak* bungalow at its entrance as our base camp, whilst Amadoo Wagnoo would do the rest of the *bandabust*. I mentioned the idea one evening at the Club in Srinagar. Enthusiasm was intense. In no time at all I had more volunteers to come with me than I could deal with, of whom I chose five. First of all there was Bill Grace, ULIA with the HLI, who was destined for an Indian cavalry regiment, and was sharing the houseboat with me. Twig had returned to duty. The others were George Trench, also from the Kohat Mountain Bty, George Young, an Army vet, and Mike Scott from the Royal Ordnance Corps. Finally there was Frank Mittendorfer, a civilian *box-wallah* up on leave from Calcutta, who as a real live Austrian, I thought, must know something about mountaineering. Aged about 30, Frank was the hairiest man I have ever seen in my life. When he took his shirt off, he was as hirsute as a bear. Starting with a collar just below his neck, he had a thick black pelt of which any Himalayan bear could have been proud. In his bathing trunks Frank was the sensation of the year on the Nagim Bagh and the Dal Lake. His pelt also ended in tight frills around his wrists and ankles, from which bare hands and feet stuck out incongrously. His head, on the other hand, was balder than a coot's. Our porters on the Zoji La held him in extreme awe, as half-man, half-beast, and I am persuaded that it was he who was the origin of the Yeti myths.

Back on the houseboat we told Amadoo Wagnoo to have everything ready for climbing a mountain in two days time. We managed to hire the odd ice axe or two. I had my own, and bought some rope in the bazaar. What would have happened had it been put to the test, I quiver to think. We had to cross a very long glacier at 18,000 feet to get to the foot of the final climb to the summit. If anyone had fallen into a crevasse, probably me as I was leading, nobody would have had the faintest idea what to do. It was an expedition in true British amateur style, but in those days practically everything was run that way, including the Army. The Zoji La is about 100 miles from Srinagar. The first 30 we could do by native bus, but the rest we had to walk, across the lovely Sonamarg meadows, to the *dak* bungalow at the foot of the Zoji, where we set up our base. None of us had the proper clothes for such an adventure. In fact few even had climbing boots, whilst Mike Scott, unused to marching, had feet raw from blisters. We never reached the summit, but despite it all, managed to get to over 20,000 feet. Fifty years later, all of us, save the hairy Frank, met for a reunion. We had survived the war. Mike Scott had finished up as a Major General and George Young as a Brigadier. My chief recollection of Mechoi was what a happy time it had been, and how well everybody got on with each other. As for Frank Mittendorfer, he was a charming companion, but, if that were possible, he knew even less about mountaineering that we did.

The Munich crisis that September passed us by without much effect. Relief at its outcome was tempered by the belief that it could never have led to war, or that Britain and France had the bottle to stand up to Nazi Germany, or even to Mussolini for that matter. They had not done so when Italy invaded Abyssinia in 1935 and drove out somebody called Highly Delighted, the Emperor. In fact most people believed the Italians had done the Abyssinians a good turn at that, and they would now have good roads, trains running on time and clean water to drink. The methods used to conquer them, however, were considered distinctly unsporting, especially the spraying of mustard gas, which not only burnt the people most savagely, but even worse, was cruel to the sheep which ate the contaminated grass. We could not, by any stretch of the imagination, have even contemplated employing mustard gas against the Pathans. Pansy Cox would have had a fit at the mere idea. In any case, Hitler seemed to have made a habit of taking over some fresh part of Europe every autumn or spring. Czecho-Slovakia appeared to be normal practice.

We had other more pressing matters nearer home. People were

drifting back to Peshawar at the end of the leave season; a new batch of girls was arriving from England. Everyone was getting prepared for the rigours of the forthcoming cold weather, the last of its kind in peace-time, in fact the last of its kind ever. An era, an epoch, had come to an end, and however hard people tried, things could never be the same again. In only a few short years, the British would have gone for good, and the North-West Frontier would be part of a new country called Pakistan. No-one could have dreamt of such a thing that autumn.

There was good news. Someone called Hore Belisha, hitherto famous for his road crossing beacons, had become Minister for War, and had speeded up promotion in the British Army, so that it was automatic for officers to become Captain after eight years service, and Major after 14. The 74th Mess suddenly became bright with new stars and crowns. Some like George Wallace, for instance, went straight up to Major, having completed over 14 years as a Lieutenant. There was much rejoicing at this good news and many a party thrown in the bungalows along the Mall. The most talked of undoubtedly, was that in which Veronica ffinch-Bewdsley's rather voluptuous right breast slipped out of her dress and peeped coyly out at the side. Blissfully unaware of the reason for the sensation she was causing, she carried on in some amazement at suddenly having become the centre of such overwhelming male attention, even though she was as dishy a girl as you could wish to see, and personally I can think of no better way to liven up an otherwise rather dull cocktail party.

Napoleon is reported to have said 'There are no bad battalions, only bad commanding officers'. The 74th Highlanders were a magnificent battalion with, in Lt Colonel Berney-Ficklin, an outstanding Commanding Officer, who knew the nuts and bolts of his craft as a plumber does his trade. With Fortescue-Green he had an excellent though unimaginative Adjutant. Our Captain (Quartermaster) 'Ginger' McInness was a genius of supply. Morale of the whole unit was sky high. Led by RSM McIver, the Warrant Officers and NCOs had been long in their jobs, and knew them inside out. The Jocks were all seasoned soldiers and the Battalion up to full strength. Many had been on the Frontier for ten years, first at Razmak and then in Peshawar, during which time they had taken part in two small tribal wars. The officers were ready at any time to set an example in dying, with the added advantage of having a Warrant Officer or Platoon Sgt always handy to tell them what to do. There was a current joke about the Cameronians in Landi Kotal, when a subaltern on being asked by an inspecting General whether he or his Sgt ran his Platoon, replied, 'My Sgt, Sir, but dammit! Do you know, for the life of me, I cannot remember his name.'

Thus we were overjoyed in October to hear that we were to leave India in ten days for Palestine, where for some reason the Arabs had been giving trouble, most inconsiderately objecting to their land being handed over to Jewish refugees from Hitler's Germany, whom nobody else seemed to want or have room for. It was Active Service at last, and sufficiently dangerous to make it exciting. As Surtees wrote of foxhunting, 'the image of war with only ten per cent of its danger'. There was frantic packing of our baggage, selling our horses, cars and all superfluous possessions for whatever we could get for them. Finally the evening came when we fell in for the last time on the parade ground at Roberts Barracks. With the pipes skirling and the drums thudding at our head, we marched, or rather swaggered, proud as Lucifer, down the Mall, with the rest of the garrison lining the streets, to embark on the train for Karachi, from where we would take ship to face an uncertain future.